Mastering Scientific Presentations

Barbara Hey

Mastering Scientific Presentations

Unlocking Your Communication Skills

Barbara Hey
Leibniz Centre for European Economic
Research (ZEW)
Mannheim, Germany

ISBN 978-3-658-44183-8   ISBN 978-3-658-44184-5 (eBook)
https://doi.org/10.1007/978-3-658-44184-5

© The Editor(s) (if applicable) and The Author(s), under exclusive license to Springer Fachmedien Wiesbaden GmbH, part of Springer Nature 2024

This work is subject to copyright. All rights are solely and exclusively licensed by the Publisher, whether the whole or part of the material is concerned, specifically the rights of translation, reprinting, reuse of illustrations, recitation, broadcasting, reproduction on microfilms or in any other physical way, and transmission or information storage and retrieval, electronic adaptation, computer software, or by similar or dissimilar methodology now known or hereafter developed.
The use of general descriptive names, registered names, trademarks, service marks, etc. in this publication does not imply, even in the absence of a specific statement, that such names are exempt from the relevant protective laws and regulations and therefore free for general use.
The publisher, the authors, and the editors are safe to assume that the advice and information in this book are believed to be true and accurate at the date of publication. Neither the publisher nor the authors or the editors give a warranty, expressed or implied, with respect to the material contained herein or for any errors or omissions that may have been made. The publisher remains neutral with regard to jurisdictional claims in published maps and institutional affiliations.

This Springer imprint is published by the registered company Springer Fachmedien Wiesbaden GmbH, part of Springer Nature.
The registered company address is: Abraham-Lincoln-Str. 46, 65189 Wiesbaden, Germany

Paper in this product is recyclable.

Foreword by the ZEW Institute Management

The scientific presentation is a central component of the research process. The work of months or years is presented in a highly condensed form, but should still be convincing, attractive and arouse curiosity. Good presentations are the starting point for discussions, collaborations and new ideas that can enrich the research presented. They enhance one's own reputation and tie a further knot in the national and international network.

Science communication is changing rapidly and moving with the times. The traditional talk is being joined by a variety of other forms of presentation and communication. The channels are becoming more numerous, the media more digital and creative, the formats faster and in some cases more informal. Completely virtual presentations have become an integral part of our everyday lives and bring with them completely different challenges.

These new possibilities result in very well-designed presentations that are exciting, informative and entertaining at the same time. This is also how science works!

This book helps to keep pace with these changes and is based on the author's many years of experience with researchers. Barbara Hey has been training, coaching and moderating for 26 years at ZEW, at other research institutes and universities in Germany and around the world, and in the research and development departments of multinational companies. She advises doctoral candidates as well as institute directors across many disciplines. At ZEW, Barbara Hey's seminars are an important part of our internal training programme, an integral part of our structured doctoral training and are aimed at our researchers and research support staff.

The book will also help you with many experiences, tips and tricks to master your next presentation and develop your own personal presentation style.

Prof. Achim Wambach, Ph.D.
President of ZEW
Leibniz Centre for European
Economic Research
Mannheim, Germany

Thomas Kohl
Managing Director of ZEW
Leibniz Centre for European
Economic Research
Mannheim, Germany

Preface

Excellent science needs professional communication.

Presentations make a decisive contribution to this and are the instrument that has significantly increased its effectiveness in recent years. In addition to appearances at face-to-face events, the visibility of scientists has increased significantly, especially through participation in virtual conferences all over the world. The demands placed on researchers and their presentations have not diminished as a result.

This is where this book comes in, providing you with a compact and comprehensive source of practical tips, techniques and tricks. You will find everything you need to prepare your presentation efficiently and effectively, tried and tested tips for the presentation and helpful strategies for the discussion. In addition, there is a separate chapter that deals with the special features of virtual conferences and presents recommendations that you can implement quickly.

What sets this book apart from other publications is the unique combination of more than 26 years of practical experience in presentation training and lecture coaching for researchers from all over the world and the latest findings from brain research.

Presentations are the basis for a successful scientific career, so the time and care you put into your research should be reflected in your presentation. That is what I wish for you.

Mannheim, Germany   Barbara Hey

Contents

1 Scientific Talks—Effective Communication that Assists with the Conveyance of Research Results 1
  1.1 The Framework Conditions for Presentations Have Changed 2
  1.2 Talks Pay off Fourfold 2
  1.3 Differences Between the Written and Spoken Word—Paper and Presentation 3
  1.4 Scientific Talk and Business Presentation—The Distinctions and Special Features 7
  References 8

2 Conference Meetings and Co.—Occasions for Scientific Presentations and Talks 9
  2.1 Formats for Scientific Target Groups 9
    2.1.1 Academic Conferences 9
    2.1.2 Academic Workshops 10
    2.1.3 Poster Session and Poster Walk 11
    2.1.4 Brown Bag Events 12
    2.1.5 BarCamp 13
    2.1.6 Lightning Talks 14
    2.1.7 Research Pitch 14
  2.2 Formats for Target Groups from the General Public 16
    2.2.1 Science Slam 16
    2.2.2 Science Cafe 17
    2.2.3 Science Speed Dating 18
  References 19

3 From the Collation of Material to the Scientific Talk—Preparation as the Key to Success 21
  3.1 Research Results, Papers, Articles and Additional Information—Collation of Material for Scientific Presentations 22
  3.2 Classical Structure of Scientific Talks 23
  3.3 General Conditions of the Talk—Audience, Goal and Time Limit 25
    3.3.1 The Audience—The Decisive People for a Talk 25

		3.3.2 Goal—What Should the Talk Set Out to Achieve?	28
		3.3.3 Time Management—(Not) a Problem	30
	3.4	Designing the Dramaturgy of the Talk—Defining the Content and the Central Theme	31
		3.4.1 Types of Information for the Presentation	32
		3.4.2 Using Scientific Storylining to Identify the Core Information for the Talk	33
	3.5	Visualisation in the Talk—Selecting and Using Media in a Targeted Manner	34
		3.5.1 Making Proper Use of the Media	34
		3.5.2 Main, Spontaneous and Permanent Media	38
	3.6	Poster—Illustrated Summary of Research	41
		3.6.1 Planning and Preparing Scientific Posters	42
		3.6.2 Use Four Important Design Elements	46
		3.6.3 Considering the Design Principles of Proximity, Alignment, Repetition and Contrast	49
		3.6.4 Designing Scientific Posters	50
		3.6.5 Tips for Poster Presentations	51
	References		54

4 Visualisation in the Talk—Design Slides in a Professional Manner ... 55
   4.1 Fundamentals of Design—Nine Rules for Better Slides ... 56
   4.2 Classical and Illustrative Visualisation Elements ... 57
      4.2.1 Classic Visualisation Elements ... 58
      4.2.2 Illustrative Visualisation Elements ... 60
   4.3 Five Principles for Effective Slides in Academic Talks ... 63
      4.3.1 Create a Separate Slide for Each Core Message and Vice Versa ... 64
      4.3.2 Arranging Text Boxes and Numbers in Tabular Form ... 69
      4.3.3 Show Charts and Other Forms of Illustrations ... 74
      4.3.4 Avoid the Use of Confusing and Unnecessary Elements ... 99
      4.3.5 Make Use of Animations ... 103
   References ... 105

5 Communicating Methods, Results and Knowledge Gains—The Talk and Presentation ... 107
   5.1 Final Preparation Activities at Home and in the Conference Room ... 107
      5.1.1 Preparatory Activities from Home ... 108
      5.1.2 Preparatory Work in the Conference Room ... 111
   5.2 Introduction—First Impression, Lead-Up to the Topic and Increasing People's Attention ... 114
      5.2.1 Three Elements Form the Basis for a Classic Introduction ... 115

		5.2.2 Tailor the Introduction with "Hooks"	120
		5.2.3 Starting With and Without Visualisation	127
	5.3	Main Part—The Actual Presentation	128
		5.3.1 Classic Structure	128
		5.3.2 A Results-First Structure	129
		5.3.3 Hourglass Structure	130
		5.3.4 Keeping the Audience's Level of Attention High	131
	5.4	Conclusion—Anchoring Core Theses and Knowledge Gain	132
		5.4.1 Summary and Visualisation of the Important Contents of the Talk	132
		5.4.2 Conclusions and Future Research	134
		5.4.3 Closing Point and Transition to the Q&A Session	134
	5.5	Question and Answer Session and Discussion	135
		5.5.1 Chairperson—Moderator and Timekeeper	135
		5.5.2 Discussant—Critic and Promoter of Understanding	136
	5.6	Follow-Up After a Scientific Presentation	137
	References		138
6	**Remarkable and Useful Things—A Toolbox for Scientific Talks**		139
	6.1	Communication and Its Impact at Talks	139
		6.1.1 Body Language in Lectures—Eye Gaze Behaviour, Facial Expressions, Gestures and Posture	141
	6.2	Stage Fright—A Human Survival Programme Between Brilliant Performance and a Mental Block	150
		6.2.1 Negative and Positive Effects of Nervousness	151
		6.2.2 Classic Techniques to Reduce Nervousness	152
		6.2.3 Techniques to Reduce Nervousness Just Before the Talk	153
		6.2.4 Techniques to Reduce Nervousness During the Talk	157
		6.2.5 Slips of the Tongue, Forgotten Points and Losing the Thread	157
	6.3	Recite the Talk Freely, Read It Out or Learn It off by Heart	159
		6.3.1 Reciting Freely	159
		6.3.2 Reading Aloud in a Talk	160
		6.3.3 Reciting from Memory	160
	6.4	Guiding the Audience's Gaze—Using Laser Pointers, Animations and Your Hands	161
		6.4.1 Guiding the Audience's Gaze Using the Laser Pointer	161
		6.4.2 Guiding the Audience's Gaze Using Animations	162
		6.4.3 Guiding the Audience's Gaze with Your Hands	162
	6.5	Hyperlinks—Provide Additional Information or Abbreviate the Talk if Necessary	163
		6.5.1 Provide Additional In-Depth Information	163
		6.5.2 Dealing with Time Constraints	163
	6.6	Steering the Discussion and the Audience	164

		6.6.1	Answering Constructive Questions and Responding to Factual Statements	165
		6.6.2	Dealing with Unfair Criticism, Killer Arguments and Deadlocked Situations	168
		6.6.3	Interrupt Deadlocked Discussions with Metacommunication	169
		6.6.4	4 Strategies for Different Situations in the Discussion	170
	References			172
7	**Mastering Virtual Presentations**			173
	7.1	Preparation		174
		7.1.1	What Remains the Same	174
		7.1.2	What is Different	174
		7.1.3	What Additional Elements Are There	175
	7.2	Shortly Before Starting the Presentation		181
		7.2.1	What Remains the Same	181
		7.2.2	What is Different	182
		7.2.3	What Additional Elements Are There	183
	7.3	Introduction		184
		7.3.1	What Remains the Same	184
		7.3.2	What is Different	185
		7.3.3	What Additional Elements Are There	186
	7.4	Main Part		186
		7.4.1	What Remains the Same	186
		7.4.2	What is Different	186
		7.4.3	What Additional Elements Are There	187
	7.5	Conclusion		188
		7.5.1	What Remains the Same	188
		7.5.2	What is Different	188
		7.5.3	What Additional Elements Are There	189
	7.6	Discussion		189
		7.6.1	What Remains the Same	189
		7.6.2	What Additional Elements Are There	189
	7.7	Follow-Up After a Virtual Scientific Presentation		189
		7.7.1	What Remains the Same	189
	References			190

Scientific Talks—Effective Communication that Assists with the Conveyance of Research Results

> Today, you are here to listen to me and I am here to talk to you. If you finish first, please let me know!

This unusual introduction by a Professor of Business Administration at Thames Valley University[1] in London to his talk[2] underlines how important it is for the presenter[3] to know as much as possible about the audience, their level of knowledge and expectations.

Nevertheless, almost every academic can cite examples of colleagues who are well trained in professional and methodical terms and who try to get through a 30-min lecture in half the time using densely written slides, unfiltered data streams and by talking at a very high speed. Such talks are often used without any adaptations as presentations for all eventualities and for different target groups. Even the most fantastic data and results are of little use if the audience does not understand them or has switched off. They run the risk of becoming a waste of time for everyone involved. Presenters have also missed an opportunity to present their current work, promote their own reputation and expand their network. Furthermore, such talks are often followed by brief discussions with few questions. This means that there is an absence of criticism and ideas from the audience for the development of the research project. Thus, a poor presentation may in some cases obstruct the dissemination of good science.

---

[1] Thames Valley University was renamed the University of West London in 2011.
[2] The terms "talk", "presentation", "lecture" and "speech" are used synonymously in this book.
[3] The generic masculine chosen in this book refers simultaneously to male, female and other gender identities.

© The Author(s), under exclusive license to Springer Fachmedien Wiesbaden GmbH, part of Springer Nature 2024
B. Hey, *Mastering Scientific Presentations*,
https://doi.org/10.1007/978-3-658-44184-5_1

1.1 The Framework Conditions for Presentations Have Changed

Why do so many academics invest so little in the preparation and delivery of their talks? An absence of time, typical patterns of thinking and behaviour in the academic field and a lack of knowledge in terms of the efficient and effective design of scientific presentations are considered to be the main reasons for this type of behaviour.[4]

The form of academic lectures has been transformed and continues to evolve. In the past, blackboards and overhead projectors were important visualisation facilities. Preparation was mainly restricted to pulling out a few pages from their dissertation onto slides and to more or less just reading them out. Nowadays, laptops, projectors, interactive white- and smartboards have found their way into scientific conference and meeting rooms. Whereas a few years ago presentation programmes, animations and colour slides were considered a sign of a lack of academic rigour, most researchers now make use of the benefits of software-supported presentations.

Running in parallel with this trend, the expectations and attitudes of the audience also changed accordingly. Slides that are difficult to read, an unstructured lecture or a style of presentation that is difficult to understand are not so willingly accepted these days. In the academic context, results and information count, but the use of anaemic and unprofessional presentation techniques is becoming increasingly unacceptable. Content tailored to the audience and presentation skills are considered by many researchers today to be a basic requirement to ensure a good academic presentation the core statements of which are well remembered.

1.2 Talks Pay off Fourfold

Presenting, for instance at a conference or project meeting, is an important form of communication for researchers, which can offer many different forms of benefits, positive effects and even career opportunities: and what's more, excellent research that is professionally prepared and presented advances not only scientists but also academic field.

1. The talk as a business card
   Each presentation provides an opportunity to bring your own results, working methods and you yourself closer to a (larger) audience. Every appearance therefore acts like a business card, a signboard that makes you better known. It ensures that you get noticed and increases your visibility.

---

[4] Answers from informal interviews in international seminars, workshops and coaching sessions of the author.

2. The lecture supports the profile and reputation building
   With each presentation, you hone your reputation in the scientific community and increase the likelihood of people being able to put a name to your face. Talks are a form of publication that offers you the opportunity to establish yourself in the "scientific community" and to develop your own profile, in any direction. Good presentations positively influence your own reputation, bad presentations can have a negative effect.

3. Establishing and developing your own network
   Participation in scientific events is an indispensable tool in order to establish and maintain contacts with colleagues. Networking keeps you up to date with the latest research and facilitates collegial support where required. Without a functioning network, it is scarcely possible to embark on a successful (academic) career; in this sense, every conference is also a job interview. Social contacts and networks are also considered important resilience factors[5]

4. Your own further development and that of research
   Feedback and constructive criticism that you receive from colleagues in discussion or another form of exchange improve academic work and increase its impact. Such feedback also helps you to develop as a person and as an academic.

Figure 1.1 provides an overview of how academics can benefit from presentations.

1.3 Differences Between the Written and Spoken Word—Paper and Presentation

Every scientific talk is based on an article, paper or another form of written publication. Both forms—written and verbal communication—constitute important tools for researchers with notable differences. However, anyone who recalls presentations in which the researcher "read" verbatim from his paper will be well aware that written language is not very suitable for a presentation.

Figure 1.2 shows seven elements that characterise comprehensible language.

Scientific language has to be transparent and objective. The content and not the author form the focal point of the text. The reader's attention should be focused immediately and without any distractions on the facts presented.

The following grammatical structures are often used in scientific language in order to achieve this:

---

[5] Donya Gilan und Isabella Helmreich, "Resilienz - die Kunst der Widerstandskraft: Was die Wissenschaft dazu sagt", 2021, page 143.

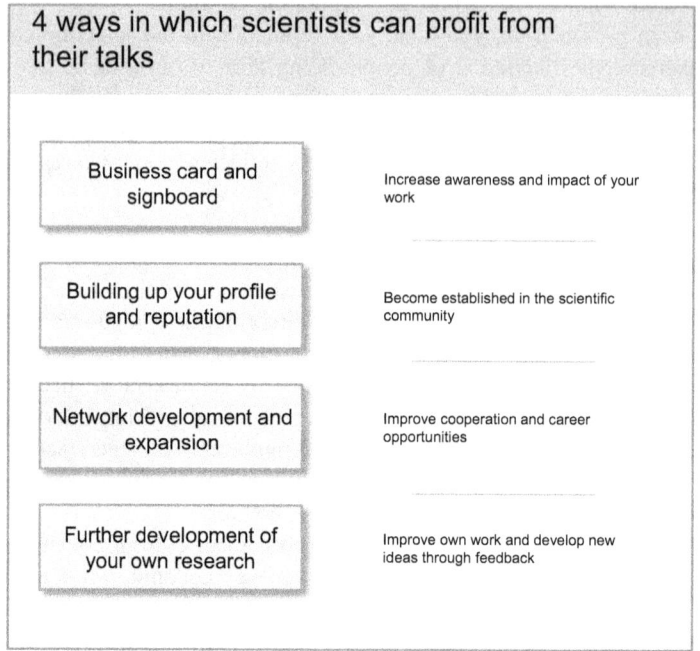

Fig. 1.1 4 ways in which scientists can profit from their talks

- Nominative style: Scientific language is characterised by substantive verbs. For example, if you use the term "measurement" instead of the word "measure", your text sounds more abstract and not linked to the author as a person.
- 3rd person singular: In scientific language, the 3rd person singular is predominantly used. In this way, researchers emphasise that the findings they have found exist independently of him or herself or other people. This emphasises why the personal pronoun "I" should only be used in exceptional cases. It is more appropriate in this case to write in the first person plural form (we).
- Passive voice: In passive clauses, as they often occur in scientific texts, the action or a fact is to the fore. People do not play a part here either.

All three patterns emphasise the neutrality and objectivity of scientific language, but at the same time make it seem cumbersome and ponderous. For this reason, written language is less suitable for a presentation. Consequently, the text of a scientific publication should not be adopted verbatim for a lecture.

This becomes even more important when researchers present to a lay audience. Especially where lectures for non-scientists are concerned, the requirements for the design and preparation of the lecture are more extensive. Researchers must also learn to present their results in a language that is comprehensible for lay people and non-specialists. To this end, it is important to present the results to different and heterogeneous audience groups, and in such a way that each audience group

1.3 Differences Between the Written and Spoken Word—Paper and Presentation

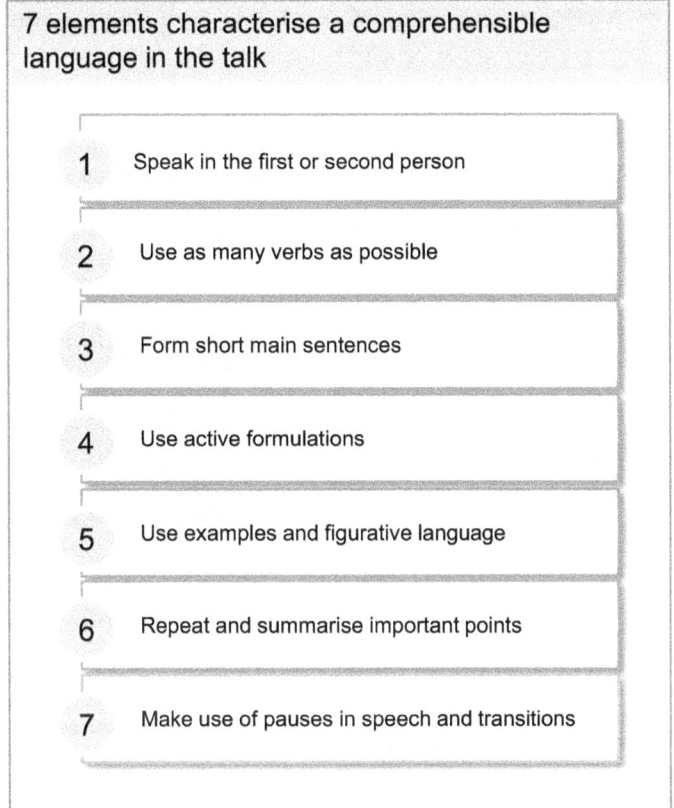

Fig. 1.2 7 elements characterise a comprehensible language in the talk

sees an informative talk that is relevant and comprehensible to them. Whereas in the past the rule of thumb was that one third of the talk did not need to be understood by the audience, today's listeners tend to expect a presentation that is individually put together for them and that they can understand.

▶ Each talk is unique, and designed or adapted for the respective target group.

Figure 1.3 clarifies the different conditions for readers and audiences of a scientific talk.

The situations of readers of a research paper and the audience of a scientific presentation vary. Readers determine for themselves where and when they will read the paper. They also determine the reading speed and the order of the individual text sections. Another important distinction from the talk is the fact that the reader

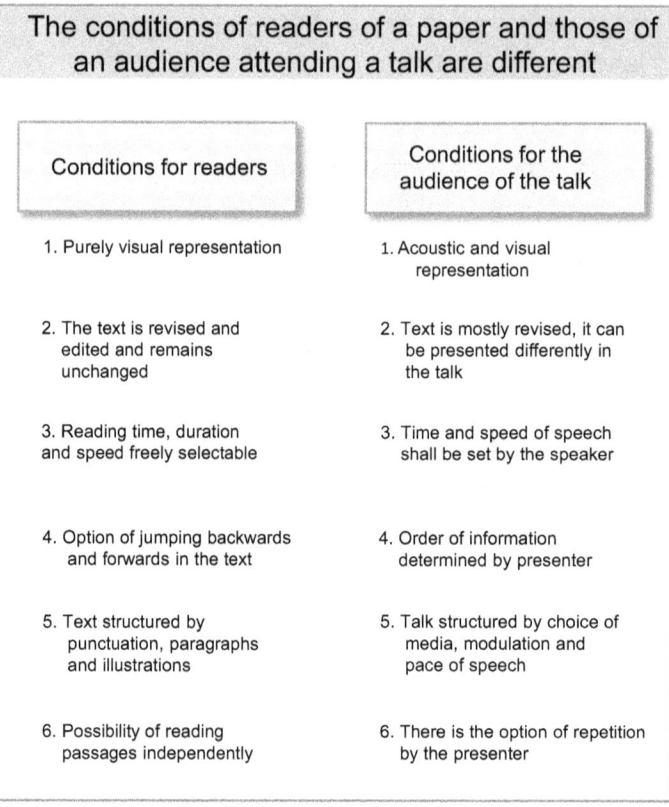

Fig. 1.3 The conditions of readers of a paper and those of an audience attending a talk are different

can study difficult passages several times if necessary and look up points for which no answer could be found.

▶ Readers of a scientific paper read it asynchronously, while the audience attending a talk absorbs what is presented synchronously.

Members of the audience at a talk do not have all these possibilities. They must understand the content determined by the speaker in a set sequence at a set time and place. Whether and what the audience understands at a conference depends on the pace of delivery of the presenter, his presentation skills, the content selected, the structure and design of the slides. Apart from that, the only option left to him is to clarify the unresolved aspects of the discussion. The audience attending a talk depends on the speaker's careful planning and preparation.

▶ It is crucial for the audience's understanding to select the content of a presentation in such a way that is specific to the target group, to structure and prepare it well and, above all, to use language that is easy to understand.

The three grammar constructions described can, when used in a talk, quickly lead to fatigue and mental blocks because they make language complicated, cumbersome and less easy to understand. This can be avoided by replacing as many nouns as possible with verbs, by using the first person or we form of address and by using active sentences. It also helps to divide up nested sentences into several short sentences and to use phrases with few relative clauses. Visualisations, such as bulleted lists or graphics, aid comprehension and mean people retain what is being said more easily.

By contrast with the reading of a text, there is no possibility of re-reading or looking up what is not understood or complicated in a talk. Therefore, it helps the audience if presenters repeat, paraphrase and summarise their statements. This makes it easier for people to make a mental note of, and comprehend, what is being said. In addition, specific examples and figurative language can deepen and anchor what is being said.

Figure 1.4 reveals the characteristics of scientific talks.

1.4 Scientific Talk and Business Presentation—The Distinctions and Special Features

By contrast with a business presentation, scientific talks are characterised by objectivity and neutrality. All statements and results must be based on the author's own scientific studies or on designated third-party scientific studies and must be presented in a value-neutral manner.

As distinct from presentations in business, researchers are rarely affected by the results and implications of their study. They also do not have to make any decisions on this basis. These reasons automatically lead to a certain distance and less emotional attachment to the lecture results than is often the case with business presentations.

Researchers are subject to these general scientific principles in their work, and therefore also during their talks. Unlike presenters in the business field, they must be objective in the selection of data or the methodological approach. Different (theoretical) directions are encouraged and discussed. While speakers at a business presentation usually adopt a position, scientists rarely take sides. Rather, they put forward arguments for both sides and provide far fewer concrete examples, which makes the talk seem more formally abstract than a classic business presentation. The latter often serves as a basis of decision-making for those responsible. The image, large sums of money and in certain instances even the very existence of a company can be at stake. This explains why the approach or assumptions that led to the figures, data and facts presented are not always fully disclosed. Some weak points are concealed. In business presentations, the main focus is usually on the possibilities and benefits of the content presented. The opposite is true for

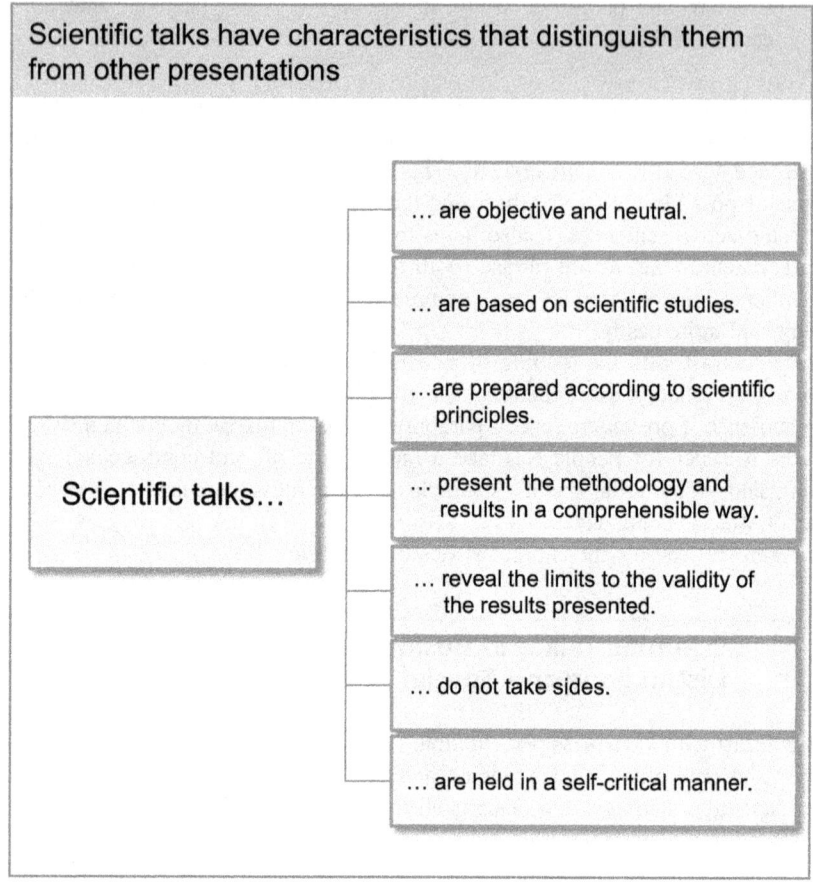

Fig. 1.4 Scientific talks have characteristics that distinguish them from other presentations

scientific talks: Here, all data are presented openly and transparently ensuring that the audience can understand the approach taken. Scientists also point out the limits of the meaningfulness of their results and take a critical look at their own work.

References

Gilan, Donya and Helmreich, Isabella, "Resilienz - die Kunst der Widerstandskraft: Was die Wissenschaft dazu sagt", 2021, 1st edition, Herder Verlag

Hey, Barbara, "Präsentieren in Wissenschaft und Forschung", 2019, 2nd edition, Springer Verlag

Conference Meetings and Co.—Occasions for Scientific Presentations and Talks

Researchers hold speeches on different events and occasions. The individual formats are usually aimed at alternating groups of participants, pursue different goals and differ in terms of their duration, size and structure. The overriding goals are to disseminate one's own work to the target group and to interchange and network with other researchers.

The classic forms of scientific communication, such as conferences, are aimed at a specialist audience within the scientific community. In addition, there are a growing number of different and unusual formats that make science and its results accessible to a broad public. For scientists, this means adapting to diverse challenges and sometimes unfamiliar conditions—an excellent opportunity for further development.

The most important forms, the respective sequence and the tasks of presenters at presentation events involving internal and external science communication are outlined in this chapter.

2.1 Formats for Scientific Target Groups

2.1.1 Academic Conferences

Goal:

- To present current scientific findings to a larger group of participants
- To exchange views on your own and other lectures
- To establish and develop your own network—seeing and being seen

Characteristics:
Conferences usually last 1 to 3 days. They usually attract larger, homogeneous groups of participants of up to several 100 people. The informal parts of the event are particularly appreciated due to the opportunity they provide of intensive exchanges.

Structure and sequence:
At the start of a conference there are usually one or more longer plenary lectures held by renowned scientists, which introduce the topic of the conference. This introduction to a topic is also called a "Keynote Speech". The introductory speech will be followed by lectures of other researchers. These contributions were submitted in advance and approved by the organiser. Conference participants will receive the abstracts of the lectures before the start of the event.

A larger conference is often made up of several parallel event sections. These so-called sessions consist of presentations by several speakers. Each session covers a specific focus derived from the general topic of the conference. This is followed by a question and discussion section. Depending on the structure of the conference, the discussion part may be moved to the end of the entire session and then be organised across the lectures.

Form of the presentation:
Classic slide presentation.

Similar formats

- Academic symposium
- Academic congress

2.1.2 Academic Workshops

Goal:

- Being able to address open questions about your own paper
- Intensive and longer discussions and exchanges with others
- Receipt of recommendations for the further progress of personal research activities

Characteristics:
The audience is limited to 10 to 20 experts, who mostly research in the same subject area. This type of event focuses on its character as a workshop. It is primarily a matter of working on one's own paper, i.e. addressing open questions or receiving recommendations for the further progress of one's personal research work. In order to allow for an intensive debate, the discussion part in particular is assigned considerably more time than at classical conferences.

There are also forms of academic workshops that bring together a small group of like-minded scientists with different skills and specialisms to achieve a larger goal.

Structure and sequence:
At academic workshops—especially at internal events—working papers that are still incomplete are often presented. Renowned professors—usually proven experts in the topic of the workshop—often take part in external workshops.

Form of the presentation:
Classic slide lecture, working together on blackboards or smartboards.

Similar formats
Brown Bag Seminar.

2.1.3 Poster Session and Poster Walk

Goal:

- To obtain a rapid overview of numerous research papers
- To provide a larger group of conference visitors with an overview of your own research
- To discuss things informally and in a small group in an open, unstructured setting.

Characteristics:
Posters, in the same way as the talk, follow the classical structure of scientific papers. Poster presentations are a form of visualisation that is condensed to the core statements. This relaxed way of presentation provides the audience with a rapid overview of the individual talks. The limited presentation space of the poster necessitates a careful preparation and consideration of the content.

Structure and sequence:
In the case of a poster presentation, all posters are displayed at the same time and for the duration of the session—usually one to two hours—the presenters stand next to their poster to present their work to interested parties, answer questions and discuss things.

Classic poster presentations can also be combined with a so-called pitch. For this powerful short introduction of the content to all conference participants, researchers have only a few minutes to promote their poster and their research. These short presentations make it easier for the audience to decide which posters in the exhibition to take a look at.

Another presentation format for posters is the so-called poster walk. Posters will be selected during the submission process and presented and briefly discussed in moderated tours. The moderators visit the posters together with interested conference visitors and the presenters have the opportunity to introduce their poster in three to five minutes. Presenters thus have the security of knowing that they will definitely be able to present their poster and their work and discuss this in greater depth later with interested colleagues.

Posterwalks are a special form of presentation both in face-to-face events and in virtual or hybrid conferences or poster sessions.

Form of the presentation:
Poster Presentation, Pitch.
Similar formats
E-Poster presentations.

2.1.4 Brown Bag Events

Goal:

- To receive feedback and recommendations on papers at an early stage of research
- To save time by linking food and work
- To gain presentation experience in a more sheltered setting

Characteristics:
A brown bag event is an informal and casual gathering among colleagues where scientists present an unfinished research project. Compared to the actual lecture, a large part of the time is reserved for questions and discussion. During the meeting, the food brought along will be eaten.

The focus of these meetings is not the quality of the presentation, but what is presented and which questions are asked. No one anticipates a polished talk or robust data here. Communication, collaboration, criticism and support are important to move the paper and the researcher forward.

Brown bag events are usually offered as a series and organised by the interested parties themselves. The name is derived from the brown bags in which Americans transport their lunch.

Structure and sequence:
The basic structure is based on that of scientific conferences, consisting of a talk followed by a discussion. Often the works are not yet progressed so far that a classical presentation can be shown. In these cases, the discussion commences following a brief overview of the current status and, if applicable, the challenges of the research project.

Form of the presentation:
Short slide presentation, free speech without visualisation, whiteboard.

Similar formats

- Lunch Lecture
- Lunch and Learn
- Lab Meeting Presentation

2.1.5 BarCamp

Goal:

- Open, autonomously organised exchange on jointly defined topics
- All participants can and should actively participate
- All participants meet on an equal footing

Characteristics:
BarCamps or "unconferences" are open, usually two- to three-day events the programme of which is not planned in advance, but is determined jointly by all participants at the beginning of the BarCamp. The main topic of the event is generally fixed, although it can also occur that the meeting starts in a completely open manner and the participants then decide on the topics. This format deliberately dispenses with the roles so typical of classic conferences, such as chair, presenter or discussant. There is also no audience, as those present can take on any of these roles. Only at the beginning of the BarCamps is it the task of the person who has sent the invitations to initiate the start.

In German-speaking countries, "Wissenschaft im Dialog" (WiD), a non-profit GmbH founded by leading German science organisations, has introduced the term Scicamp[1] for BarCamps.

Structure and sequence:
The person sending the invitation starts the Barcamp and then the participants create the programme together. Everyone is free here to propose a contribution, lead a session, request a topic or simply start the exchanges on a specific question. Everyone is free to decide whether, where and how they contribute. The schedule of a BarCamp is completely open and always varies, as each participant sets their own priorities.

Form of the presentation:
Free speech with and without visualisation on pinboards or whiteboards.

Similar formats

- Scicamp
- Open Space Technology

---

[1] https://www.wissenschaft-im-dialog.de/projekte/scicamp/

2.1.6 Lightning Talks[2]

Goal:

- To accommodate as many speakers as possible in a short period of time
- To induce speakers to get to the point quickly
- Making presentations more interesting for the audience

Characteristics:
Lightning Talks are suitable for an expert audience as well as for participants from other disciplines or the general public. The aim is to present one's own research without being able to go into detail. Stylistic devices such as humour and unusual stories are desirable to inform the audience and keep their attention high.

Structure and sequence:
In five minutes or less, speakers explain their research using a limited number of slides. After that, they immediately hand over to the next presenter. As a rule, there is a signal announcing the imminent end of one's presentation time after four minutes.

Form of the presentation:
Slide presentation.

Similar formats

- Ignite Talks
- Pecha Kucha
- Open Space Technology

2.1.7 Research Pitch

Goal:

- To be able to present the most important aspects of one's own work in a very short space of time
- To have a motivating entry point for a conversation with other researchers, potential supervisors or interested persons and to open the door for further exchange
- Arousing the audience's curiosity at events

---

[2] https://www.nature.com/articles/d41586-021-01674-9.

2.1 Formats for Scientific Target Groups

Characteristics:
A research or science pitch is an informal, very short, entirely oral form of communication lasting one to three minutes. The aim is to present one's research and experiences concisely in a short time window, leaving a positive impression that makes it easy for the counterpart to recall it.

Pitches are also—where adapted accordingly—very suitable for use at events for the interested public.

Structure and sequence:
Pitches can be used as a kind of universal tool for entirely different purposes. Researchers can use pitches at a poster session to promote their own poster and motivate audience members to attend, or if they want to speak to a renowned professor at a conference. A pitch also helps during rounds of introductions at project meetings or chance encounters at academic events.

Regardless of the intended use, short presentations of this kind must be prepared carefully and appropriately for the target person. The following structure supports the preparation of the research pitch:

1. Say your name so slowly and clearly that your counterpart or the audience can understand it well.
2. Briefly describe in one sentence your academic background and experience.
3. Outline in a few words the problem, challenge or research question you are addressing.
4. Say why this is important and interesting.
5. Make clear how your work might be relevant to the other person or how your work contributes to the discussion in your research field.

It takes some practice to be able to deliver a pitch confidently and authentically. Video recordings and feedback from other researchers are valuable sources for the finishing touches.

When presenting a pitch during a meeting, academics should be courteous and respectful. This includes asking potential interlocutors if they have time, and addressing them by name if possible.

Form of the presentation:
Brief oral presentation.

Similar formats
Elevator Pitch.

2.2 Formats for Target Groups from the General Public

2.2.1 Science Slam

Goal:

- Presenting science in an entertaining and generally comprehensible manner and getting people excited about it
- Extending one's presentation skills in a competition beyond classic conferences
- Increasing your own visibility and expanding your network

Characteristics:
The slogan of the German science slam scene: "Concentrated science in 10 min"[3] aptly describes this communication format. The aim is to present scientific results in the most varied, engaging and scientifically correct manner possible outside of the classic conference rooms. The presenters are free to decide how they wish to design this. The special thing about the Science Slam is its competitive nature. All the speakers compete against each other in a tournament. Jokes, live experiments and unusual utensils are used intentionally and help add to the special atmosphere. Science Slams take place in unusual venues such as pubs or warehouses, where the audience acts as the jury in a relaxed setting and chooses the winner over a glass of beer or wine.

How far this can go in the best case scenario is illustrated by the example of the medical doctor Giulia Enders, whose book "Darm mit Charme" (Bowels with Charm) was number one on SPIEGEL's bestseller list for paperback non-fiction books after a science slam performance in 2014.[4]

Structure and sequence:
A moderator briefly introduces the participants and guides them through the event. As a rule, the order of presentation is drawn by lot in front of the audience. The appearances of the individual academics then follow. Ultimately, there is a vote in which the audience decides the winner.

Scientists face more stringent conditions compared to the Science Slam at the Famelab. In this case, the protagonists have three minutes for their presentation. The use of slides is not permitted and only aids that the speaker can bring onto the stage himself may be used. The winner will be determined by a separate jury.[5]

Form of the presentation:
No prescribed form; mostly slide-based talk with entertaining and partly interactive elements.

---

[3] https://www.spektrum.de/index/science-slam/1495883.
[4] https://en.wikipedia.org/wiki/giulia_enders
[5] https://www.britishcouncil.de/en/famelab

Similar formats
Famelab.

2.2.2 Science Cafe

Goal:

- Open, autonomously organised exchange on jointly defined topics
- All participants can and should actively participate
- All participants meet on an equal footing

Characteristics:
At a Science Cafe, interested people meet at a venue organised by the party issuing the invitation. The relaxed atmosphere of a street café is recreated here. All those present will have the opportunity to discuss the topic(s) among themselves and with the academic in a casual setting. In order to facilitate this, a coffee house style room is chosen and equipped for group discussions. Usually there is a host at each table who moderates the discussion and remains seated at "his" table during the event while the participants (can) move to other tables. In this way, different small groups are formed again and again, which promote exchanges between them and opens up the possibility of permitting many people to discuss several different topics.

Structure and sequence:
There is usually a brief talk or video on the announced topic. Following this, all those present are divided into groups of four to five people and can casually discuss the details of the main topic at small tables. The host aids the discussion and all participants note down aspects of importance to them on the paper tablecloths or on pinboards provided. After a set time, the groups move to the next table where they learn from the moderator what the previous group has discussed and noted down. On this basis, there are further exchanges and notes are added to the tablecloths. At the end of this process, the moderators present the results to everyone and discuss them with the scientist.

Some Science Cafes dispense with the table switching and get to grips with the discussion with the scientist more quickly.

Form of the presentation:
Short slide talk or film on the topic.

Similar formats
World Cafe.[6]

---

[6] https://en.wikipedia.org/wiki/World_caf%C3%A9_(conversation)

2.2.3 Science Speed Dating

Goal:

- To make science more tangible
- To obtain new impulses through questions and feedback from the participants
- To develop your own presentation skills in a special environment

Characteristics:
In science speed dating[7] research organisations offer people interested in science the opportunity to discuss a defined topic with scientists for a personal exchange within a defined period of time. Participants can ask different researchers questions in a personal discussion, give feedback and also express their opinion. The events are usually organised in the same way as speed dating, where participants meet several scientists one after the other. There are also formats, such as "Book a Scientist",[8] where a fixed meeting is arranged with an expert for a more detailed discussion for the exchange of ideas within a set period of time.

Structure and sequence:
Interested parties register with the organisation offering the exchange. In this case, they state the question(s) they have concerning it. On site, they meet their expert for the first speed dating session. After the time has expired, they move on to the next free scientist. The design of the room varies. There are often two rows of chairs with some space between them. Sometimes there is also a kind of open booth for the discussions. It also sometimes occurs that the meetings take place in separate rooms.

Form of the presentation:
Discussion

Similar formats
Meet-a-scientist.[9]

Figure 2.1 illustrates an overview of the different occasions involving talks.[10]

---

[7] https://www.wissenschaftskommunikation.de/format/science-speeddating/
[8] https://berlinscienceweek.com/event/book-A-scientist-2/
[9] https://www.wissenschaftskommunikation.de/format/meet-the-scientist/
[10] Own representation.

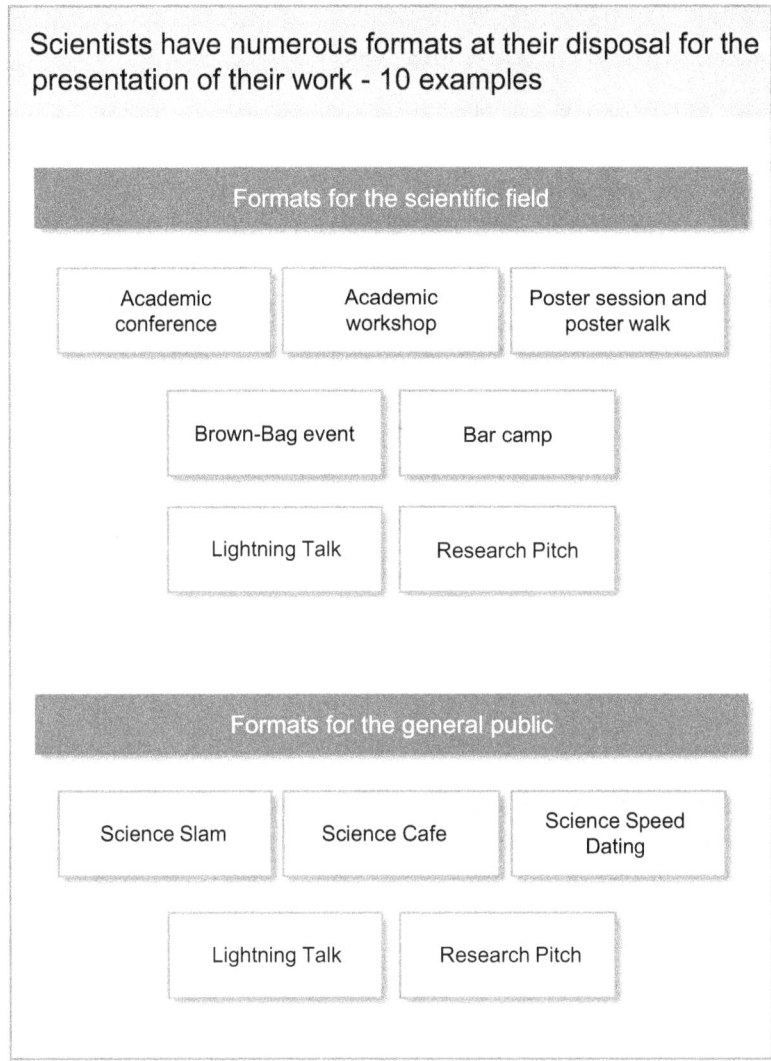

Fig. 2.1 Scientists have numerous formats at their disposal for the presentation of their work—10 examples

References

British Council Germany, 2021, FameLab, https://www.britishcouncil.de/en/famelab, last retrieved: 29.12.2023

Leibniz-Gemeinschaft, 2022, Berlin Science Week, https://berlinscienceweek.com/event/book-a-scientist-2/, last retrieved: 29.12.2023

Nationales Institut für Wissenschaftskommunikation (NaWik) gGmbH (publisher): Leitfaden Präsentieren, Karlsruhe 2021

Spektrum.de, no year stated, Science Slam, https://www.spektrum.de/index/science-slam/1495883, last retrieved: 29.12.2023

Wikipedia, 2022, Giulia Enders, https://en.wikipedia.org/wiki/Giulia_Enders, last retrieved: 29.12.2023

Wikipedia, 2022, World café (conversation), https://en.wikipedia.org/wiki/World_caf%C3%A9_(conversation), last retrieved: 29.12.2023

Wissenschaftskommunikation.de, keine Jahresangabe, Science Speeddating, https://www.wissenschaftskommunikation.de/format/science-speeddating/, last retrieved: 29.12.2023

Wissenschaftskommunikation.de, keine Jahresangabe, Meet the Scientist: https://www.wissenschaftskommunikation.de/format/meet-the-scientist/, last retrieved: 29.12.2023

Wissenschaft im Dialog, keine Jahresangabe, Scicamp - die Konferenz, die keine ist, https://www.wissenschaft-im-dialog.de/projekte/scicamp/, last retrieved: 13.03.2023

Woolston, Chris, 2021, Lightning talks: science in 5 minutes or less, https://www.nature.com/articles/d41586-021-01674-9, last retrieved: 29.12.2023

From the Collation of Material to the Scientific Talk—Preparation as the Key to Success

3

Excellent research requires an equally professional form of presentation. Talks are considered a classic opportunity to present one's own research to a larger audience, to discuss it and to increase one's own profile. Conferences, workshops and seminars are popular science communication formats that can be beneficial for academics in many ways. In addition to enhancing one's own reputation, further developing one's own research and exchanging ideas with colleagues, numerous networking opportunities also arise. For these reasons, it is worthwhile for every researcher to reflect on what might interest and captivate the audience. Strictly speaking, each talk is unique, as the audience is different and varying levels of knowledge and expectations should be taken into account. Consequently, it is correct and important to revise, adapt and, if necessary, redesign your presentations accordingly.

The basis for the appealing design and convincing presentation of the talk is its individual preparation. This should not start just before the conference visit by you hurriedly putting together some slides. On the contrary: many researchers collect ideas, images, articles and the like in their everyday scientific work, which they later use for different presentations. This helps to minimise the time needed for the actual preparation and to provide the presentation with a more individual touch.

The following chapter reveals the path from the collection of material to the design of slides to the finished scientific presentation and lists the steps upon which effective preparation are based.

▶ Prepare well, it helps when facing the biggest challenges! This is because: Scientists, regardless of their nationality, discipline and experience level, have been expressing the same concerns in presentation seminars and coaching sessions over many years: Questions from the audience, a blackout and technical problems.

© The Author(s), under exclusive license to Springer Fachmedien Wiesbaden GmbH, part of Springer Nature 2024
B. Hey, *Mastering Scientific Presentations*,
https://doi.org/10.1007/978-3-658-44184-5_3

3.1 Research Results, Papers, Articles and Additional Information—Collation of Material for Scientific Presentations

In academic practice, the creation and regular maintenance of a permanent collation of material on one's own topic has proven successful. In this pool of ideas, scientists record all information on their subject area, such as the (preliminary) results of research activities, current discussion papers as well as articles in journals and articles, quotations or results of other researchers, but also further links or demonstration objects. Together, this information material forms the framework for the design of the talk.

Collections of material are inspiring, help to save time for the preparation and ensure that nothing important is forgotten. They can be subdivided into three categories.

1. Own material:
    Own results, publications and experiences as well as notes on audience reactions to one's own presentations and slides.
2. Other people's material:
    Results, thesis papers and literature of other researchers.
3. General material:
    Visualisation elements such as pictures, graphics, diagrams, films and humour.

> **Practical tip**
> Always note down ideas on your research topic or feedback on your talks right away. A small notebook that you can easily carry with you is perfectly sufficient for quick handwritten notes.

It is essential that sources and references are recorded directly in full to prevent laborious reference work later on and to be able to mark and prove quotations as well as analogies in the presentation and thus to follow the recommendations for ensuring good scientific practice.[1]

The material in the third category helps to make abstract scientific topics clearer and easier to understand and to increase the attention of the audience. Sayings, anecdotes and caricatures—if they are related to the topic—are increasingly used in scientific presentations to make them more attractive. If the material is recorded

---

[1] https://www.dfg.de/en/principles-dfg-funding/basics-and-principles-of-funding/good-scientific-practice

promptly and in a pre-sorted manner, the workload is kept within limits. The collection of materials remains clear and up to date or you sort them out on a regular basis.

▶ Quote correctly and always designate the thoughts of other scientists. Always reveal how the data was collected. Never make any data corrections.

3.2 Classical Structure of Scientific Talks

Scientific presentations primarily serve to present one's own research to a larger audience. As with any other scientific work, they follow a classical structure. On the one hand, this includes the elements that ensure that the presentation is objective, comprehensible and verifiable. This reduces the likelihood that the presentation will be incomplete in a scientific sense. In addition, a predominantly uniform presentation structure is frequently anticipated, especially at conferences.

On the other hand, oral presentations and written publications differ.[2] Readers of an article and listeners at a talk have different conditions. For example, readers can read complex parts several times and at their own pace. Conference visitors do not have this option. In return, they have the opportunity of addressing the author personally in the discussion or over a coffee. Speakers, in turn, are usually subject to strict time constraints that can force them to limit the content shown. Researchers also have other ways of setting up their presentations at their disposal besides the classic structure. The structure chosen depends on the goal of the presentation, the composition of the audience, the time available, the occasion and the speaker himself.

> **Practical tip**
> A classical structure is expected at many conferences. If you have no other information, follow the standardised structure of an academic talk.

Figure 3.1 reveals the classic structure of academic talks.[3]

Introduction
The introduction marks the start of an academic talk. It has a psychological character as well as a professional one and assists scientists in establishing first contact with the audience. The audience is put in the right mood for what is to follow. This indispensable element of the talk—used correctly—helps to raise the audience's

---
[2] Barbara Hey: "Präsentieren in Wissenschaft und Forschung", 2019, page 19 et al.
[3] Barbara Hey: "Präsentieren in Wissenschaft und Forschung", 2019, page 122.

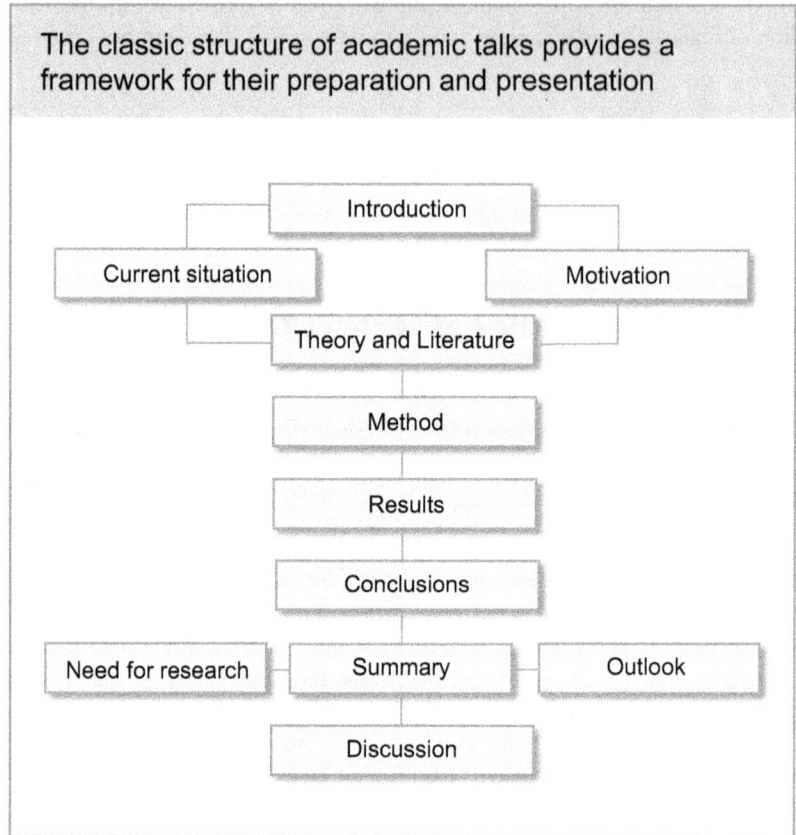

Fig. 3.1 The classic structure of academic talks provides a framework for their preparation and presentation

attention. In addition to the welcome, it includes the introduction of the speakers, co-authors and the topic of the talk, unless this has been done by a third party.

Motivation and current situation
Using the elements of "Motivation" and the "Current Situation", researchers reveal why they are working on this topic or question and also provide the audience with a view of the bigger picture of the current (research) situation. At this point, speakers also clarify the extent to which the work is of interest (to the audience).

Theory and literature
In a classic talk, the work is classified in the literature at this point and, if necessary, a new theoretical approach is explained and how it differs from previous approaches.

Scientists often dispense with these components due to time constraints, as the results can be understood without this information and an expert audience usually knows the relevant literature. Appropriate notes in the talk documents are sufficient in many cases.

Method, model or experiment
In this part, scientists describe their methodological approach. It is important that the auditorium understands the results and how they came about. The novelty, the specialness of a process, a method or an experiment is always of particular interest.

Results
The description of the methodological approach is followed by the presentation and interpretation of the study results. This part is of particular importance because this is where the knowledge gain is presented. For this reason, some speakers present their results and implications at the beginning of the presentation.

Summary and transition to the discussion
At the end of each talk, there is a summary of the most important statements—i.e. results and conclusions. Researchers also cite research gaps or weaknesses in their own research at this point. It provides an outlook on the possible further development of the research field and on future research needs. After thanking the auditorium, the actual presentation is over.

> **Practical tip**
> Use the summary of your presentation to improve your scientific standing. Point out your other papers (there should be more than one) and publications.

3.3 General Conditions of the Talk—Audience, Goal and Time Limit

The size and composition of the audience, one's own objectives and the time available play a decisive role in the selection of the content of the talk. These three aspects shape not only the selection and sequence of the presentation content, but also all other steps from the preparation to the delivery of a talk.

3.3.1 The Audience—The Decisive People for a Talk

Delivering a talk is not an end in itself. All participants come to this talk with a certain level of expectation. They would like to see these fulfilled—at least in part—in order to be able to draw a benefit for themselves from the talk. A talk is, in a figurative sense, a trade involving the audience investing some of its time.

They expect something in return for this. At the beginning of the preparation, therefore, there is a crucial question that speakers should ask and answer:

> What knowledge gain or benefit does my presentation offer to the audience?

The answer to this question helps researchers to better adapt to the audience and, together with their own objectives, forms a good basis for an effective talk. A pleasant side effect is also the fact that an introductory part to the presentation is worked out at the same time.

3.3.1.1 Gaining an Impression of the Audience

First of all, presenters should consider the professional background or level of knowledge of the audience and how much they know about the topic. It is important to reflect as precisely as possible which technical terms, abbreviations, variables or methods can be assumed to be known or must be explained so that the audience understands the talk. The second step involves identifying the scientific, i.e. professional interests of this group as far as possible.

Afterwards, it helps to consider the attitude of the audience towards the speaker on the one hand and the topic, methodological approach or results, on the other. This provides early indications of possible reservations, criticism, resistance and perhaps even attacks that scientists must expect in the talk or during the discussion. These assumptions can be taken into account in the course of the further preparation for the formulation of arguments or in-depth explanations.

This is followed by considerations of whether there are one or more people in the audience who are of particular importance to speakers and their work—for example, people with great reputations or funders for a research project. If it is appropriate and makes sense, it is a good idea to arrange the talk or parts of it accordingly. This should be well-considered because there is a risk of "losing" the rest of the audience.

> **Practical tip**
> Do not give a standard talk for different occasions. Prepare individually for each event.

There are several ways to obtain information about the audience:

- Take a look at the current list of participants and the conference programme.
- Ask colleagues or participants you know from previous events or similar conferences.
- Track publications about the event on the web (organiser's homepage, articles in trade journals, posts on social media).

3.3.1.2 Target Group-Specific Preparation in the Case of a Rather Heterogeneous Audience

Where the audience is rather homogeneous, it is relatively easy to compile the interests and expectations of the talk. It becomes more challenging when the audience is heterogeneously structured and has different interests as well as levels of experience or knowledge about the topic of the talk.

> **Practical tip**
> The larger and more heterogeneous your audience is, the more result-oriented your talk should be. Basically, all the audience should, if possible, understand your motivation, the results and the conclusions drawn from them.

As a rule of thumb: The introduction and summary should be structured in such a way that everyone can understand them. The main part is designed in such way that it is interesting for experts. In the case of longer talks, this approach is recommended for each individual part of the presentation. It ensures that even the non-experts understand the results of the study without the experts getting bored. In this way, researchers manage the balancing act when dealing with the different levels of knowledge on the part of the audience.

In the event of a smaller audience, scientists also have the opportunity to visualise basic information—for instance, the detailed explanation of variables of a formula that are not known to all present—on a whiteboard or a flip chart. Those who need the input use the additional medium. Those who have the necessary knowledge to understand the talk ignore it. This action alternative has the advantage that the speakers provide the necessary information without losing time for the actual presentation.

> **Practical tip**
> You are better off taking another two steps back in your thought process. Reflect on whether someone can follow your talk who has not spent the last few months on the topic. This is because, in contrast with your audience, you are still at the heart of the matter because you have only recently finished dealing with it. Therefore, you may tend to speak in a very technical way or with too much attention to detail, so that your listeners can no longer follow. Find a balance between the need for content and the interests of the audience.

3.3.1.3 Experts in the Audience

It is usually the case that the audience has less knowledge of the topic than the experts holding the talk. However, the opposite constellation also arises. A specialist (or even several specialists) is/are sitting in the audience who knows a lot and possibly more about the current issue than the speaker himself. Here it helps to familiarise yourself with the expert's publications on the topic and to be prepared for possible questions.

> **Practical tip**
> Stay calm and relaxed. The audience—including professors—is often benevolent. Go ahead and present yourself with an appropriate level of self-confidence, after all, you have been working on the topic. Show respect towards others. Keep two basic elements in mind: Politeness and diplomacy!

3.3.1.4 Compile Possible Questions from the Audience

While the content, structure and visualisation of the presentation are in the hands of the speaker, he can have little influence on reactions from the auditorium. Therefore, it makes sense to compile potential audience questions and formulate answers to them. The following questions upon which to reflect help to prepare for possible audience reactions.

- What would I ask myself, if I was a member of the audience?
- What would other people ask? (ask colleagues for help with this)
- Which questions have I been asked about this topic so far?
- What are the divergent opinions and hypotheses on this topic?
- Where are the weaknesses in my work?

If you want to further enhance your feeling of security, rehearse the answers for particularly critical situations and even learn them by heart in an emergency. Often the compilation of possible audience questions provides the presenter with information about what information is important for the talk.

Detailed hints and tips for dealing professionally with questions from the audience and steering the discussion follow in Chapter 6.

3.3.2 Goal—What Should the Talk Set Out to Achieve?

The specific objective serves as a compass and determines the "common thread" of the talk. A clear formulation of goals and expectations of the audience constitutes a key building block of a successful presentation and help researchers select content and information that serves this purpose.

The goal of the talk should be formulated as specifically and as verifiably as possible.

▶ Complete the following sentence starters to formulate your goal:

- I would like to achieve the following with my talk....
- I realise I have achieved my goal when ...

3.3.2.1 Goals That Are Not Verifiable or Difficult to Verify

"Bad" goals are characterised by the fact that their achievement is difficult or impossible to verify. Furthermore, they do not provide orientation and help for the content structure of the talk. They are often tasks rather than goals. The following examples illustrate the weaknesses of the goals formulated:

- *"I want to motivate the audience to listen to me."*
  Is that all the talk should set out to achieve? Is it really enough if the audience just listens?
- *"I want to get the most important points across.""*
  What are the most important points of your talk? Why do you want to "get across" precisely these points?
- *"I want my audience to know what the content of my research is."*
  What exactly do you want the audience to know following the talk?
  Is it enough if the audience knows the content or does it also have to be understood?

3.3.2.2 Verifiable Goals

The following goals of academic talks are verifiable and assist in the design of the presentation:

> *"I want my talk to help the audience learn and understand the three main differences of the new survey method compared to the previously known methods."*

> *"I want to stimulate a strong discussion with my arguments and get new impulses for the further development of my research."*

In addition to the official purpose of the talk, there are often additional unspoken expectations that scientists want to achieve through the presentation. This so-called "hidden agenda" usually includes goals that have less to do with gaining knowledge or scientific exchange and more to do with recognition and raising the profile of the speakers. Ideally, the goal of the talk, the objectives and the expectations of the audience are highly congruent.

▶ Your goal of the talk should only be "to get through" in absolutely exceptional cases.

3.3.3 Time Management—(Not) a Problem

"Unfortunately, due to time constraints, we cannot go into this interesting aspect any further." Statements like these are typical in everyday scientific presentations. In many presentations, time is considered the critical factor. In the scientific context, in particular, the urge for completeness is pronounced and speakers want to present their work in as much detail as possible and in all its facets. This is an understandable wish, considering how much time is invested in research projects and how important the communication of one's own scientific activities is for researchers. At the same time, the talk is not the paper. To be able to present the essence of an 80-page paper in 20 minutes, it is necessary to identify the parts of the work that are crucial for the audience and the achievement of the goal.

Even though most presenters find it easier to go into detail about their topic than to present the key messages in a short time, focusing on the essentials offers some advantages. A high density of detail and information often leads to a high rate of speech. This makes it more difficult to understand the talk. The audience's levels of interest, attention and retentiveness are very likely to decrease. Slower speech and pauses in speech are a welcome way for listeners to follow and understand what is being said. A quote from Voltaire aptly rounds off the statements:

▶ The secret of being a bore is to tell everything!"

Hardly any talks go as planned. There are always interruptions, previous speakers who overrun their time, technical problems or unforeseen things that take up more time. Time problems can be reduced through good planning.

The following recommendations help you to remain within the allotted time frame:

- Rehearse your talk and time it.
  Also present it in front of colleagues, friends or the camera to get a better sense of time and to calm your nerves.
- Allow a time cushion of 20%.
  This time cushion makes it possible to get by without cutting content if any problems arise and to stay within the given framework. If everything proceeds normally, you have the opportunity to go into more detail and be able to provide the audience with interesting additional information. Besides, no one will be upset if the talk ends a few minutes early.
- Plan to include your most important information relatively early in the talk.
  If you have to shorten your presentation due to time constraints or are interrupted by the chair, then you have still illustrated your most important points.
- Include hyperlinks.
  Such shortcuts are ideal to be able to skip slides without having to fade them in and then skip them. Using such a link, you can go directly to the last or most important slide of your presentation in case of an emergency or pressure of time.

This saves the quick click-through to the end, where viewers would see what they were not presented with and thus prevents frustration or disappointment. You can see more on this in Chapter 6.
- Use a presenter with an alarm function.
  Modern presentation pointers can be programmed to alert you in good time to the end of the speaking time with a light vibration alarm—that is imperceptible to others.
- Ask a friendly colleague in the audience to give you a sign when 50% of the time is up.

Practical tip
Never underestimate the amount of time you will require. Find out in advance how much time you will have. Make yourself aware of how short a time of 15 minutes (or 20 to 30 minutes) is. Stick to the time constraints, i.e. do not go into too much detail. Restrict yourself to thematic sub-aspects and do not pack too much into your talk. Exceeding the time limit—possibly even in spite of a request—quickly leads to antipathy on the part of the audience. Repeat important aspects, speak a little slower and plan time for both.

Figure 3.2[4] illustrates an overview of the three influencing factors for the planning and implementation of talks.

3.4 Designing the Dramaturgy of the Talk—Defining the Content and the Central Theme

"We don't pay attention to boring things".[5]

This quote by molecular biologist John Medina underlines how important interesting and appropriate content, a clear structure and a varied presentation style are for the success of a talk. The self-evident and the familiar, on the other hand, do not help to attract people's attention.

Therefore, it is important for researchers to realise that they have more knowledge on the subject than they can actually show. The art of holding a talk is to find the information that allows the audience to gain knowledge, at the same time serves one's own goal and fits within the given time frame. It is helpful to this end to know the different types of information in a talk and to have a good technique for identifying the appropriate content. Both are described below.

---

[4] Own representation.
[5] https://brainrules.net/attention/

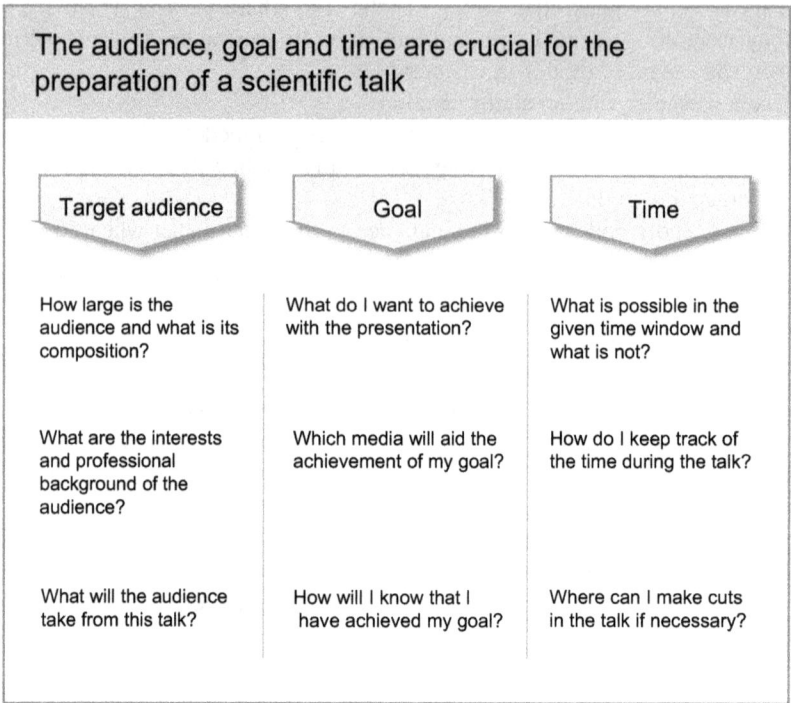

Fig. 3.2 The audience, goal and time are crucial for the preparation of a scientific talk

3.4.1 Types of Information for the Presentation

Determining the common thread of a talk serves to ensure a logical and audience-oriented structure. The audience should be able to follow the speaker's approach and understand his results. To this end, it is important that all information builds on each other and breaks are avoided. The audience also understands a scientific presentation and its results more easily if scientists, when determining the content and its order, ensure that one idea has been thought through to the end before a new one is pointed out. The contents of an academic talk can be subdivided into three categories:

– Core information
    is imperative to ensure the audience understand the talk. This includes the research question, required input on the methodological approach, and the main results and conclusions of the study.
– In-depth information
    provides in-depth know-how and additional input, such as specifics on the methodological approach or concrete examples. In-depth information underpins core information and ensures a better understanding.

- Detailed information
    is specific or special "nice to have" hints that speakers mention where time permits or it is specifically requested. These are usually so special, particular or peculiar that they are more easily remembered.

3.4.2 Using Scientific Storylining to Identify the Core Information for the Talk

In order to develop a scientifically correct, logical and comprehensible presentation, it is advisable to introduce the elements of a classic scientific talk like a story as a basic framework. This structure helps the audience to better understand the content and contexts and serves as a common thread for speakers. It is also called storylining[6] and is often used in a similar form in business presentations. The storyline can also be used wonderfully well for academic talks. A tried and tested form[7] that has also been adapted for researchers is presented below.

▶ An effective storyline starts with the slide titles. These are formulated in such a way that they state the most important message of the respective slide.

Unlike classical structuring forms, the structure of a science storyline for your own talk does not begin with the content, but with the headings of the slides. This is because concise headlines motivate and they provide the audience with a rapid orientation. Instead of generic or general slide titles—such as "motivation" or "methodology"—it is important to find headings that summarise the core message of the respective slide in one sentence. These headlines are also called "talking headlines"[8] or "action titles."[9] Strung together, they form the storyline of the talk. A good storyline not only serves as a helpful basis for the production of the talk, it can be used as an abstract, executive summary or pitch and prevents researchers from getting lost in the details. The storyline forms the backbone of the talk. In further steps, the content is supplemented and necessary additional slides are created.

▶ A good storyline forms the basic structure of a talk and can be used for many purposes. It is easy to further build upon it and easy to retain.

---

[6] Graebig Markus et al.: Wie aus Ideen Präsentationen werden, page 127.
[7] Own adaptation.
[8] Origin could not be reliably clarified.
[9] Origin could not be reliably clarified.

3.4.2.1 Example of a Scientific Storyline

The following example[10] from the field of economics illustrates how a storyline for scientific talks can be created in five steps. The sample presentation chosen here deals with different aspects of the integration process after mergers or acquisitions of companies (Mergers & Acquisitions, in short: M&A).[11] The focus here is on the integration process of the research and development (R&D) departments after the merger of three companies.

The five steps of the storyline:

1. Take a sheet of paper or create a computer document.
2. Start with the classic or other appropriate structure for scientific talks and draw the individual structure points as the basis for your storyline. Figure 3.3 shows an example of this.
3. Use reflective questions, identify the key message for each structure point, as shown in Fig. 3.4
4. Formulate each core message as a meaningful headline (talking headline). Figure 3.5 shows an example.
5. Read all the headings in succession and check the logic and completeness of your storyline

With the storyline as a basis, the next steps are easier. The focus is now on in-depth and detailed information that researchers add to complete the manuscript.

3.5 Visualisation in the Talk—Selecting and Using Media in a Targeted Manner

In his 12 Rules for the functioning of the human brain,[12] molecular biologist John Medina names two factors that play an important role for talks in general and visualisation in particular. Medina says that all human senses want or should be stimulated and that sight trumps all other senses.[13] The visualisation elements and media of a talk appeal to the human eye and support the spoken word. They help people to better recall the most important statements and make it easier to understand what is being said. Varied presentations with attractive visual aids make a talk more interesting and appealing.

3.5.1 Making Proper Use of the Media

▶ The information must be easily readable from every seat!

---

[10] Talk by Thomas Zwick, Julius-Maximilians-Universität, Würzburg.
[11] http://wirtschaftslexikon.gabler.de/Definition/mergers-acquisitions.html
[12] https://brainrules.net/introduction/
[13] https://brainrules.net/vision/

3.5 Visualisation in the Talk—Selecting and Using Media in a Targeted Manner

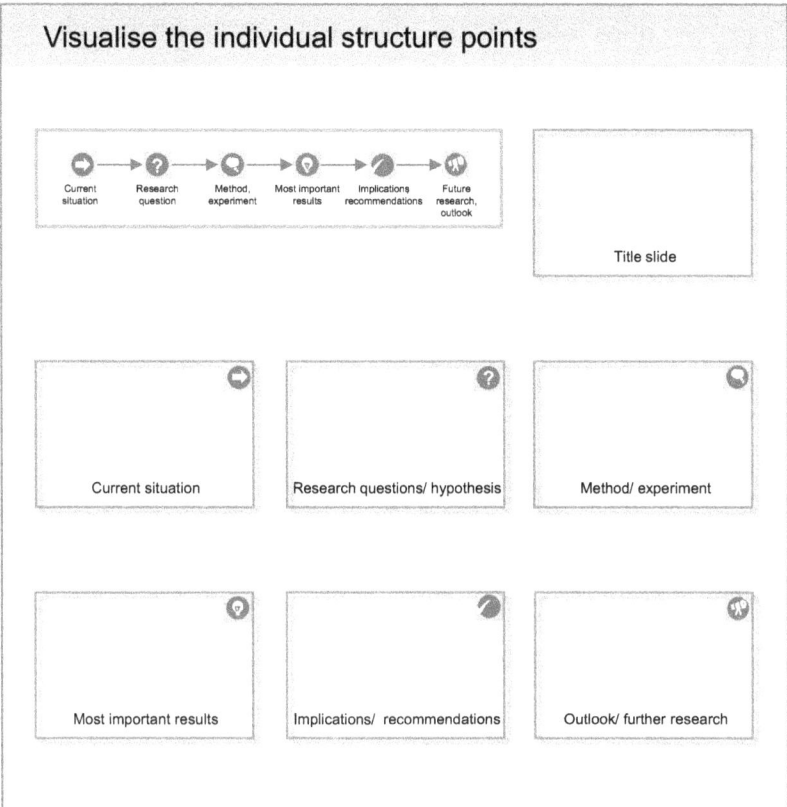

Fig. 3.3 Visualise the individual structure points

As self-evident as this sentence may sound, it is neglected or ignored in some academic talks. Presentational bankruptcy statements such as

"You probably won't be able to see it in the back rows, so I'll read it to you briefly"
or

"I have summarised all the data in this table. It's not so easy to read now, but I wanted to show it to you anyway!"

are not among the exceptions at conferences. Media that are unsuitable for the size of the group or visualisations that are difficult or impossible to decipher are pointless and frustrate the audience in the long run. They also cost time because they have to be explained in more detail. No less serious are the disadvantages for the speakers themselves associated with the selection of inappropriate media and visualisations:

– An absence of benefits:

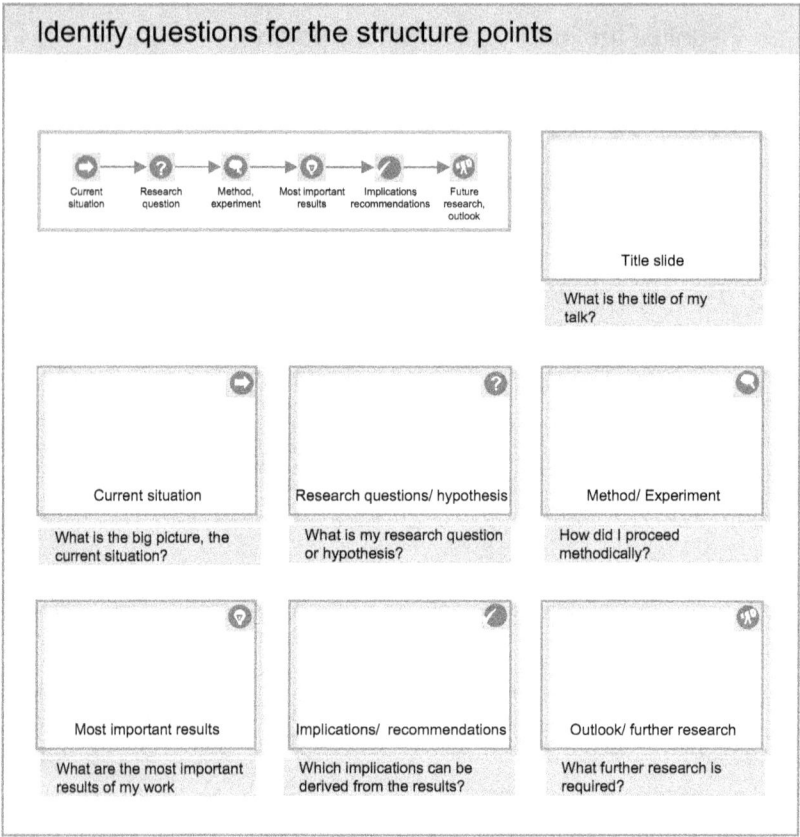

Fig. 3.4 Identify core messages of the individual structure points

An unreadable/poorly readable slide makes the presentation more difficult to understand, as the audience focuses more on deciphering the slide than on the presentation.
- Difficulty in achieving goals:
  Unreadable visualisation elements of a talk do not support the spoken word and thus the achievement of the goal.
- Bad reputation:
  Poorly readable media and visualisations do nothing to enhance your scientific reputation. They are rather evidence of unprofessional, or a lack of preparation, and possibly indifference towards the audience.

Targeted use of media and the combination of different media enliven a talk. They assist in presenting content more comprehensibly. Many combinations of different media are conceivable. But beware, because: twice as much is not always twice as good. When in doubt, researchers should use too few media rather than too many.

3.5 Visualisation in the Talk—Selecting and Using Media in a Targeted Manner

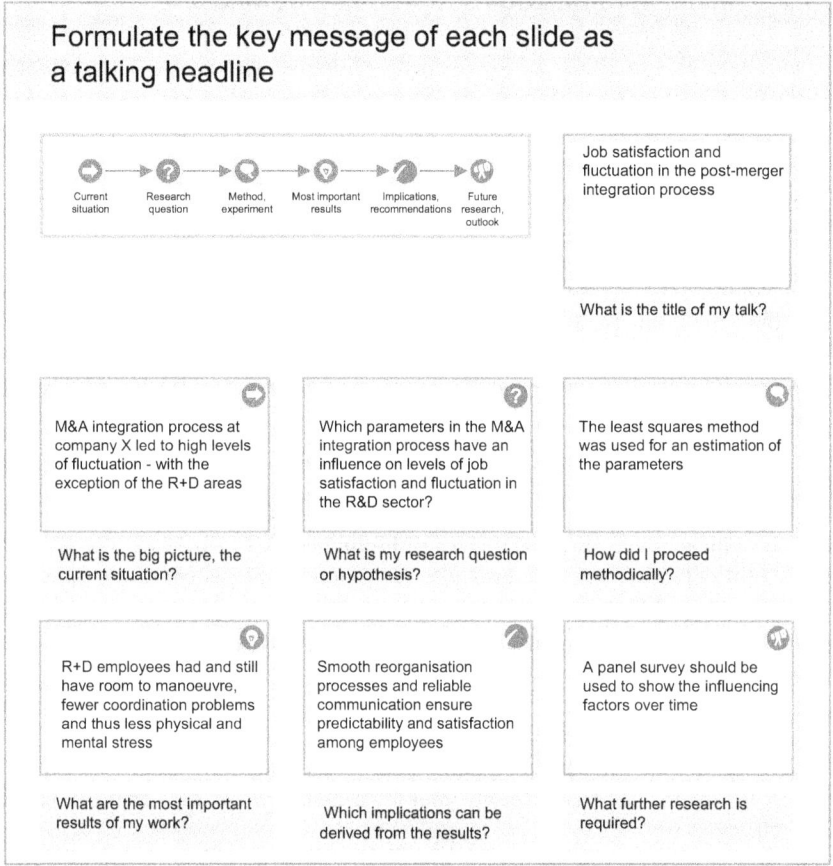

Fig. 3.5 Formulate the core message of each slide as a talking headline

What is permitted and useful is what aids understanding and the achievement of goals.

Rules of thumb for the use of media and the combination of media are:

- Only use media that you are proficient in.
- Check your media before the talk to make sure it is in working order.
- Only use more than two media in one talk in exceptional cases.
- Only combine media if it aids understanding.
- If possible, only use slides that you have created yourself or that you have helped to produce.

3.5.2 Main, Spontaneous and Permanent Media

Visualisation aids in a talk can be divided into main, spontaneous and permanent media.

The main medium is the medium that presenters use for most or all of their talk. In the vast majority of cases, this means the laptop and projector.

A spontaneous medium is used by speakers for smaller groups. Detached from the planned sequence, a detail or a special feature is sketched spontaneously. These unplanned additions can be shown on a board or flipchart.

By contrast, the permanent medium is visible in the room from the beginning and offers the audience the opportunity to access information that is helpful for the entire talk, such as the agenda, important formulas or definitions and variables. Boards, flipcharts and interactive whiteboards or smartboards can be used as permanent media.

3.5.2.1 The Projector

The projector or beamer, in combination with a computer, is now considered a reliable main medium in most scientific disciplines. It can be used for all group sizes, but it is predestined and unrivalled for groups of 35 people or more, because its projection surface can grow with the number of participants. It also transmits sound, images and videos as distinct to other media. Ideally, bright and quiet projectors should be used.

It is now the case that more wireless presentation systems such as ClickShare and wireless projectors are being used. In this way, organisers are complying with the wishes of many scientists of being able to present using their own computers. To be on the safe side, bring your own adapters for the different beamer connections.

A large projection surface and lots of bright light attract the audience's attention. This is why presenters should make sure that the projector does not dominate their presentation.

▶ In certain situations, it is a good idea to use a key combination on the computer or the presentation mouse to briefly turn the screen black without shutting down the computer.

3.5.2.2 Smartboards

A smartboard combines communication, collaboration and presentation functions in one. In the case of presentations to smaller groups or in hybrid settings, it is suitable for supplementing existing illustrations and creating new ones. Errors can be corrected, new ideas incorporated, results saved and immediately shared with all participants. If necessary, you can continue working on this at a later date.

3.5.2.3 Flipchart, Pinboard, Whiteboard and Blackboard

Flipcharts, pinboards and all forms of blackboards are rarely used as the main medium of talks, with a few exceptions. They are ideal for use as a permanent or spontaneous medium and can be used as a supplement to the beamer for small to medium-sized groups.

3.5.2.4 Spontaneous Use of Flipcharts, Pinboards and (Digital) Boards

Flipcharts and (digital) boards make a talk more interesting because their use breaks up the classic structure of the talk. Such media leave a special impression on the audience because they mark a change from the normal course of talks and are created specifically for the audience group. The handmade illustrations provide the audience the impression of being offered something special—something that goes beyond the normal content of the academic talk. Everyone appreciates this. Precisely because the visualisation is created by hand in the case of permanent media, and even in front of the eyes of all the audience in the case of spontaneous media, they appear less sterile than computer-generated slides or posters. This makes them ideal tools for attracting the audience's attention and highlighting things. They also support a more interactive style of talk.

In addition to these more psychological aspects, there is another reason to use spontaneous media in a scientific talk. They are an excellent tool to explain complex relationships step by step and thus facilitate understanding. The scientist has the option, for instance, of introducing a difficult formula "bit by bit" or to present an experiment successively.

3.5.2.5 Permanent Use of Flipcharts, Pinboards and Blackboards

Permanent media can be used to permanently display complex formulas, a picture of the object of the talk or the summary at the end of the talk. They provide the audience with detailed information, that they can read again and again to facilitate a better understanding and orientation. Interruptions to clarify comprehension issues can thus be reduced. In the case of rather heterogeneous audience groups in particular, permanent media help to bridge existing knowledge differences or gaps. Permanent media also lend themselves to homogeneous audiences. In addition, they can be used very well as a relaxing or dramaturgical element in the presentation and discussion. For example, speakers have the opportunity of lightening up their talk structure by pointing out and referring to the contents of the permanent medium.

▶ When using spontaneous media, the room layout, the number of participants and the expectations of the audience must be taken into account.

Academics using flipcharts, pinboards or whiteboards should first check with the organiser concerning the lecture room, their talk space and seating and consider the following:

- Spatial conditions

    Depending on the length and width of the lecture room, it is possible that only those people in the front rows can see the medium in its entirety. Audience members sitting further back will only see the top half of the visualisation because of the people sitting in front of them. A podium or u-shaped seating can help here.
- Group size

    Blackboards or flipcharts cannot be used for any number of participants because the visualisation area is smaller than that of most screens. Depending on the space available and the font size, the limit is probably reached at the latest when audiences of more than 30 people are present. Basically, the following applies: The bigger the group, the bigger the font size/writing or the sketch has to be and the less can be shown on one medium.
- Legible writing

    Anyone who wishes to use spontaneous or permanent media does not have to have beautiful handwriting, but legible handwriting. Those who tend to write cryptically should practise or have someone else prepare their spontaneous medium and add simple visualisations, such as arrows, numbering or highlighting, by hand in the presentation. Drawing skills are an advantage, but not essential. Many things can be represented with simple symbols or additionally explained with words. The audience are involved in the creation of spontaneous media from the very beginning and can thus follow every step—even if it was not perfectly represented visually.

    Anyone planning a separate presentation using the flipchart should practise beforehand. In this context, it is important to note that thick moderation pens are best suited for this type of visualisation. A broad line can be seen more easily than a narrow one and, on top of that, thin lines often look more wobbly. Researchers who regularly use spontaneous media use their own pens so as not to be dependent on items that have more or less dried-up at the talk venue.
- Expected standard of presentation

    Apart from the spatial conditions and the size of the group, the use of spontaneous or permanent media also depends on the occasion of the talk and the expected standard of presentation. At highly official or festive events, such aids are rather inappropriate. Exceptions are highly respected and reputable scientists who are allowed to break with conventions and whom the public respects for such breaches of taboos.

3.5.2.6 Videos

Videos represent a special form of media use at academic talks. Especially in the field of natural sciences, film sequences are used to show experiments or simulations. These cinematic contributions are characterised by the fact that moving images make a talk more lively. They give the audience the feeling that they are virtually live in a scientific experiment, and they seem more authentic and real than pictures or pure text. The audience can see the experimental set-up and the results for themselves. Complex or complicated processes can be presented more vividly using moving images. Videos are popular because they offer a departure from the standard, more speech and text-intensive sequence of the talk. They are ideal for heterogeneous audience groups. Regardless of their level of knowledge, every listener sees what has happened. Experts can also identify specific details.

As with all media, films must be easily recognisable. Shaky or barely decipherable material is unsuitable and should only be shown in exceptional cases—for example, when a non-repeatable trial has been recorded. Film sequences should be used sparingly and, above all, only briefly. Videos, shown over several minutes can have a soporific effect, especially if the lights are also turned off. Besides which, long films are risky because presenters lose contact with the audience. Where possible, they should comment on and explain their video themselves.

For all its importance, one thing is crucial when using media in a presentation: the linchpin remains the results presented and the speaker himself. Technology and media must not dominate the talk. It is the scientist who, as an expert on the subject, can provide new scientific knowledge and make the talk special using the selected content and his personality. Presenters run the risk of losing the overview and the common thread when there is too much media.

It is inappropriate and even frowned upon at academic events when speakers hold presentations with a considerable amount of multimedia tools and thus want to create the impression of a particularly high quality of talk. All too often this gives rise to the suspicion that the speaker is trying to conceal a lack of content through the use of technology and effects. A lack of scientific quality cannot be substituted by the presentation style, the media or a professional design.

▶ Rehearse your talk and media use and don't try to be perfect!

3.6 Poster—Illustrated Summary of Research

Poster presentations have become an increasingly important and popular medium of scientific communication. A poster, when designed professionally, presents complex contents and contexts in a condensed and simultaneously clear way. Due to its open dialogue character, it is more often a starting point for conversation and exchange with other researchers than is the case after a talk. Presenters are less likely to give a monologue and more likely to discuss matters with interested and interesting colleagues. This is also an opportunity to receive more detailed feedback and fresh impetus for one's own research project. Sometimes cooperation or career opportunities arise from the personal conversation. Poster sessions ensure that the conference is more varied and does not mutate into a marathon talk.

Posters are used at conferences in the so-called poster sessions. After the short presentations by the presenters, the participants can choose the topics on which they would like to learn more from the respective speaker and whose poster they would like to visit—as described in more detail in Chapter. 2.

3.6.1 Planning and Preparing Scientific Posters

Scientific posters follow the same structure as all other scientific papers and should therefore ideally also be created individually for the respective audience. As distinct from the classic talk, scientists at a poster session have the opportunity to make this individual adjustment in interchanges with visitors through oral explanations.

Figure 3.6 summarises the 8 most important rules for the design of scientific posters.

3.6.1.1 Gather Important Information Beforehand

First of all, it is important to find out from the organiser what the general guidelines are and what they are regarding the format and size of the poster. Scientists should also ask what the spatial and organisational conditions will be like on site. For

Fig. 3.6 The design of scientific posters in a nutshell

instance, if the presentation is conducted in a standing or sitting position, when, where and how are the posters attached? It helps to know how many people will be displaying their posters and which interesting people will be attending the event with whom a meeting could be arranged before the conference.

3.6.1.2 First Steps in the Preparation

Posters are media with a high density of information on a small surface. Even more so than with slides, the content and design elements should be designed in such a way that they serve to convey the core message and do not tend to distract people. Whether the work presented attracts interest or is even noticed depends on the visual impression it conveys. The design and layout should therefore visualise the information in such a way that the message is immediately understandable to the audience.

The subsequent form of presentation also plays a part in the design of the poster. The format should be chosen depending on whether the presentation will be made before a seated or standing audience. For instance, it is more comfortable for an audience seated in front of the poster if the poster is designed in a landscape format. A portrait medium would be difficult to read from a seated position from the second row of chairs in the lower section. In turn, such a poster would take up a lot of (too much) space in a poster session with standing visitors.

▶ Before starting to design the poster, think about the composition of your potential audience and the goal you want to achieve with your poster.

It is also important to determine what purpose the poster should serve. The design depends on this to a large extent. If it is a poster that will stand alone, then it must be created in a correspondingly self-explanatory and more detailed manner. If the focus of the medium is on supporting a poster pitch and for exchange with visitors the poster will get by with a significantly smaller amount of (detailed) information and using a design that is much less dense.

▶ Design the poster in an eye-catching and original way if you want to provoke interesting questions and reactions.

It is crucial that a poster is designed to be as easily comprehensible as possible. Abbreviations, foreign and technical terms should only be used if they can be assumed to be generally known or are explained in the presentation to the audience.

Those things that apply to talk also apply to posters: a storyline provides the professional framework for the preparation, presentation and exchanges.

3.6.1.3 Creating Posters Yourself

Students in particular often choose to create and print their own poster for reasons of time and cost. Common and easily available presentation programmes can be used for this purpose. Corresponding graphics programmes are more recommended and professional.

It is best to generate the poster in DIN A-4 format on the computer. Only when printing should the poster be transferred to the desired format. The easiest way to do this is to send the poster as a PDF file to a suitable copy shop or print shop.

Posters that are made up of many individual DIN A-4 sheets to form one large poster are less well suited and rather unprofessional. As a rule, such loose-leaf collections do not work very well and appear unconvincing. Where possible, researchers and students should only choose this form of poster production for informal talks. In most situations, it is worth investing in a computer-generated and professionally printed poster.

A special form of scientific poster is the handwritten poster. The selected content is presented on a flipchart sheet. Such posters have a special aura because they really are handmade. The other side of the coin is that they can also appear less professional at the same time.

The advantages of the form are certainly that it makes the speaker stand out from other posters, that it is inexpensive to create, that mistakes can be easily corrected and that modifications can be easily added. However, handmade posters usually do not meet the expected standard of presentation and thus do not suit every target group or every talk event.

If you want to use a handwritten poster, you need clean and secure block letters and a certain talent for drawing.

3.6.1.4 Creating Paper Posters and Having Them Printed Professionally

There are good reasons for having things printed by professionals. A poorly printed medium, with badly legible type, unclear illustrations and photo with altered colours can hardly leave a positive impression. The correction and time requirements are correspondingly high. For such time as paper posters—despite the great competition they face from e-posters—are used and an accepted means of communication by the scientific community, it makes sense to produce and print them professionally.

▶ If you want to be on the safe side, consult graphic designers during the design of the poster and commission them directly.

For the printing of the poster, there are some points that academics should know and consider to facilitate the production of a professional poster. To this end, it is first of all of great importance that the format specifications of the organiser are adhered to. Pictures of posters that partly extend to the floor because of their size or that overhang sideways demonstrate why compliance is necessary. A lot of research organisations also have their own corporate design, which—almost always—has to be used.

Photos must be in high resolution (at least 300 dpi), otherwise they weaken the effect of the poster or even reverse it. Motifs that are not, or barely recognisable, hardly motivate people to look at them (for a longer period).

For the printing, the poster should be saved as a PDF. In terms of the colour profile, CMYK is recommended (RGB works better for presentations). Finally, it is important to ask the printer concerning the bleed margin. This is the area that extends beyond the final format for processing reasons. This avoids white edges on the poster.

3.6.1.5 Creating an E-poster

In the following sections, the most important design elements and principles as well as basics for the layout are presented. E-posters are enjoying increasing popularity, due to the fact they provide numerous benefits that classic paper posters cannot offer. This starts with the high printing, paper and possibly postage costs that are not incurred with the electronic version. Visualisations can be easily enlarged to allow detailed views. Corrections and adjustments are no longer possible in the case of the printed poster, whereas the development process of a scientific project, for example, can be presented in e-format on a daily basis. Strictly speaking, the complete research process could be displayed on request. This form of presentation provides huge possibilities. It can conceivably be used for almost any occasion, in face-to-face events, virtually, for a scientific or a general audience. There is much to suggest that e-presentations will constitute the dominant form in the foreseeable future.

Using an e-poster, researchers can display many times more information, illustrations, photos and videos with links. There are then a large number of other pages behind the poster. Some researchers use the poster as a kind of overview page from which, in the discussion with interested conference participants, individually suitable pages can be accessed—offering a maximum level of target group orientation. The price for this is an enormous amount of time involved in the creation and maintenance of such a personal research database. Furthermore, researchers must somehow ensure that they know the structure of their presentation in order to navigate safely between the slides.

The e-poster, with a maximum of one additional page for source references, is currently frequently found in virtual presentations in an academic context—together with electronic versions of the paper poster. Both variants are more manageable and easier to control for the presenters and audience, reducing the challenges that virtual events bring (see Chapter 7).

The creation and design of e-posters follows the same rules that apply to classic posters and which are presented in the next section. Theoretically, smaller texts or images could be placed on electronic formats due to the zooming option. This is not recommended.

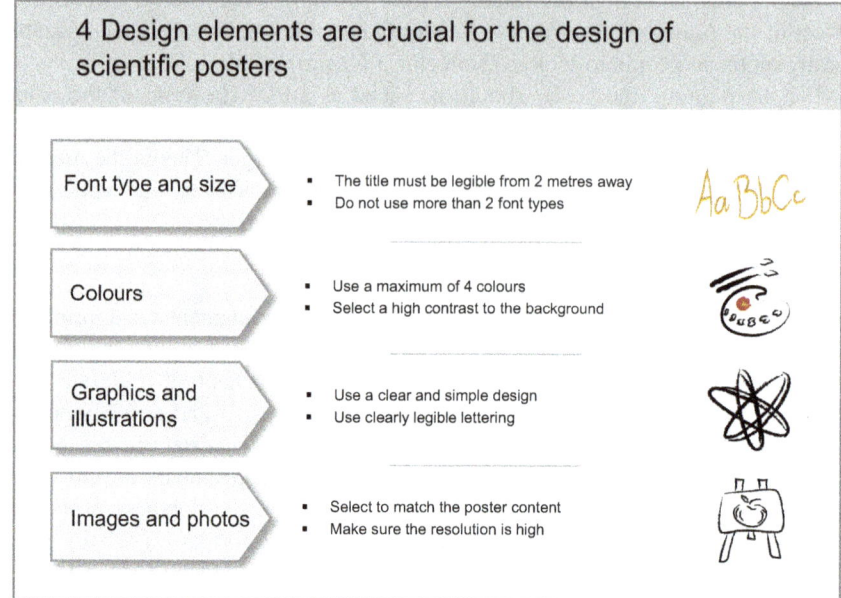

Fig. 3.7 Design elements are crucial for the design of scientific posters

3.6.2 Use Four Important Design Elements

Typically, the design includes the headlines, descriptive text and visualisations. Graphic elements, such as arrows or frames, are used for structuring and orientation. The combination of these elements is what makes a poster attractive. In addition, the reading direction from left to right and from top to bottom must be observed. Researchers should definitely mark deviations with arrows or at least by numbering them.

The four most important poster design elements are shown in Fig. 3.7.[14]

3.6.2.1 Font Type and Size

The font type is an indispensable element for posters. Sans serif fonts such as Arial and Helvetica are suitable for this purpose. They are easier to read even from a distance. One or two fonts are enough to ensure a professional appearance. More fonts complicate people's perception and confuse them. Different fonts help to emphasise a word or passage. Please note: both fonts should be completely different to achieve the best effect. The most effective and largest font should be used for the poster title. This should also be legible to passing participants from a distance of two metres, have a font size of between 80 and 100 points and be

---

[14] Own presentation.

placed in a prominent position on the poster—this can also be in the centre of the poster. It is important to highlight the poster's message and motivate participants to stop and ask questions. All other headings should also stand out from the rest of the text in terms of size, spacing and, if necessary, colour. For the content, academics choose a font size of between 24 and 32 points. Additional information, such as bibliographical references, does not have to be readable from a greater distance and can be written in a smaller font size to save space.

A sufficiently large line spacing ensures better readability and gives the poster a clearer appearance. Likewise, longer texts should be broken down into columns and breaks should be avoided. This improves the readability because viewers can focus on the text better and do not get lost in long lines. Left-aligned typesetting looks better, usually has fewer holes than justified text and is more up to date than centred alignment. It is also advisable to dispense with most of the distinctive features of a typeface because of their detrimental effects:

- Italics: Has low contrast to the normal font type and is not very suitable for posters because the difference is barely perceptible.
- Bold font: In the same way as colours, it immediately catches the eye and, when used selectively, is suitable to emphasise important things. If too much text is set in bold, it can appear like it is shouting at viewers.
- Capitals: Words and text that only consist of capital letters are more difficult to read and should only be used sporadically and with larger spacing between them.
- Underlining: Seems like a relic from the age of typewriters, it is better to use bold or colours to highlight things.

3.6.2.2 Colours

There is a multitude of—in some cases contradictory—tips and advice for the choice of colours in poster design. Much of this is a matter of taste and judgement. Readability is the decisive criterion. Colours structure the poster and attract people's attention. They are particularly suitable for highlighting and demarcation. They help visitors to orientate themselves more quickly with regard to the poster and to distinguish between what is important and what is less important. Therefore, they should be used consistently. For example, if you have decided to write titles in blue, you should keep this consistent for the entire poster.

It is important to use colours selectively and in moderation. This concerns the number of different colours, the frequency with which they are used and how rich in contrast they are. Too many colours and too much use of colour distract the viewer and are therefore usually counterproductive and can have an oppressive effect. Poster backgrounds with stripes, patterns, gradients or watermarks achieve a similar effect. They distract from the content and therefore do not facilitate an easier understanding of the poster.

In overall terms, it is advisable not to use more than four colours and to ensure a high contrast between the font and background—i.e. light font on a dark background and vice versa.

> **Practical tip**
> Remember: if you use too many colours, then no one single thing is highlighted any more, everything is colourful.

3.6.2.3 Graphics, Illustrations and Diagrams

Using graphics, illustrations and diagrams, scientists have a tool to hand with which they can visualise information and text and thus make their poster clearer and more appealing. These visualisation options serve as eye-catchers and can present complex things more simply than is possible with text. This is important because experience shows that less text usually means more visitors. A clear and simple design together with easy-to-understand labelling, form the basis for effective and enriching illustrations.

Ideally, researchers design their graphics, illustrations and diagrams so that they are self-explanatory. If the scientist cannot be at the poster for a moment, visitors still have the opportunity to gain an impression of his/her research. Legends and inscriptions are correspondingly important.

3-D graphics, distracting graphic, decoration or gradients should be avoided.

3.6.2.4 Photos

Scientific posters tend to be text-heavy. Visualisation elements such as graphics, illustrations and diagrams, but above all photos, break up long passages. The following applies to all of them: they must be sufficiently large and have legends. Photos appeal to emotions, are usually a unique selling point and therefore easily attract visitors. They are almost always a powerful way of standing out from other posters. They arouse people's curiosity, increase their levels of attention and are more easily remembered.

There are four points to consider when using photos:

1. When selecting photos, it is imperative that the image fits the theme of the poster.
2. In order to be able to print photos in high quality, researchers must ensure that the resolution is printable (at least 300 dpi).
3. Photos from the internet usually have a lower resolution.
4. Most illustrations and photos on the internet are protected, which poses the risk that copyrights could be infringed.

▶ Depending on the research discipline, scientists have samples, specimens and prototypes to attach to posters or to place in front of them.

In Chapter 4 you will find more in-depth information on design elements.

3.6.3 Considering the Design Principles of Proximity, Alignment, Repetition and Contrast

These four principles help in the layout and arrangement of the design elements on the poster and on other visualisations.[15]

3.6.3.1 Proximity

Elements that have a close proximity are perceived as belonging together. For this reason, components that belong together in terms of content should also be arranged close to each other on the poster. This helps to organise the information and creates a visual unit. Conversely, parts that do not belong together in terms of content should be clearly separated spatially on the poster.

This provides the layout with a logical structure, it appears orderly and clear. The necessary white space is created and the viewer can orientate himself more quickly at first glance.

3.6.3.2 Alignment

No part of a poster should be randomly or haphazardly placed. The uniform alignment of elements provides a (subtle) visual link between the elements of the poster. It conveys a sense of order and guides the eye of the person viewing it. This makes the poster look more structured and professional. Central alignment is often chosen for headlines in particular, but this is not always effective. For instance, left or right alignment makes the poster look tidier because it creates an invisible connecting line.

3.6.3.3 Repetition

Recurring elements might be the same fonts, colours, accentuations and graphic elements. This creates a certain constancy that makes the poster appear calmer and generates a recognition value. This creates a uniform and consistent impression and makes it easier for the viewer to find their way around.

3.6.3.4 Contrast

Two elements that are not the same should be clearly distinguishable from each other, i.e. have a marked contrast. Contrasts increase the visual impact and thus arouse the viewer's interest. Contrast can be created using different colours, sizes and shapes.

The clear highlighting of important elements makes them more interesting. Thus, it helps to structure the information in such a way that the important content can be distinguished from the less important content and a clear hierarchy is created. A marked contrast must be selected, especially for the background and font.

---

[15] https://www.sciencedirect.com/topics/computer-science/gestalt-principle

3.6.4 Designing Scientific Posters

3.6.4.1 Creating a Sketch of the Layout

The design of a poster starts with a sheet of paper. The computer is not needed at this point. In the first step, scientists list the content and visualise the order of the individual elements—a storyline is useful for this, as it is for the talk. Following this, produce a rough sketch of the poster by dividing up space on the sheet. To this end, the researcher positions placeholders for the individual information blocks and illustrations in such a way that priorities and focal points are visualised.

One of the most important principles related to poster design concerns the unprinted space of a poster or other visualisation. Experience shows that this white space is too small on most posters and slides because most researchers want to place as much information as possible on them. White space reduces distractions on the poster, provides space and air to what is important and forms the basis for the individual points of a visualisation to be perceived better and to come into their own. This makes it easier for viewers to grasp the content. Effective posters require a sufficient amount of white space.

▶ The ratio of text, illustrations and white space should be approximately: 50% - 30% - 20%.

3.6.4.2 Integrating Content Within the Poster

The contents of the poster are added to the sketch in the second step. This includes the elements of the storyline and a strong headline that displays the poster's core message. Talking headlines are predestined for this. They immediately catch the eye, motivate people to come closer, and save space that would otherwise have been used for the generic title. Tables and formulas should be used sparingly and a frame does not have to be drawn around all elements. Now the poster can be created on the computer.

In addition to research-related content, academics should also think about the following supplements:

- Your name and affiliation with the logo
- The names of your co-authors
- The funding body, if applicable
- References
- Short acknowledgement, if applicable

Figure 3.8 shows steps to complete a poster sketch.

3.6 Poster—Illustrated Summary of Research

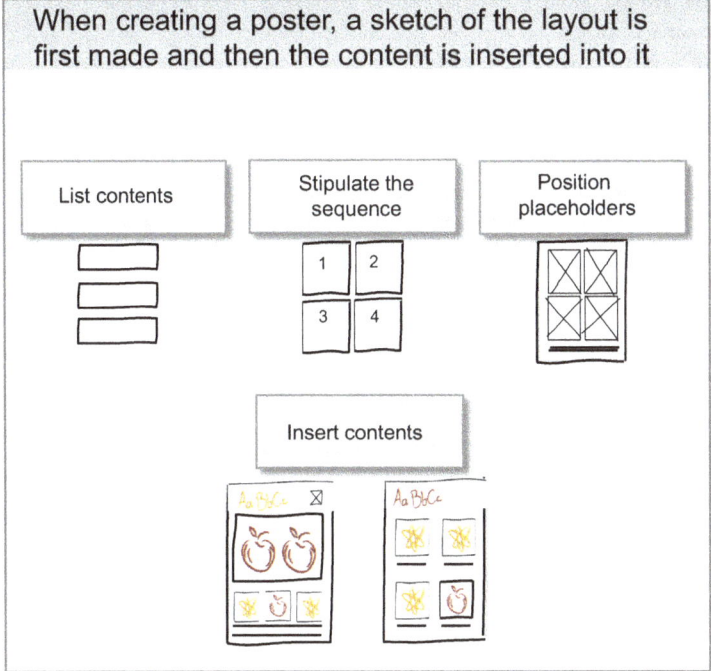

Fig. 3.8 When creating a poster, a sketch of the layout is first made and then the content is inserted into it

3.6.5 Tips for Poster Presentations

The presentation of the poster differs from that used at a classical scientific conference. In academic talks, presenters are subject to a (strict) time limit, while in poster sessions the participants determine how long each talk lasts. Unlike at classical conferences, where researchers have the attention of a larger audience in their time slot, at a poster presentation they speak to just a few people, sometimes only one person. On the one hand, this offers the opportunity to interchange ideas more intensively, to discuss details and to expand the network. On the other hand, scientists compete for the audience's attention at poster sessions.

Scientists should prepare themselves for this. The checklist shown in Fig. 3.10 with the most important things scientists should take with them for a successful exhibition and the eleven tips for professional and effective behaviour at a poster session will help in this regard.

1. Reflect on how you can capture the attention of conference goers who are moving around and are exposed to many distractions.
2. Stay by your poster as long as possible and take advantage of this opportunity, even if the given attendance time is over.

3. Stand next to your poster and offer a friendly look to people passing by.
4. Actively approach and invite interested people.
5. Just briefly (!) present yourself.
6. Use your poster and pitch as conversation openers.
7. Structure the exchange with visitors mainly as a dialogue and to a lesser extent as a presentation.
8. Refer to the elements of your poster and guide the visitor's gaze.
9. Actively request assessments or feedback from your visitors and note them down.
10. Carefully and in a manner that saves face make sure that visitors have understood your presentation and information.
11. Distribute printouts of the poster or your business cards to interested people who do not have time for a (longer) conversation.
12. For the follow-up and subsequent contacts, write down the dates of interesting interviewees and a few key words about the content.

Figure 3.9 shows the poster of an economist who was awarded the Best Poster Award 2018 at the European Association of Labour Economists (EALE) in Lyon.[16]

A checklist of the most important things for a successful poster session can be found in Fig. 3.10.

---

[16] Terry Gregory, Senior Researcher at Leibniz-Zentrum für Europäische Wirtschaftsforschung [Leibniz Centre for European Economic Research] (ZEW). Conference of the European Association of Labour Economists (EALE) in Lyon, 2018.

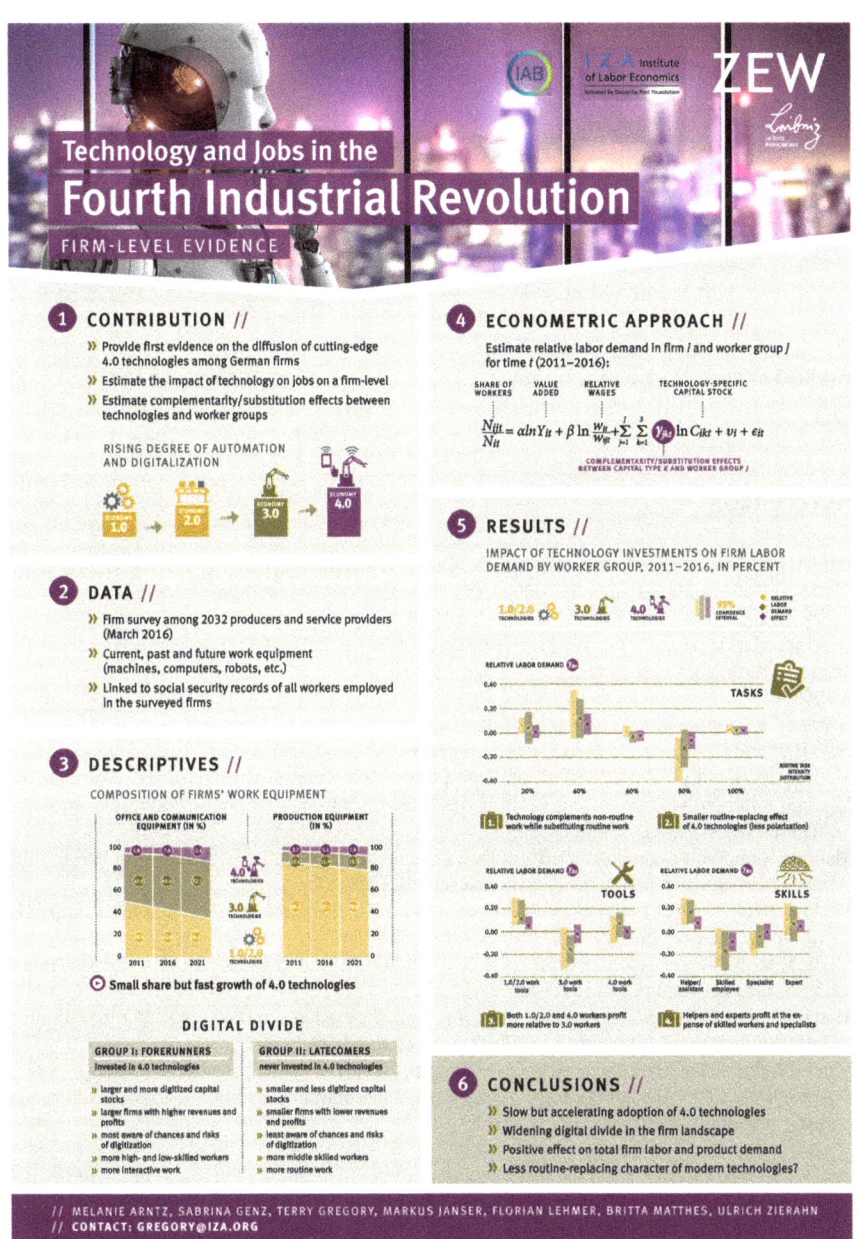

Fig. 3.9 Award-winning example poster

CHECK LIST FOR POSTER SESSIONS

- ☐ The poster in a protective poster roll
- ☐ Double-sided sticking tape, masking tape, scissors and pins
- ☐ Samples, prototypes and examples
- ☐ DIN A4 printouts of the poster with contact details on the reverse side
- ☐ Copies of the paper and other relevant own papers
- ☐ Business cards with current contact information

Fig. 3.10 Checklist for poster sessions

References

Deutsche Forschungsgemeinschaft, 2022, Good research practice, https://www.dfg.de/en/principles-dfg-funding/basics-and-principles-of-funding/good-scientific-practice, last retrieved: 29.12.2023

Graebig, Markus et al.: "Wie aus Ideen Präsentationen werden", 2011, Gabler Verlag

Gregory, Terry: Conference of the European Association of Labour Economists (EALE) in Lyon, 2018

Grimpe Christoph: No date indicated, Talk, Kopenhagen Business School

Hey, Barbara: "Präsentieren in Wissenschaft und Forschung", 2nd edition, 2019, Springer Verlag

Medina, John, No year indicated, Brain Rules, https://brainrules.net, last retrieved: 29.12.2023

Medina, John, No year indicated, Brain Rules Excerpt: Introduction, https://brainrules.net/introduction/, last retrieved: 29.12.2023

Medina, John, No year indicated, Brain Rules—Rule #4: We don't pay attention to boring thing, https://brainrules.net/attention/, last retrieved: 29.12.2023

Medina, John, No year indicated, Brain Rules—Rule #9: Stimulate more of the senses, https://brainrules.net/sensory-integration/, last retrieved: 29.12.2023

Medina, John, No year indicated, Brain Rules—Rule #10: Vision trumps all other senses, https://brainrules.net/vision/, last retrieved: 29.12.2023

Mietzner, Mark: 2018, Mergers & Acquisitions, https://wirtschaftslexikon.gabler.de/definition/mergers-acquisitions-41789/version-265148, last retrieved: 29.12.2023

Minto, Barbara: The Pyramid Principle, 3. Edition, 2021, Financial Times Prent. Verlag

ScienceDirect, 2023, Gestalt Principle https://www.sciencedirect.com/topics/computer-science/gestalt-principle, last retrieved: 29.12.2023

Visualisation in the Talk—Design Slides in a Professional Manner

Hardly any scientific talk can be a success without visualising the content. This visual support serves two purposes. On the one hand, it makes it easier for the audience to grasp, understand and retain information and, at the same time, it acts as a memory aid and guide for the presenter. The most frequently used medium at scientific events is the slide.

Despite the very frequent use of slides, they often fail to achieve the desired effect. Instead of helping people to take in the content of the talk and making the presentation varied, they often achieve the opposite effect: they tire or confuse people. This effect is fuelled by the understandable desire of many scientists to show as much of their own work as possible and the numerous technical options of the current presentation programmes. It is no coincidence that the martial-sounding term "Death by powerpoint"[1] has emerged for business and academic talks. This often includes too many slides with too much information and too many bullet points (!). Whether slides help or hinder the talk depends to a large extent on how they are structured. Well-designed slides help people to understand science better and avoid misunderstandings. To this end, it is important that scientists understand how people perceive things and how the brain functions in these situations.

▶ Everything presented in a talk must be related to the topic of the presentation and the talk's objective. It must also be created in a manner that suits the audience, be easy to read and be presented in a way that is as easy on people's brains as possible.

---

[1] https://www.smallbusinesscomputing.com/software/death-by-powerpoint/.

Drawing on these findings from the fields of the psychology of perception and brain research, this chapter shows what it takes to create effective slides for scientific talks. It first introduces important basics of design, then illustrates classical as well as illustrative visualisation elements and concludes with five tried-and-tested layouts for (scientific) slides.

4.1 Fundamentals of Design—Nine Rules for Better Slides

Human perception has adapted to living conditions over the course of evolution, producing cognitive abilities that help us recognise patterns, orient ourselves and grasp complex images more easily. It is precisely these so-called gestalt principles or laws[2] that speakers should know about and use when creating their slides. Nine of these rules are of particular importance and are briefly outlined here.

1. Contrast
   Contrast ensures that objects can be seen. The higher the contrast, the more they stand out from the background and the better they can be perceived. When designing the slides, it is therefore important to ensure clear differences in font sizes and the colours of objects and lines. Backgrounds should be light or dark and presented without gradients or the like.

2. Quantity
   The larger the amount of text or illustrations, the longer viewers need to grasp and understand content. At the same time, this ensures that they tire more quickly and their interest wanes. Presenters should show as little text as possible.

3. Proximity
   Human perception captures elements that are close together, all belonging together. Speakers can therefore show what belongs together (proximity) and what does not (distance) in a simple and effective way through the geographical distance of the objects.

4. Colour
   Colours are probably the best way to emphasise differences, what belongs together, what is special or important. When using slides, people's attention is immediately drawn to things that are highlighted in colour. This should be used carefully, as the effect of colour weakens and even disappears completely if it is used too often. Colour assignments should be kept consistent within a slide set.

---

[2] http://www.scholarpedia.org/article/Gestalt_principles.

5. Size
   Size has a similar effect on people's perception as colour. Differences in importance and significance are (also) visualised via the size and changes to it. This is how the development of data over a period of time can be visually represented. When using text in particular it is important to define levels of structure and thus a hierarchy with different sizes.

6. Shape
   Forms can be used to illustrate togetherness and differentiation. Similarly to colour and size, the viewer very quickly perceives and pays attention to differences in form. Shapes rank among the things that can be visualized using images that are more easily recognised and understood than text.

7. Alignment
   Neatly aligned elements make a slide clear and give the viewer a good level of orientation. Carefully aligned objects make the relationships between them clear and the slide appears less irritating and stressful.

8. New and unexpected things
   If you present or do something new or unexpected, you increase your audience's level of interest in a flash. People like surprises and are curious about what is coming. Speakers can increase and hold people's attention with unexpected elements. New and unexpected things should only be shown very selectively, perhaps even only once in the talk.

9. Movement
   Films and other forms of moving images are among the best attention grabbers available to speakers. They are more detailed and precise than static forms of visualisation and make it much easier to understand a slide. In addition, animations can also be used to control the audience's attention when elements are faded in one after the other (Fig. 4.1).[3]

4.2 Classical and Illustrative Visualisation Elements

Four classic and four illustrative building blocks are available for the design of slides. The core of these forms of visualisation is briefly outlined below. In the second section of this chapter, you will find tips and examples for the coherent use of these and other ways in which to design slides for scientific talks.

---

[3] All illustrations in this chapter are own representations or labelled with a source.

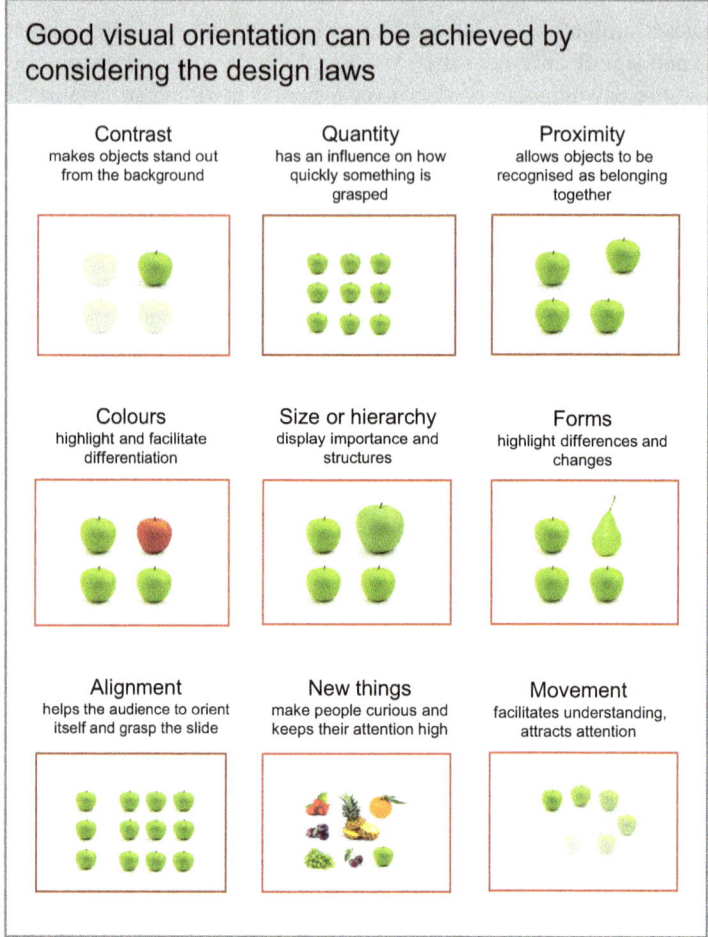

Fig. 4.1 Good visual orientation can be achieved by considering the design laws

4.2.1 Classic Visualisation Elements

Researchers tend to use classic visualisation methods such as texts, tables, diagrams and structural images for their talks. This is supported by the fact that these forms of presentation help to create an objective and factual impression, which is in line with the general understanding of science. In addition, the classic components are relatively easy to create and they show the content of the talk in a straightforward, functional and sober way (Fig. 4.2).

4.2.1.1 Text Images

Text images are used (too) frequently in scientific talks. They constitute the first choice for headlines, descriptions, text-based overviews or bulleted lists. It is only

4.2 Classical and Illustrative Visualisation Elements

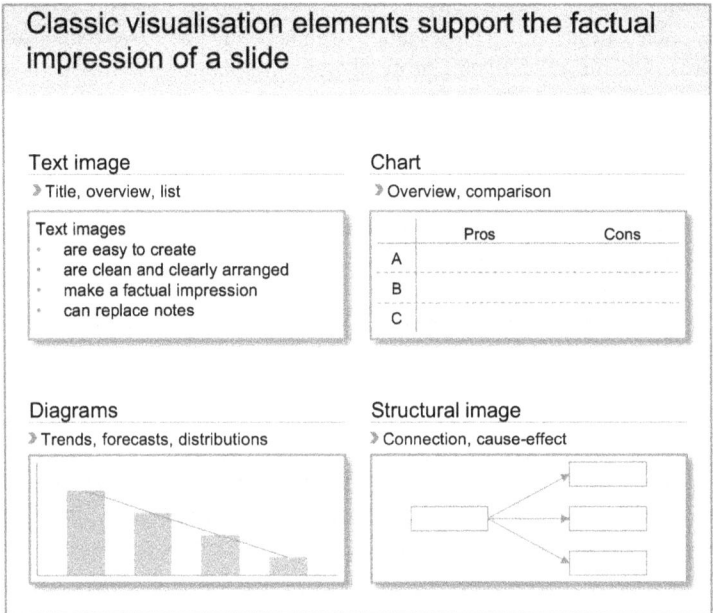

Fig. 4.2 Classic visualisation elements support the factual impression of a slide

possible to replace them with other visualisation elements in a few situations. Using the format templates of the different presentation programmes, uniform slides can be produced in a short time. It is important to ensure that the templates fit the occasion and—if available—take into account the corporate design of your own research organisation.

Text images are not images in the true sense of the word. Text and images are processed in different areas of the brain and text causes a significantly greater increase in the cognitive load than is the case with images. Too much text early on has a detrimental effect on the audience's concentration and attention.

Add to this the fact that there is a certain seductive character of presentation programmes. These make it easy for presenters to quickly create a few more text slides just to be on the safe side. If you only present text, you run the risk of just reading it aloud and your presentation becoming monotonous and tiring. Experienced presenters like to call such slides "reading tracks".

4.2.1.2 Tables

In almost all scientific disciplines, data is displayed in the form of tables. They facilitate a detailed and systematic presentation of many individual values in rows and columns. Tables are very suitable when precise values or a detailed presentation of many individual values as well as their correlations should be presented. In this process, a lot of information is summarised, for instance, in order to depict frequencies or correlations of variables. However, this is precisely the reason why tables in scientific presentations often mutate into overloaded numerical graveyards. On the other hand, professionally prepared tables help to condense large amounts of data and structure them more clearly. They thus reduce detailed descriptive text and usually form the basis for diagrams and charts in scientific presentations. Capturing the data usually takes more time than is required for pictorial representations. Tables can be used as the sole form of data presentation or combined with other types of visualisation—such as text or diagrams.

4.2.1.3 Charts

Charts are the tool of choice when it comes to the graphical representation of statistical data. They clarify relations to other results in addition to quantitative correlations between variables. Charts are also very suitable for illustrating developments, forecasts or for changes over a certain period of time. The use of charts is recommended especially in those cases where several or complicated sets data or several complicated sets of data are to be compared or the use of tables would be too confusing. Visualised data in charts appear to be clearer and more descriptive than those displayed in tabular form or as text and can be grasped more quickly by the audience. Professionally designed charts that take into account human perception patterns are a prerequisite in ensuring diagrams are not misleading, and are better understood and retained.

4.2.1.4 Structural Images

When sequences, processes or dynamic systems are simplified, reduced to the most important things and clearly presented in scientific presentations, structural charts are often used. They reduce the complex and complicated aspects by displaying a general, rough sketch that illustrates the parts of the system and their relationships and interdependencies. The individual components are visualised with differently labelled geometric shapes or symbols and the connections are clarified using lines and arrows. The advantages of structural images lie in their simplicity, which facilitates a rapid overview and focus less on details and more upon the whole. They are not appropriate for detailed and in-depth descriptions

4.2.2 Illustrative Visualisation Elements

"The human being, creature of eyes, needs the image." Leonardo da Vinci summed up the importance of pictorial representations in this way and illustrates why science should definitely use pictorial visualisation alternatives in addition to the classical visualisation elements. These enrich presentations and make them more comprehensible, varied and memorable. The following section presents four frequently used illustrative elements. Figure 4.3 presents the most important illustrative elements at a glance.

4.2 Classical and Illustrative Visualisation Elements

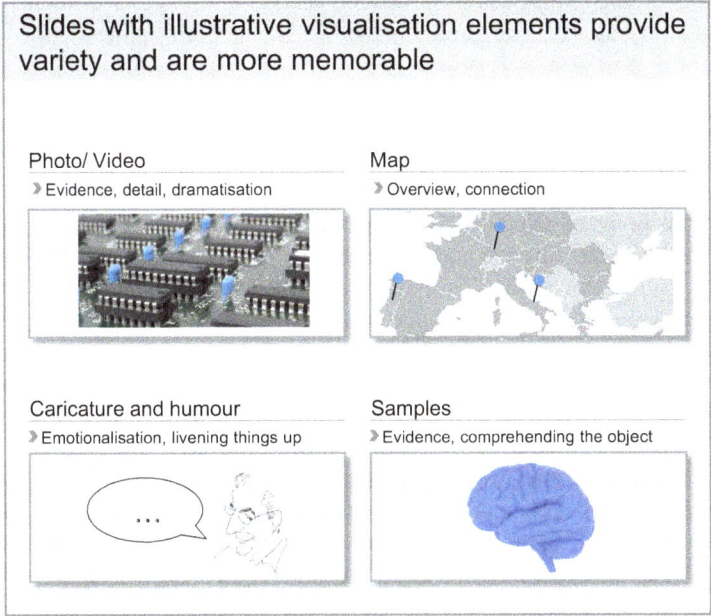

Fig. 4.3 Slides with illustrative visualisation elements provide variety and are more memorable

4.2.2.1 Photos and Videos

Photos and videos enable presenters to share their research with the audience almost up close and personal. Both have long been used in science. To this day, film sequences in particular are the most powerful tools to visually substantiate the data, display the set-up of an experiment and present observable results, processes or details to the audience. Both videos and photos can be used for different purposes.

In the case of a picture or a film sequence, academics have forms of visualisation at their disposal with which they can make a talk more realistic and lively. They combine a high level of probative value and persuasiveness and provide variety in a presentational daily routine that is dominated by text. (Moving) images are suitable for all target groups for the science communication and can thus address a much wider audience—ranging from scientific specialists to all groups of the interested public.

4.2.2.2 Maps

Maps depict conditions, objects and processes to scale and explain them. This form of visualisation facilitates the understanding of complex spatial relationships in a talk. Maps can present a lot of content in a very condensed way without having to write a lot of text. This can be both an advantage and a disadvantage at the same time. A lower level of detail can improve clarity, but can result in misinterpretations. Maps can be structured according to various criteria. They are used with varying frequency in the individual research disciplines.

4.2.2.3 Caricatures, Cartoons and Comics

At first glance, caricatures or comic character do not seem very suitable for use in scientific presentations. By way of a general understanding, talks should be factual, reliable and limited to the essentials. The critical outlook of many researchers, even to the point of rejection, is not without justification. Humorous interludes can be misinterpreted by the audience and give the impression that there is a lack of due scientific earnestness. Despite all the justified reservations, caricatures and comics are valuable tools to enhance one's own talk. First and foremost, they do, when employed correctly, make the speaker's job easier, because the atmosphere is more relaxed. They also offer the audience points of reference and things they can associate with. This helps people to better understand and retain what is said.

4.2.2.4 Samples and Demonstration Objects

This form of visualisation does not directly form part of the slide design, but it can complement it well. Samples and demonstration objects offer scientists a special opportunity to present the results of their work and increase the public's interest in it. Therefore, before a presentation, researchers should consider which physically tangible objects (such as a three-dimensional model of a person's internal organs or a sealing profile made of a new rubber compound) might fit the occasion, goal and audience of the talk.

In most talks, the speaker addresses the visual and the auditory perception channel of the audience. If he also provides an object that the audience can touch and test, he additionally addresses the haptic channel. This gives the audience the opportunity to "grasp" the object, the sample or the specimen. In this way, interested parties can gain their own impression of the structure, composition, weight or functioning of the object and are not exclusively dependent on the description of the speakers.

The use of objects is particularly useful with smaller groups of spectators. Poster sessions are very well suited to providing the interested audience with an object, such as a prototype. At large events or where there are many visitors at a poster presentation, it is less advisable to let a sample wander through the rows. That would be very time-consuming and would create a constant source of unrest that the scientist would have to react upon. In such cases, the object can be displayed at the end of the talk in an easily accessible place for interested parties. If this is not possible, the researcher shows the object to the audience, even if this means that the effect of touching is lost in the process.

4.3   Five Principles for Effective Slides in Academic Talks

The importance of effectively designed visualisation in academic talks (and not only these) can be well illustrated by the typical reactions of the audience at such events.

If many text-dominated slides with formulated sentences are presented at a conference, it can usually be observed that one part of the audience listens, another reads the text, a third group jumps between the spoken and written word and the remaining people are busy with something else. In a nutshell: The focus of the conference participants is is directed towards different points on the slide. This kind of situation is difficult for speakers to navigate around and the question remains: What will the audience talk from this talk?

▶   It is crucial for presenters to capture and maintain the attention of their audience so that their work can be seen, understood and developed.

At this juncture, the cognitive load theory of the Australian educational psychologist John Sweller provides valuable clues. It states that people only have a very limited ability to process new information.[4] The cognitive load is the total amount of power required to do this. These processes take place in people's working memory, which, unlike the long-term memory, is limited both in terms of its capacity and in the length of time it stores information. If the working memory reaches its load threshold, information can no longer be (correctly) stored. Once this point has been reached, hardly any, and in the worst case no message from the speaker can be taken in. The affected people in the audience switch off or turn to other activities. They are very unlikely to take anything away from the talk and will probably not contribute to the discussion.

What can scientists do to counteract this? The decisive part where the cognitive load is concerned, is played by the difficulty and complexity of the information on the one hand and its presentation and design on the other. This means that talks and the way of presenting have to change. Researchers should therefore be aware that they have a strong influence on whether and how the information is received by the audience by means of the design of their slides and the way they present content. This is equally important for all presentations, but becomes even more significant where this is a heterogeneous or lay audience against the backdrop of external science communication events.

Where the slide design is concerned, five strategies have proven effective in reducing the cognitive load and turning slides into useful visualizations. These are presented below (Fig. 4.4).

---

[4] https://www.sciencedirect.com/science/article/abs/pii/B9780123876911000028.

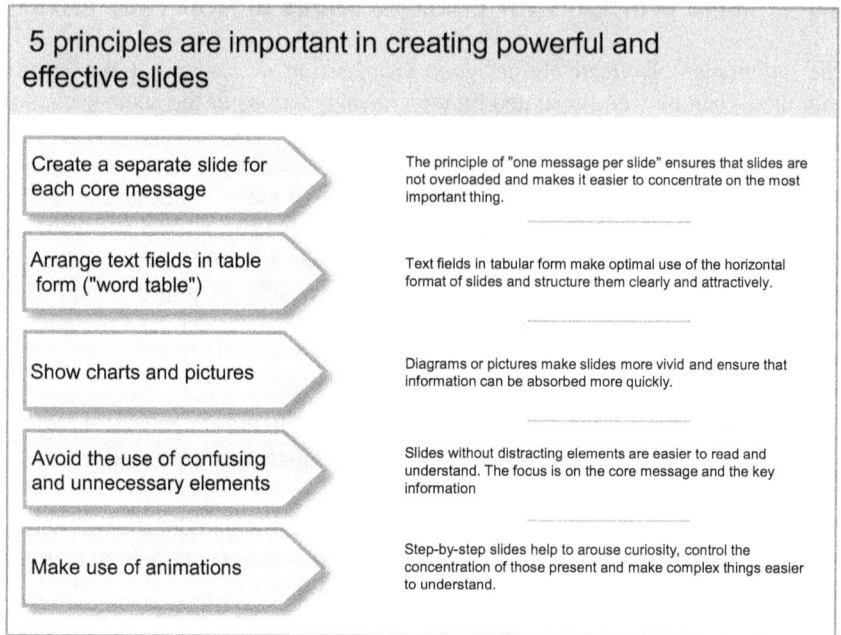

Fig. 4.4 5 principles are important in creating powerful and effective slides

4.3.1 Create a Separate Slide for Each Core Message and Vice Versa

Many details and especially large amounts of text heard and read at the same time increase the cognitive load for the viewer. They make it difficult for people to understand and retain what is presented. This is especially true when presenting complex or complicated content, or when speaking quickly and without pauses. In this context, it is interesting to note that experience shows that it is not the number of slides that makes a lecture exhausting for the audience, but rather the amount of information per slide.

▶ Remember: A rather low density of information suitable for the audience and readability from all seats in the auditorium are the guiding principles that apply to any form of visualisation.

The principle of "one message per slide" applies here. The idea is to create a separate slide for each important point of a lecture, where the information about it is broken up and presented in small, easier-to-digest pieces. On the one hand, this ensures that the slides are not overloaded and that the audience can thus concentrate on one aspect. Both contribute towards reducing the cognitive load. At the same time, this principle allows researchers to allow their most important

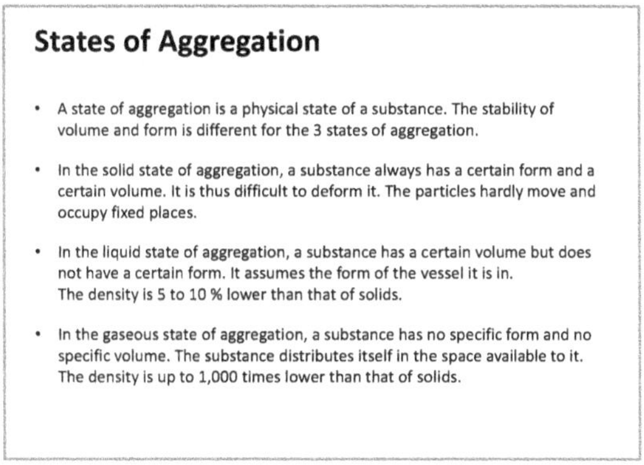

Fig. 4.5 Generic titles are less specific and concrete

> **States of Aggregation**
>
> - A state of aggregation is a physical state of a substance. The stability of volume and form is different for the 3 states of aggregation.
> - In the solid state of aggregation, a substance always has a certain form and a certain volume. It is thus difficult to deform it. The particles hardly move and occupy fixed places.
> - In the liquid state of aggregation, a substance has a certain volume but does not have a certain form. It assumes the form of the vessel it is in. The density is 5 to 10 % lower than that of solids.
> - In the gaseous state of aggregation, a substance has no specific form and no specific volume. The substance distributes itself in the space available to it. The density is up to 1,000 times lower than that of solids.

message sufficient space on the slide. This makes it less likely that other, subordinate information will take the visibility and impact away from the core message. The presenter formulates this as a concise sentence, which is placed as a title in the header. Following this, the slide is supplemented with all the necessary information, graphics, pictures or other required elements.

4.3.1.1 Core Message as Slide Title—Talking Headlines

The larger an object is in relation to others, the more attention it attracts. Interestingly, this is true even when the large object is completely irrelevant, as Michael J. Proulx of Queen Mary University of London notes in a study.[5] Here it becomes clear how important it is to mark important things about size as such. From the point of view of perception psychology, the title line of a slide is a good place to put the core message. On the one hand, in the default setting of most presentation programmes, the font is significantly larger than that of a slide text and labels of tables or diagrams. Moreover, this is the place where the viewer's gaze first rests (top left). It is important to make use of this prominent position.

Descriptive headings that succinctly summarise the most important message of the slide are suitable for this purpose: The Talking Headlines (see also Chapter 3). Unlike generic or abstract titles such as "Literature" or "Motivation", Talking Headlines are specific and allow the audience to (more) quickly grasp and retain what this slide is about.

The following figures demonstrate the different impact of a generic title (Fig. 4.5)[6] by contrast with talking headlines (Fig. 4.6) and the principle of one message per slide.

Talking headlines do not only offer advantages to the audience but also to the presenters themselves. In addition to the clarity, the focus on the most important statement and the easier perception, they also represent a pleasant orientation aid. If you have lost the thread or have been distracted for a moment, you will find the

---

[5] https://journals.plos.org/plosone/article?id=10.1371/journal.pone.0015293.
[6] https://studyflix.de/chemie/aggregatzustand-einfach-erklart-4087.

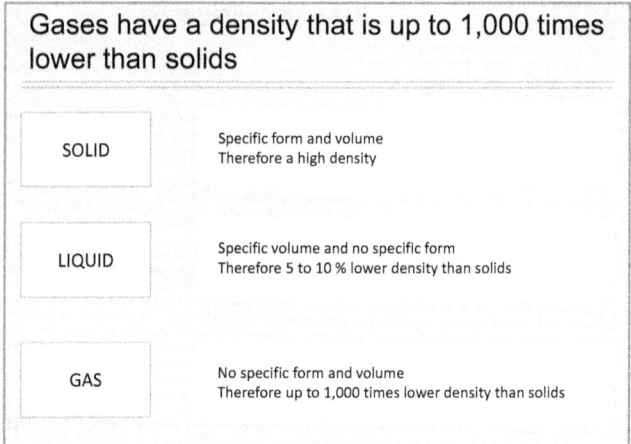

Fig. 4.6 Talking headlines articule the key message of a slide

red thread again more quickly with the heading "One message per slide ensures that slides are not overloaded" than with the general title "Lecture headings" (Fig. 4.7).

Talking headlines should ...

- ... be self-explanatory.
- ... be relevant to the audience and related to the topic of the slide/tallk.
- ... should use as many words as necessary and as few words as possible.
- ... include results, special features, challenges, unusual or new features.
- ... ideally state the key message of the slide.

4.3.1.2 Assertion-Evidence Approach—Supporting Key Messages with Visual Evidence

In this context the Assertion-Evidence Approach (AEA) by Michael Alley, professor of technical communication at Pennsylvania State University, who researches the effectiveness of different designs for presentation slides, is very interesting and helpful.[7] The AEA works according to the "one-message-per-slide principle". In the case of the AEA, the headline consists of a concise statement, the core message, in the form of a talking headline. In the large text field of the slide, (preferably visual) evidence supports and substantiates this statement and therefore this approach is also very suitable for scientific presentations. Compared to bullet

---

[7] https://www.assertion-evidence.com/.

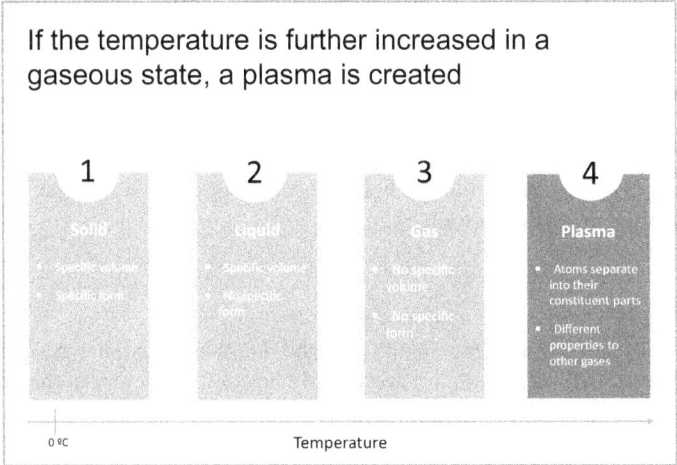

Fig. 4.7 Key message of the slide as a title—If gas is further heated, a plasma is created

point lists, forms of slide design such as the AEA help the audience understand and retain significantly more information.[8]

The default settings of presentation programmes such as PowerPoint consisted for a long time of a short heading and a large text field with little difference in font size, prompting bullet points of text and thus violating the basics of perception described above. Microsoft has responded by adding an AEA template to PowerPoint in 2022.[9]

4.3.1.3 Number of Slides

Reducing the amount of information on a slide is an important step in keeping the audience's level of attention high. Nevertheless, the number of slides must not be completely neglected. In some scientific talks, the aim seems to be to show as many slides as possible in the allotted time. In consultations and training sessions, this repeatedly leads to questions about the number of slides that may be shown per time unit or how long one should spend talking on each slide. It is obvious that researchers should adapt the amount of slides shown to the time window and the receptiveness of the audience and reduce it in case of doubt. It is just as obvious that adhering to a meticulous specification does not really help anyone in the talk. If you are constantly clicking through your set of slides, you will miss the actual purpose of the talk, no matter how slim the number of slides.

There is a lot of information about this in books and on the internet, and the correct answer is: It depends on:

---

[8] https://www.researchgate.net/publication/286042632_How_the_Design_of_Presentation_Slides_Affects_Audience_Comprehension_A_Case_for_the_Assertion-Evidence_Approach.

[9] https://www.assertion-evidence.com/templates.html.

- what type of slide is displayed - orientational or content slide
  You cannot have the same amount to say about each slide and not all of them serve the same purpose in a talk. Slides that are used as a transition to the next part of the talk or to introduce the agenda only need to be displayed for a few seconds. They serve as a guide to the audience and any detailed explanation is unnecessary. The situation is different in the case of content-related slides, for instance with regard to the methodological procedure or the results. Detailed explanations are mandatory here.

- how deeply engaged the audience is in the topic
  In the case of an audience with a sound knowledge of the research aspect being presented, fewer slides are usually needed to describe the basics and the literature than for a lay audience.

- how familiar the audience is with the form of presentation
  More slides can be presented if, for instance, the structure of a table or an algorithm is familiar to the audience or all the variables are known and do not need to be explained separately.

- how large the allocated time window is.

  ▶ The following applies as a rough rule of thumb for the number of slides in the talk: Anyone who cannot speak for about a minute on a slide with content should question the necessity of this transparency and, if necessary, delete such a meaningless slide.

4.3.1.4 Format of the Slides

The readability of a slide can also be influenced by the choice of format. In the days of physical slides slides in science were often labelled and presented in portrait format. In the meantime, horizontal use has become the norm, and this provides several advantages. For one thing, it is considered the more eye-friendly format because it provides a larger active image area. And secondly, this allows for more projection surface to be used, especially in rooms with low ceilings. The so-called "favourable reading area" in the middle part of the slide is larger. In rooms where the audience is seated at ground level and the screen has not been raised, it is difficult for the audience in the back rows to see the lower part of the slide. For this reason, it is recommended to visualise results, implications and recommendations further in the upper part of the slide and, to the extent possible, to leave the lower edge of the slide free. The principle of "one message per slide" helps here.

4.3.2 Arranging Text Boxes and Numbers in Tabular Form

Text is a frequently used element in slide design that is produced quickly and often used in an inflational manner in presentations. While photos or graphics are relatively easily grasped by the audience, (too) many words can result in a high cognitive load. Good readability, a reduced amount of text, a clear structure and uniform alignment of the elements of a slide make an important contribution as an orientation of the audience and faster comprehension of content. Text boxes in tabular form are a good way to make the most of the horizontal format of a slide and to structure the slide in a clear and appealing way.

▶ Do not write down everything that you are going to say on the slides. Keep your slides lean. Instead, verbally add what might be additionally interesting for the respective audience.

The following tips are important for the design of text:

1. Use a maximum of three structuring levels and distinctly different font sizes to create a hierarchy that facilitates orientation. Visualise as few bullet points as possible.
2. Indent the 2nd and 3rd structuring levels to the right and assign a fixed distance from the left margin to each structuring level. Align the text with bullet points to the left if possible so that the text image appears neat and not "tattered". Centred alignment is only suitable in exceptional cases.
3. Assign a separate bullet to each structuring level. These should be easily distinguishable and as simply designed as possible, so as not to distract from the text.
4. Choose a sans-serif font that is as large as possible, such as Arial or Helvetica, so that the typeface is clear and easier to read.
5. Ensure that the spacing between the individual text blocks or paragraphs is significantly greater than the line spacing within a block. They thus make it easier for the audience to read and understand the slide because individual text elements are easier to recognise.
6. Use keywords or half-sentences that you use as visualisation aids for yourself and your audience and that prevent you from reading aloud instead of reciting. Refrain from writing out transitions from one point to the next. Instead, leave enough room for purely oral additions to give the presentation a personal touch and keep the audience's attention high.
7. Create the slides in the language in which the talk is held. In this way, they make the presentation easier for you and also make it easier for the audience because the spoken and written language are identical. You also prevent unattractive language mixtures, where, for example, verbs of one language are conjugated in the grammar of the other.

4.3.2.1 Readability—Text Size and Quantity

Something that is not legible is of no value for the audience. Basic requirements for an easily readable slide are an appropriate font size and amount of text. The chosen font must be large enough to be easily deciphered even in the last row.

In the case of slide titles, the font size is best selected between 28 and 36 point, while the text of a slide should ideally be between 16 and 24 point. Headings in the text box should be at least 4 points larger than the text.

For slides, a sans serif font such as Arial is recommended. Serif fonts like Times New Roman are suitable for closely written texts in books or articles because the serifs provide orientation for the eye when reading. In the case of talks with much less text per page or slide, the small squiggles of this font are irritating.

Text should be used sparingly in order to not tire or bore the audience. Slides with lots of words also tempt presenters to read them out loud. Therefore as a rule of thumb: just as much text as is absolutely necessary for the audience. Only important figures, data and facts as well as corresponding questions should be visualised in writing. Other, supplementary information is best added orally by speakers.

▶ Make use of the options offered by the current presentation programmes: make a note of any necessary information as speaker notes that are invisible to the audience.

4.3.2.2 Present Text in Tabular Form or as Bullet Point Lists

Text can be placed on the slide in different forms. Lists with bullet points are among the classics for presenting text. In the meantime, they often have the reputation of being boring and monotonous. This is probably due to the fact that—also because of the corresponding default setting in PowerPoint—the creation of bullet points is simple and quick. Negative examples showed a long series of bullet points supplemented with phrased sentences from the research paper.

It is important to keep the number of bullet points, their length and information density per slide low so that it does not appear overloaded. Furthermore, bullet points do not have to consist of complete sentences. They should be relatively short to attain the maximum impact.

▶ Bullet points are suitable for short lists for which no longer descriptions or explanations are necessary.

For the visualisation of texts, scientists have numerous other—interesting and unusual—enumeration variants at their disposal. For a start, it helps if instead of using the small black dots, other simple symbols—such as pictograms—are used in a different colour. It becomes more varied with tabular representations, i.e. a kind of "word table". Here, shapes such as rectangles, circles, stars and arrows, in which a generic term is written, replace the bullet point. A text field with a short description is added to the right of each generic term. Colour coding and animations provide the audience with additional orientation. A good example of a word table is shown in Fig. 4.4 of this chapter.

It is also conceivable that you might arrange the text fields, for instance, in a circle or as a star, if it aids comprehension. Word tables can be produced in their simplest form without any great effort. More elaborate presentations, such as a matrix with different colours and animations, take more time to produce but make it easier for the audience to follow the presentation.

▶ Text fields in tabular form make optimal use of the horizontal format of slides and structure them clearly and attractively.

Neatly arranged and aligned text fields—preferably in tabular form—provide an orderly and clear arrangement of visualisation elements that makes it easier for the audience to stay attentive. The eye of the beholder is provided with an (invisible) eye guide. Frames and lines clearly demarcate the individual blocks from each other. Different font sizes of title and text clarify the respective outline level. Colours highlight what is important or illustrate what belongs together thematically. White space divides the visualised content into easy-to-read sections.

▶ Many scientists are only interested in the asterisks (*) in outputs. Condense the information in the table in such a way that ideally only the relevant data is displayed.

A lot of text on slides can be useful in exceptional cases if:

– the topic is completely new to the audience and a more detailed written description is necessary to understand the scientific work presented.
– the set of slides is to be used not only for the talk, but also as a document or reference work by people who were not personally present at the presentation.
– it is being presented in a foreign language and difficult passages or technical terms can be presented confidently in this way.
– the specifications of the research discipline stipulate this.
– this is the only way to overcome your nerves.

4.3.2.3 Classic Number Tables

Very few conference visitors can probably recall a table. Viewers are more likely to remember interesting images and diagrams. For this reason, tables only belong in the summary of a talk in exceptional cases.

Tables, used correctly, are a concise yet detailed form of presentation that can be helpful for the talk, provided that the amount of data shown remains manageable or is made clearer with orientation aids (e.g. colour coding or arrows). It is extremely rare that all values are required for the talk. Experienced presenters choose their values in the table according to their importance or meaningfulness and question which of them are necessary for the audience to understand the data. If you find this difficult, you should put yourself in the shoes of the audience and answer the following questions:

> Which values are interesting for my audience?
> Which values could I leave out and still ensure that the audience can follow my presentation?

Whenever researchers want to provide as thorough a presentation as possible, they run the risk of delivering columns of figures that are difficult to read or process by the audience for quantitative reasons. As a result, not only is information lost due to the large amount of input, but the connection to the topic of the talk often suffers as well.

Most tables created with common statistics programmes have a font size that is (too) small. These are not suitable to be shown on a slide. A simple way to help the audience grasp the content is to use coloured borders or arrows to highlight important information. Individually designed tables are more professional and more pleasant for the viewer. It is worthwhile to select the data of a table for this purpose. Scientists should share only the information that is relevant to the audience and transfer it to a separate table (Fig. 4.8).

Influence of further training on job changes

Variable	Coefficient	Standard error
Further training before 1997	-0.092*	(0.046)
Number of employees	0.275**	(0.016)
Vocational experience	-0.057**	(0.008)
Vocational experience ^{2}	0.001**	(0.000)
Unemployment	0.438**	(0.036)
Without a professional qualification	-0.155**	(0.055)
Axis section	-0.138**	(0.206)
Number of observations	9335	
Log-Likelihood	-3676,619	
$\chi^2_{(49)}$	1,682,093	

Significance levels: *:5% **:1%

Fig. 4.8 Table adapted to the target group

4.3 Five Principles for Effective Slides in Academic Talks

Table 1: (A0) Does training affect Labour mobility?

Variable	Coefficient	(Std. Err.)
Training before 1997	-0.092*	(0.046)
Individual Characteristics		
Number of Employers	0.275**	(0.016)
Professional Experience	-0.057**	(0.008)
Professional Experience Squared	0.001**	(0.000)
Unemployment	0.438**	(0.036)
Age	-0.037**	(0.006)
East Germany	0.095*	(0.046)
Without Professional Degree	-0.155**	(0.055)
University	0.225*	(0.092)
Partner Employed	-0.104†	(0.056)
child6to17y	0.107†	(0.064)
child>18y	0.171*	(0.075)
Other Controls		
(Married, Household size, Sex, School leaving certificate dummies, Vocational degrees, Professional position, Children dummies, etc.)		
Intercept	-0.138**	(0.206)
N		9335
Log-likelihood		-3676.619
$\chi^2_{(49)}$		1682.093
Significance levels : † : 10% * : 5% ** : 1%		

Fig. 4.9 Original stata output

To do this, the scientist[10] selected the information of interest to local politicians from the output of the statistics programme, as can be seen in Fig. 4.9.

It also makes sense to use uniform values as well as units of measurement. It also helps to take into account the usual reading directions, e.g. to right-justify amounts in monetary units. Those able to do so, dispense with disproportionately high levels of accuracy by rounding their values. In most cases, small rounding errors have no influence on the significance of a table. A table should be dispensed with if the information can be summarised in a few sentences.

The following hints will help when creating tables:

▶ 1. Only show data relevant to the audience. Review your target group analysis and select the necessary information for your table. Check whether a separate table created for this group of viewers would be useful and important.

---

[10] Anja Kuckulenz, ZEW – Leibniz-Zentrum für Europäische Wirtschaftsforschung GmbH [Leibniz Centre for European Economic Research] Mannheim.

2. Use a font size that is easy on the eye for the audience and ensure legible and clear legends and captions. Where possible, you should take into account the usual reading direction (e.g. money amounts right-justified) and thus make the slide more appealing.
3. Write units in the column and row headers and highlight crucial values with colour animations. Also make sure you have sufficient spacing between columns and rows (e.g. white space or bold lines) for better clarity.
4. Formulate a succinct table title. If possible, decide on the key messages in the form of a talking headline.

4.3.3 Show Charts and Other Forms of Illustrations

Well-designed slides are clear, easy to understand and easy to recollect. Visualisations such as diagrams[11] and photos reduce the audience's cognitive load and thus ensure that information can be grasped more quickly than with a text. John Medina justifies this by saying that reading is inefficient for humans. The brain perceives words as individual pictures and has to recognise the characteristics of the letters. As a result, reading takes significantly more time compared to the perception of images.[12]

> ▶ People are incredibly good at recalling images. When they hear a snippit of information, they remember 10% of it three days later. If you add a picture, they recall 65% of it.[13]

The Picture Superior Effect describes this phenomenon of the superiority of pictures. Pictures increase people's ability to remember things compared to purely verbal cues.[14] Pictorial visualisation is even more effective when its elements are large and especially when they move. Imposing and dynamic visualisations attract viewers' attention and hold it longer than images or even text. The more unexpectedly and rarely this happens, the greater the effect. Presenters who cannot show film sequences have the option of using changes to characteristics of the illustration—such as a table or a graph—to attract the viewer's attention. They achieve

---

[11] All figures in this subchapter are the authors' own representations and are based on fictitious data.
[12] John Medina: "Brain Rules (Updated and Expanded): 12 Principles for Surviving and Thriving at Work Home, and School", April 2014, page 183 et. al.
[13] John Medina: "Brain Rules (Updated and Expanded): 12 Principles for Surviving and Thriving at Work, Home, and School", April 2014, page 183 et al.
[14] https://www.researchgate.net/publication/247213377_The_picture_superiority_effect_in_recognition_memory_A_developmental_study_using_the_response_signal_procedure.

this by changing colours and sizes or by making elements of their visualisation appear or disappear with the help of animations.[15]

▶ Surprise your audience and make selective use of size, colour and movement for the elements of your slide to attract and hold the audience's attention.

4.3.3.1 Charts

Charts are means of presentation that turn numbers into pictures during academic talks. They can make all the difference in the presentation. The use of charts is recommended especially in those cases where several items of data are to be compared or where tables would be too confusing. Without them, science would in many cases be more difficult to understand. An appropriate amount of time should therefore also be devoted to the design of diagrams. Considering how much time is spent on obtaining the data, it would be negligent to present it inadequately through poor or misleading design.

Most charts are mapped in a rectangular cross of axes, the Cartesian coordinate system. Charts are suitable for visualising trends, forecasts, distributions or correlations. Researchers can also use them to map developments over a period of time. The use of charts is recommended especially in those cases where several items of data are to be compared or where tables would be too confusing.

There are a variety of chart types and combinations of individual types, Therefore, it is important that presenters on the one hand have a precise idea of which data they want to present and with what aim, and on the other hand that they know which chart form is best suited for this and which is not.

Eight frequently used diagrams are presented below.

– **Vertical Bar Chart**

The vertical bar chart is one of the most frequently used chart types in the scientific field. The data are displayed proportionally to their value in vertical areas, the so-called bars. As a rule, the individual bars do not touch. Some space is left between them to ensure better readability. Grid lines facilitate orientation and ensure improved comparability of values with smaller differences. They should be easily recognisable, but paler than the colours of the individual columns to avoid any confusion.

Bar charts are used to show frequencies and trends of variables at a certain point in time or over time. They can also assist in ranking the individual values. All values from zero to the final value are displayed visually and are particularly suitable when only a few measured values are compared. Experience has shown that, if possible, no more than eight values should be deducted. The bar chart otherwise becomes confusing and the clarity suffers (Fig. 4.10).

---

[15] John Medina "Brain rules for work", 2021, page 199.

Fig. 4.10 Vertical bar chart

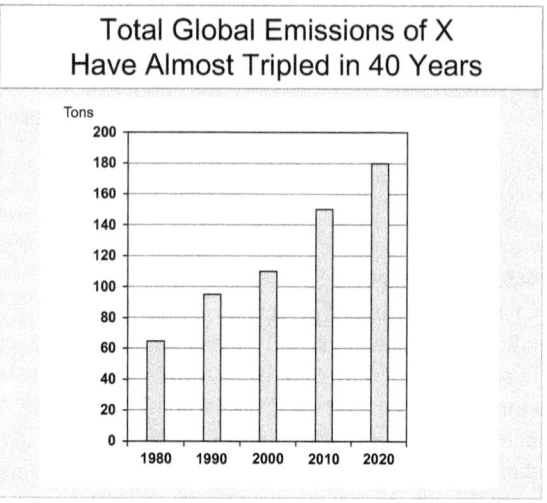

A grouped bar chart can also be used to display several values of a category for comparison. The columns of these values are displayed next to each other (grouped together) so that they can be directly compared with each other over time. In the example in Fig. 4.11, two values of a category are compared over a period of 40 years.

Fig. 4.11 Grouped vertical bar chart

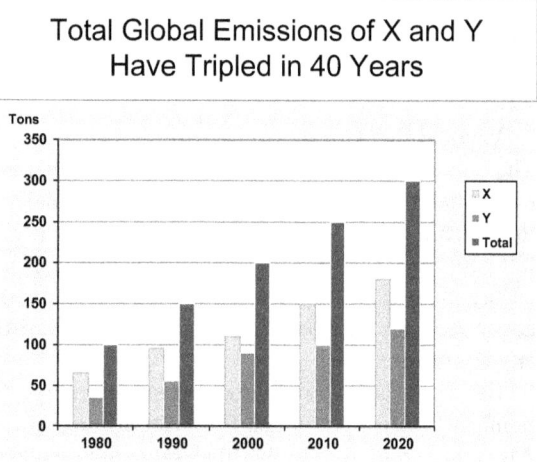

4.3 Five Principles for Effective Slides in Academic Talks

Reading and comparing aggregated data, on the other hand, is difficult with grouped bar charts. A stacking diagram is a good way to do this. Here the individual values are arranged on top of each other and the column represents the total value. This allows the viewer to read off the total values for the individual time periods and compare the composition of these over the period under consideration. Any number of values can be represented using a stack diagram. Nevertheless, clarity suffers when a large amount of data is stacked. The columns become very colourful and individual elements can become so small that they are only unequally larger than lines. The stack diagram is less suitable for reading off the changes in the mapped parts. Figure 4.12 displays the aggregates of two values over a period of 40 years in a stack diagram.

- **Horizontal Bar Chart**

The bar chart is a horizontal column chart in which the data series are displayed as horizontal bars. Many researchers use the word "bar chart" as a generic term and distinguish the two forms as horizontal and vertical bar charts. Both forms offer similar advantages.

Bar charts represent data series in horizontal bars. By contrast with column charts, the values are typically plotted on the x-axis.

The advantage of a horizontal bar chart is that the labels are easier to display and read.

In all bar charts, trend lines and the values can be added as precise numbers at the end of the bars. Especially when only a few data series are shown, the audience benefits greatly from this additional information. However, if there are too many bars, there is a risk that the individual values will be difficult to read due to the amount of detailed information and due to the fact the presenter is forced to reduce

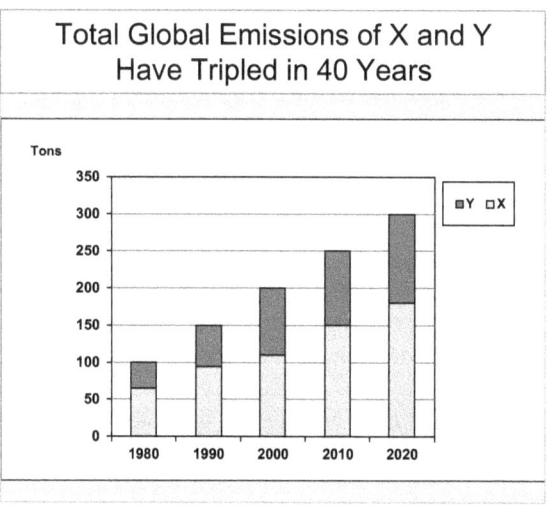

Fig. 4.12 Stacking chart

the size of the bars and font in order to accommodate all the information on the slide.

In principle, scientists should weigh up whether the additional indication of the numerical value is useful. Besides the increase in the amount of information, there is another weakness in this approach: the researcher provides redundant information. If the speaker's aim is to provide a general overview or to illustrate the "lead" of the top value, then an exact indication of the numerical value - possibly even down to several decimal places - does not provide the audience with any additional benefit. In such a case, it should be waived. If the differences in expression are small in individual data series or if the scientific investigation is concerned with the minimal differences, it is, on the other hand, advisable to also, or only, visualise the numerical value.

If you decide to do this, you should ensure that the numerical information is displayed either completely inside or outside the bars, because their border lines can obscure parts of the numerical value. Dark and bold grid lines also pose this risk. Numbers should only be written in the bars if all bars are long or wide enough to write out the value in them.

Bar charts work best when they are filled with colours over a wide area. Colours should be chosen and used with a great amount of contrast, uniformity and care. Shrill colours can be unintentionally visualised completely differently on the screen depending on the projector. Therefore, classic colours such as blue, brown and dark greens and greys are recommended. Patterns and hatching are not suitable for use in bar charts. Patterns often irritate and make the image harder to grasp. Only in situations where there are not enough colours available to mark the bars should scientists consider using simple patterns. Figure 4.13 shows an example.

– **Histogram**

A histogram is a chart that displays the frequency distribution of a characteristic. Yet, despite its similarity, it is not a bar chart. It differs from the bar chart because it is not the height of the columns but the area of the columns that depicts the absolute and relative frequencies. In addition, the data must be divided into classes of equal or different sizes for the creation of the histogram. The areas of the individual columns are proportional to their frequency. Figure 4.14 displays a histogram with classes of different sizes.

– **Line Diagram**

This diagram form is suitable if several data or measurement points should be displayed over a period of time. These points are plotted on the ordinate and connected with a line. They depict the development and functional relationship of the values. Line diagrams or also curve diagrams are mostly used for a time series comparison and for the illustration of trends at selected points in time. It is about showing changes over time and changes within a time period for several

4.3   Five Principles for Effective Slides in Academic Talks

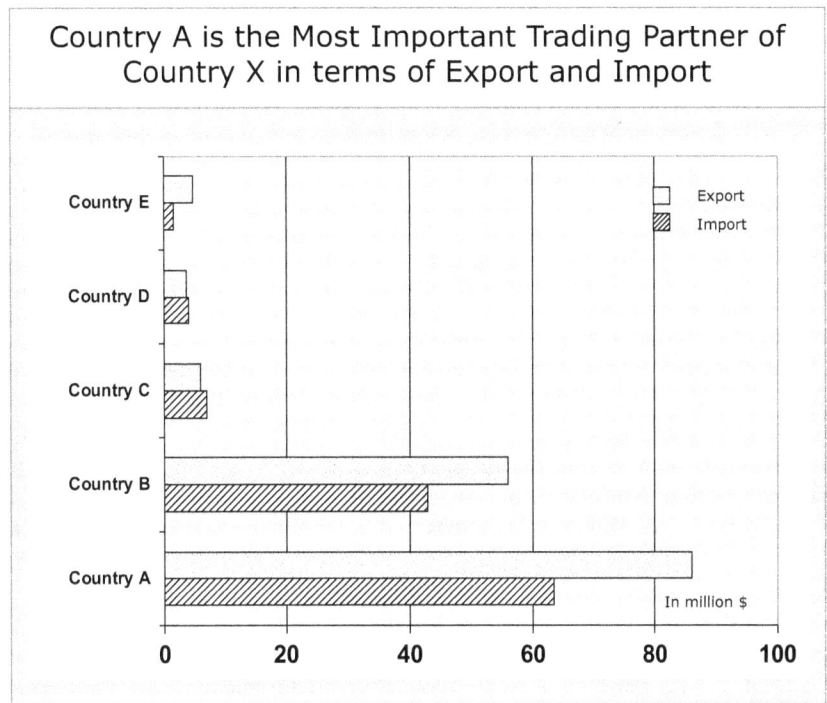

Fig. 4.13   Horizontal bar chart with pattern

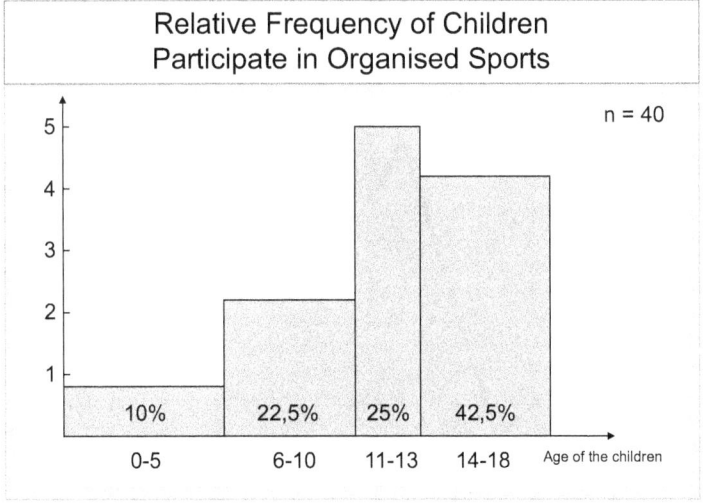

Fig. 4.14   Histogram

groups. They illustrate the stability or dynamics of phenomena. Consequently, line diagrams do not aim at visualising the single value. This diagram type is therefore also suitable for comparing several time rows. The following Fig. 4.15 shows a diagram with two rows of date.

▶   If possible, do not display more than seven data lines in a chart to keep it clear.

In the case of line diagrams in particular, there are some dangers lurking in terms of the selection of line colour and width. This section shows how the thickness or colour of lines and background affect the perception of the diagram. Basically, the diagram lines should be visualised broadly and in contrasting colours to each other and to the background. Both simplify the perceptibility for the viewer. For instance, if the grid lines are the same width as the chart lines, it is more difficult to distinguish between the individual lines. The same applies to diagram lines that are too thin. Thus, they no longer serve the purpose for which they were originally intended. This effect is intensified by backgrounds that are too dark and from which the diagram lines stand out only slightly. Reading and comparing rows of data becomes more difficult or even impossible.

In addition to contrast and line width, the choice of colour plays an important role in this chart form. When preparing a talks, scientists should take into account that bright and glaring colours are more difficult to perceive than darker ones,

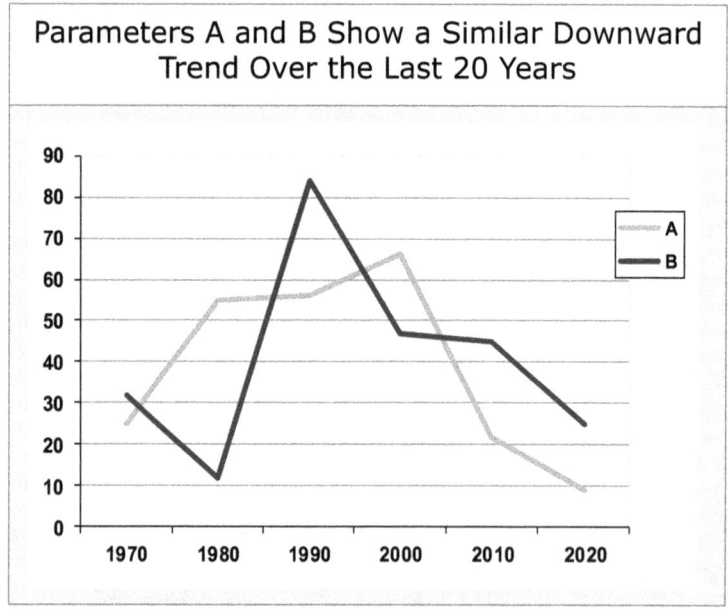

Fig. 4.15 Line diagram with to rows of date

4.3 Five Principles for Effective Slides in Academic Talks

can fluctuate and can be changed by the projection. In addition, certain colour constellations can cause problems for people with colour vision deficiencies.

▶ During your preparation of the talk, take into account that some of your audience may suffer from colour vision deficiencies. Those who suffer from these deficiencies can only recognise red, green or blue with difficulty, or not at all.

The use of bold data series lines in contrasting colours provides a clear, easy to grasp display. The effect of less thick lines significantly complicates the perception of the chart and is much more strenuous for the viewer, as illustrated in Fig. 4.16.

The comparison of many data series also challenges the viewer more. The delineation of the individual rows should be performed using easily distinguishable colours and bold lines to make the diagram easier to read. Figure 4.17 clearly shows how important this becomes when comparing now four rows of data.

This form of diagram sometimes uses different line patterns instead of colours for the data visualisation. This strategy has similar pitfalls as the choice of colour. Depending on the similarity of the patterns or the number of lines, the viewer finds it difficult to distinguish between the individual lines. If academics use several dashed and/or dotted lines, they may irritate and "misdirect" the audience. Compared to continuous lines, interrupted variants are more difficult to perceive, as the example in Fig. 4.18 shows.

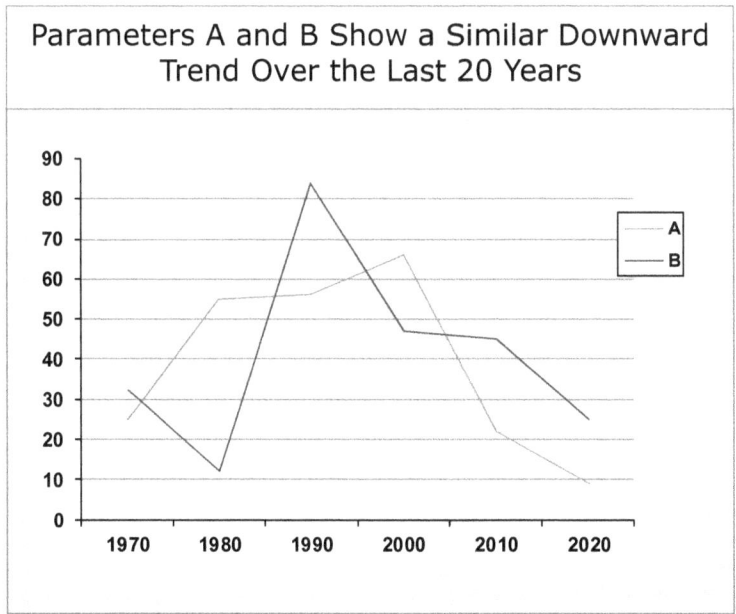

Fig. 4.16 Line chart with thin lines

82 4 Visualisation in the Talk—Design Slides in a Professional Manner

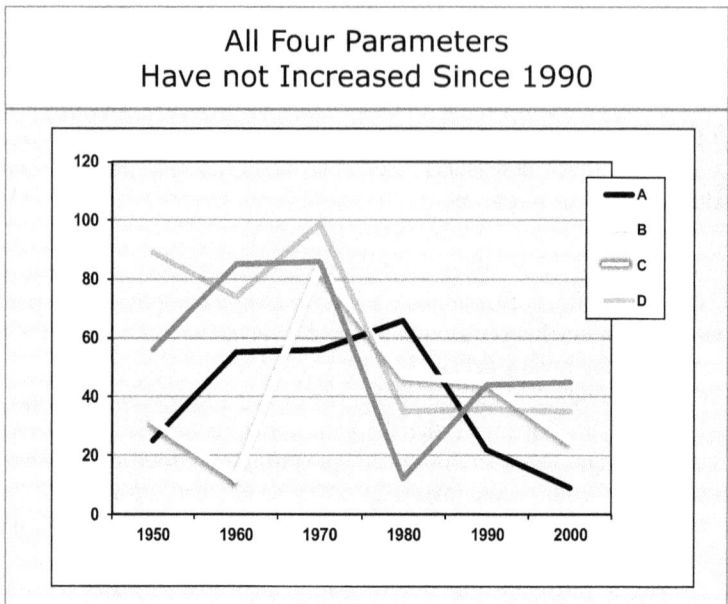

Fig. 4.17 Line chart—comparing 4 rows of data

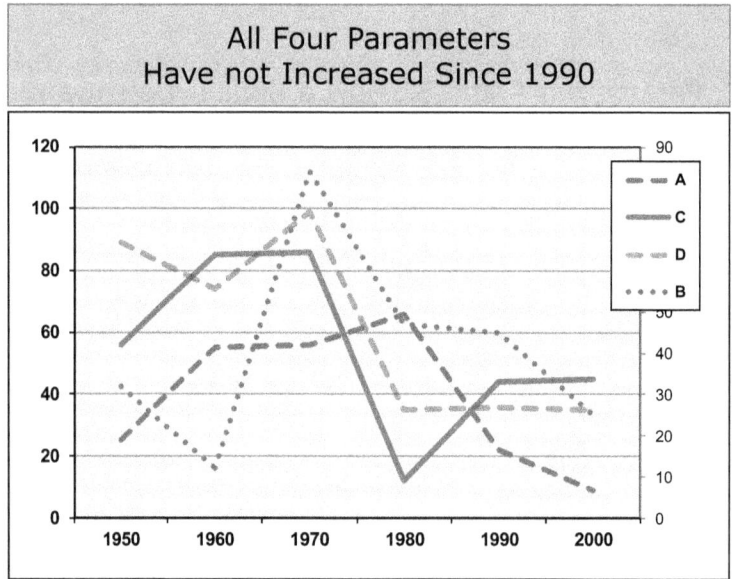

Fig. 4.18 Line chart with 4 dashed lines

4.3 Five Principles for Effective Slides in Academic Talks

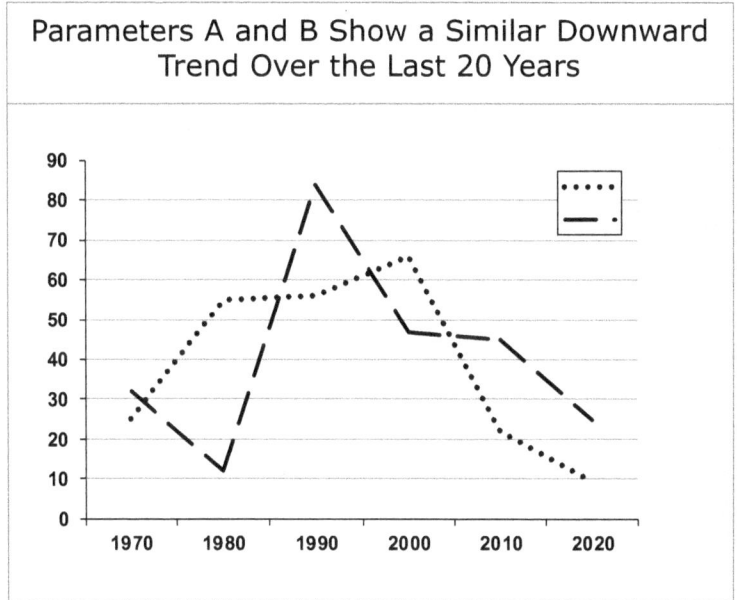

Fig. 4.19 Line chart with 2 dashed lines

With a small number of values and a strong line width, diagrams with broken lines can certainly be used for scientific presentations. If you want to avoid colouring the lines, you should work with different shades of grey and - preferably with no more than two - line patterns. It goes without saying that the shades of grey must stand out clearly from each other and the line patterns must not bear any resemblance to each other (for example, dots and dashes) as can be seen in Fig. 4.19.

Ideally, speakers choose a mixture of solid and broken lines and make sure that lines with patterns do not lie next to each other or cross. The example in Fig. 4.20 demonstrates how a chart with solid and one broken data line can be visualised in a legible way.

It is important to take note of the axis scalings and the amount of data. When scaling the two axes, unnatural and irritating compression or stretching of the lines should be avoided. This can greatly change and influence the effect of the image. Furthermore, the scaling of the x-axis of a line chart must be performed in proportional steps to exclude distortions. It helps if the values are recorded with the smallest possible time intervals so that "outliers" can be removed and are not lost. Any change in axillary scaling should be clearly indicated in the presentation.

▶ Number of lines, line colour, line type and width as well as background colours have a descisive influence on the readability of a diagram.

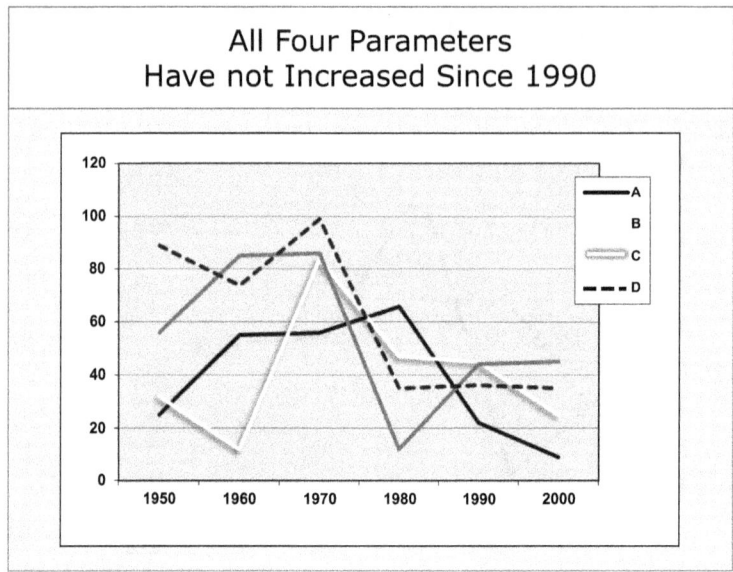

Fig. 4.20 Line chart with dashed and solid lines

- **Pie Chart and Ring diagram**

Pie charts and ring diagrams represent the relationship of subsets to a whole. Their strength lies in the fact that viewers can quickly and at a glance recognise the composition and relative proportion of the individual parts of an investigation or an object of investigation. The shares are arranged as sectors in a circle or ring, must not overlap and add up to 100 per cent of the total. The size of the individual elements corresponds to their relative share of the whole. For this reason, a pie chart is the obvious choice for the representation of proportional shares as a percentage. Figure 4.21 displays a classic pie chart.

In science, pie charts are often rejected because of their low informative value and the limited or non-existent possibility of visualising exact values. Researchers who nevertheless wish to use a pie chart for their talk should take care to give it a meaningful title, label the individual sectors of the circle with their numerical values and state the absolute total value of the chart in order to provide the audience with some orientation. It also helps if short comments on the content or other additional information are added in or at the respective sectors of the diagram. Due to the lack of axes and axis labels, this is the only way for the audience to compare data. Those who have chosen absolute values for their figure and the respective shares, must of course also indicate the total value.

The so-called ring diagram offers somewhat more possibilities in this context. It is a special form of the pie chart in which the centre is left out. This creates space to fill in missing information. Figure 4.22 shows an example that builds on the pie chart from the previous figure.

4.3 Five Principles for Effective Slides in Academic Talks

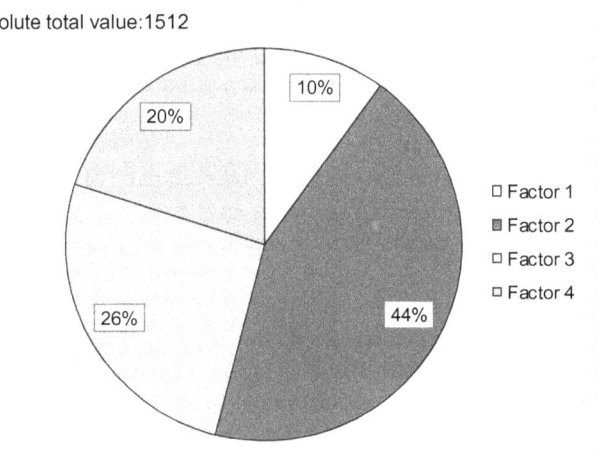

Fig. 4.21 Classic pie chat

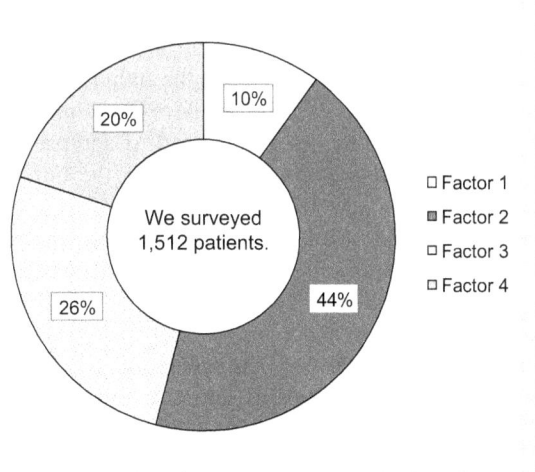

Fig. 4.22 Ring diagram with additional information in the centre of the circle

As with all other charts, it is also true in the case of pie charts and ring charts that a large contrast between the colours of the segments is important and hatching or patterns should be reduced to a minimum, not used in adjacent sectors and ideally only once per chart.

As with all other forms of representation, pie charts become confusing if they depict too much data - in this case sectors. As a rule of thumb, speakers should use no more than seven sectors, grouping many small sectors together if possible or pulling the most important part out of the circle to highlight it.

– **Scatter Plot or Dot Plot**

Scatter or dot plots graphically represent observed pairs of values of two variables. The pairs of values are entered as points in a Cartesian coordinate system. The position of each point on the vertical and horizontal axis shows the value of the individual data point.

The sum of the points results in a cloud whose direction of progression shows the correlation and the dependency structure between the two characteristics under investigation. This often involves examining how an independent characteristic affects a dependent one. This correlation is usually additionally clarified by a line, the so-called correlation line. For better orientation, grid lines are drawn in in the case of larger data sets. In this simple graphical representation of a bivariate data set, by contrast with the line chart, there is more than one pair of values. Figure 4.23 displays a dot plot.

Clearly assignable and distinguishable points are the basic prerequisite for a quick grasp and understanding of the diagram. Figure 4.24 shows an example with dots that are too large and overlap, while Fig. 4.25 illustrates why thin lines and unfilled dots do not really aid visualistion.

– **Box Graphic**

The box graphic is also called a box plot or box whisker plot and is used in statistical analyses. It is a kind of summary of a data set and is used to illustrate the distribution and dispersion. Not only the individual data, but also the span of the data set is mapped. The box plot displays the minimum and maximum levels, the lower and upper quartile, the median and, if applicable, outliers of a data set. It consists of a box ranging from the lower to the upper quartile and covering 50 per cent of the data set. The median is drawn as a vertical line in the box. A box plot also includes two lines outside the box. One runs from the minimum to the lower quartile and the other from the upper quartile to the maximum. The lines are also called "whiskers" and indicate the variability outside the upper and lower quartiles. All points outside the whiskers are considered outliers. A box plot is particularly suitable when the distributions of numerical data values are to be compared between several groups. Figure 4.26 shows the structure of a box plot.

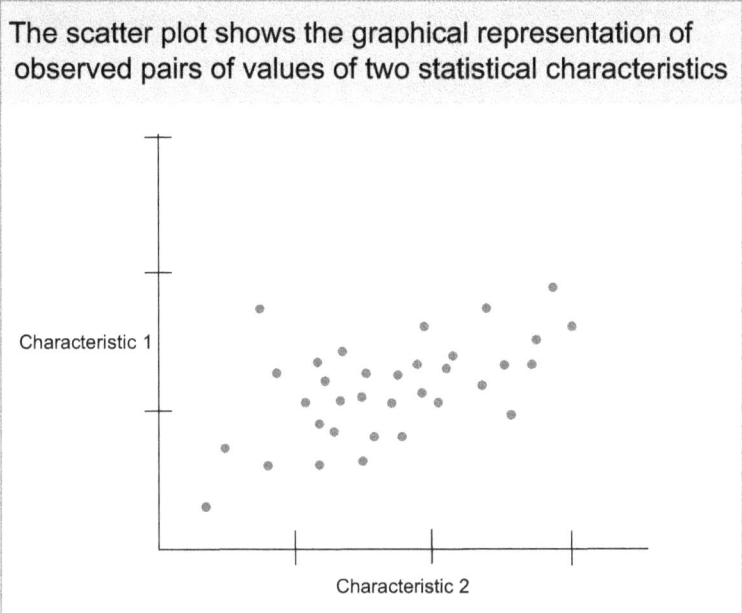

Fig. 4.23 Scatter plot

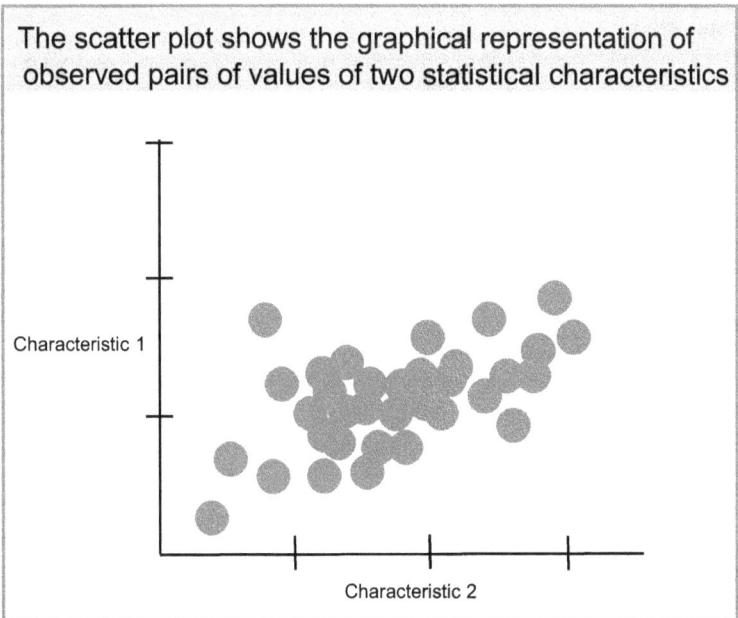

Fig. 4.24 Scatter plot with overlapping dots

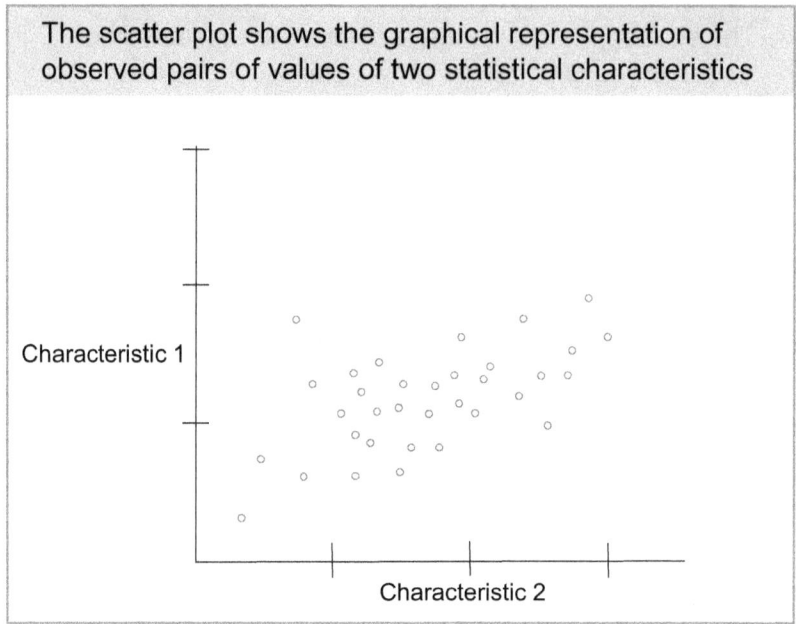

Fig. 4.25 Scatter plot with lines

– **Bubble Chart**

Bubble charts are a special form of scatter diagrams. They are used when a third dimension needs to be depicted. The values are displayed as bubbles. By contrast with other, classical 3-D images, the third information is not visualised via a third axis, but via the size of the bubble. Special features and specifics of a data set can be additionally highlighted using colours.

Bubble charts provide a quick overview, but are not suitable for precise comparisons. Large differences in the values can lead to problems in the display if, for example, the area of the slide is not sufficient. This makes the interpretation of the data difficult, not least because most people find it easier to estimate and compare the lengths of lines or bars than the sizes of areas. Especially when a lot of data is visualised, it can become confusing and irritate the viewer due to the surrounding elements. Figure 4.27 displays a bubble chart.

The following seven points show the most important steps for the design of appealing diagrams:

1. Select the appropriate chart type for the data set at hand and for your own objective. Then compile all the necessary scientific data for the visualisation.
2. Formulate a meaningful heading for the chart slide. The core message of the graphic displayed is best suited for this. The tips and hints concerning the Assertion-Evidence-Approach support you in formulating this very important element of your mapping. If you have opted for the classic form of the AEA,

4.3 Five Principles for Effective Slides in Academic Talks

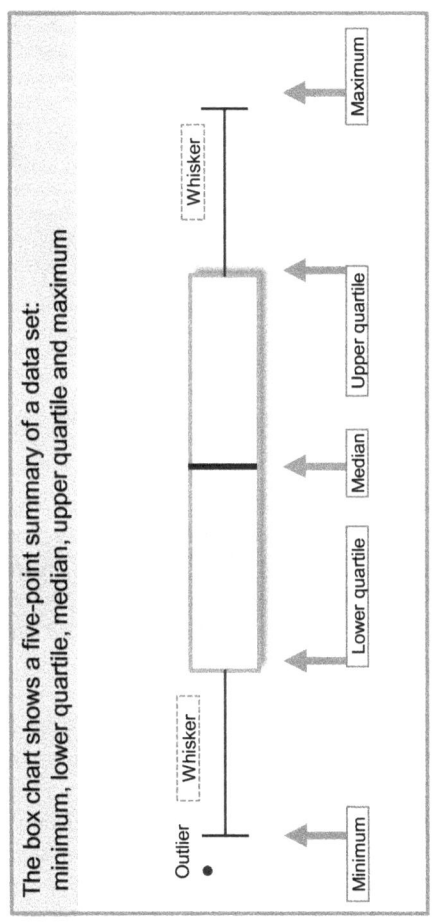

Fig. 4.26 Box chart and its structure

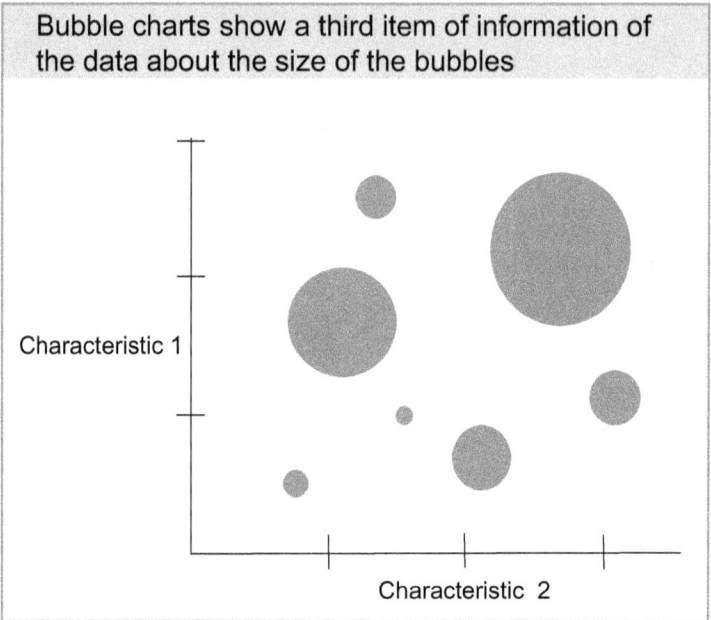

Fig. 4.27 Bubble charts show a third item about the size of the bubbles

the slide heading is sufficient. An additional title directly above the diagram is not necessary and also makes little sense, as it would be a repetition of the core statement in the title of the slide. If you want to show several illustrations on one slide, each one is given its own heading.

3. Ensure a marked contrast between the slide background, chart colours and the labelling. Refrain from using patterns and hatching so as not to irritate the audience.
4. Use bold chart lines to roughly structure the chart and finer lines to align elements of the chart. In this way, the viewers obtain a point of reference and can see which values are behind the individual data points.
5. Label axes, legends, lines, bars or sectors as well as all other elements of the graph in large letters and as horizontally as possible. Use upper and lower case letters for this text. This all serves to improve readability and makes it easier to understand the graphic.
6. In order to provide a better point of reference - especially when using complex and complicated illustrations - highlight important information, sequences and reading directions using colours, frames, arrows or animations. This helps to distinguish what is important from what is less important and to guide and focus the viewer's gaze.
7. Place your chart so it is sufficiently large, prominently positioned, well aligned and ideally without any other visualisations on the slide so that you can draw the audience's attention to it.

4.3.3.2 Presenting a Text Image, Table, Diagram or Orally

The goal of any visualisation is to present the desired core message to the audience in a quick and comprehensible manner. Presenters are faced with the question of whether to present the data and values of their study in text, table or chart form. On the one hand, this depends on which question should be answered by means of a visualisation and how complex or multi-layered the values to be displayed or their dependencies are. On the other hand, the objective as well as the experience and expectations of the audience play a role. Three different questions illustrate which considerations play a role in the decision for the table, chart or text form.

- **Presenting and Comparing Precise Values, Individual Data and Small Amounts of Data: Table**

Charts are prepared on the basis of tables. Thus, in the best case, a graphical representation can be as accurate as a table. However, it is more likely that charts are less accurate than tables due to perceptual psychological phenomena such as optical illusions, possible data overlap or reading difficulties. Even if all the potential sources of error are eliminated through the careful and professional creation of a graph, people are still able to find values faster in tables than in charts. For instance, if a scientist wants to display concrete individual data with his slide ("How much did a dollar cost exactly one year ago?"), a table is superior to a chart. Reading a number takes less time than taking in a column and the corresponding value on one of the axes. Even if the latter can be facilitated by adding numerical values to the columns, the effort of taking this in for the viewer remains high.

Tables also offer advantages over the chart when it comes to recording a single value for larger amounts of data. For instance, if the question is "When were sales of product 4 at their highest?" the viewer can read this more quickly and easily from the table. In the chart, he must first assign the products to the individual bars via the legend before he can identify the correct year.

The additional effort involved in creating a graphic is hardly worthwhile because the necessary information can also be taken from a table without any real delays. So if there is no particular reason for doing so (e.g. a small screen on which a table can no longer be read in the back rows), then researchers can dispense with the use of charts.

- **Presenting and Comparing Data Groups: Charts**

The advantages of the table decrease where many values have to be compared or relationships and dependencies between data have to be mapped. It is easier for people to discover the longest rectangle in a figure than to systematically work through a table according to the highest number. It is similar in the case of the ranking, which viewers can also grasp in graphs in a shorter space of time. Compared to tables, charts offer the simpler, more rapidly recognisable overall picture. Especially where more extensive comparisons of data groups are concerned, charts are indispensable. It is easier for the viewer to group elements from charts and compare them with others than to search for the values in tables.

- **Representing Values with Small Differences: Text or Presenting Orally**
Not every result has to be visualised using a chart or a table. Sometimes researchers get carried away and show a graph or a spreadsheet in order to produce as many statements as possible. If only a few items of data are available, presenters should refrain from visualising things using a chart or table. The same also applies if the data do not reveal any special or interesting correlations. If there is no difference or no significant difference between the values to be compared, it does not make sense to highlight this visually. Unless it specifically concerns the final result of an investigation, scientists should spare themselves and their audience the effort of having to view an additional chart. The data table does not have to be shown in all circumstances either. In many cases, it is more appropriate to supplement the result in a text image or, even better, to simply mention it verbally in one or two sentences.

- **Additional Aspects for the Decision Between Table, Chart and Text Form**
The audience's experiences and expectations regarding the three types of visualisation play a role here. There are also different (unwritten) rules and habits in individual disciplines regarding the forms of presentation. It is also important to choose the level of detail of the data to be presented based on what the audience needs to understand the results and what they don't need. It is also helpful to identify the dependencies, relationships or trends of data that are easier to tell the audience about than to show them. Ideally, scientists should take the laws of design into account when creating tables, charts and text images to ensure a good visual guide.

> Tables lend themselves to simple comparisons.
>
> Charts are suitable for comparisons of larger groups of data.
>
> Text or verbal mentions are ideal for presenting values that don't differ much.

4.3.3.3 Images, Photos and Videos

Images, photos and videos allow the audience to literally gain an impression of an issue and see science in action. They show details and subtleties, some of which would be difficult or impossible to describe. (Moving) pictures are used in the the fields of natural science and engineering in particular, because they help to present complex experiments or equipment and mark highlights at important points in the talk. In this way, they keep the audience's attention levels high and create excitement. In addition, people's distinct memory for images helps them

4.3 Five Principles for Effective Slides in Academic Talks

to process and recall more information. Scientists can also achieve similar effects with sketches or other pictorial representations.

When comparing Fig. 4.5 with Fig. 4.28, it is easy to see that pictorial representations facilitate understanding.

When taking photos and videos, it is essential to make sure that they are high resolution so that they do not become blurred or pixilated. The importance of this becomes apparent at the latest when a picture is shown enlarged. If the audience cannot recognise anything or can only recognise something with difficulty, such depictions are of little help and, in the best case, are immediately forgotten. In less favourable cases, they can annoy members of the audience. Pictures and films are only effective if they are displayed large enough so that even people in the last rows can see them well. In addition to the quality of the photo or film, the light output of the projector is also decisive.

▶ In the case of videos with sound, ensure that it can be heard well throughout the lecture room or clarify the possibilities for audio transmission with the conference organiser in advance.

Before you start the presentation, test the functionality of your video to be able to fix any technical problems in advance.

Prepare a plan B just in case.

Images, photos and videos can be produced quickly, attractively and without much effort thanks to powerful mobile phones. They show something special in lectures and should therefore not be used excessively. This is because: a flood of images in a lecture and especially on a slide reduces the impact of the individual photo. They achieve the greatest effect when they are shown sparingly, suitably and with appropriate levels of exposure.

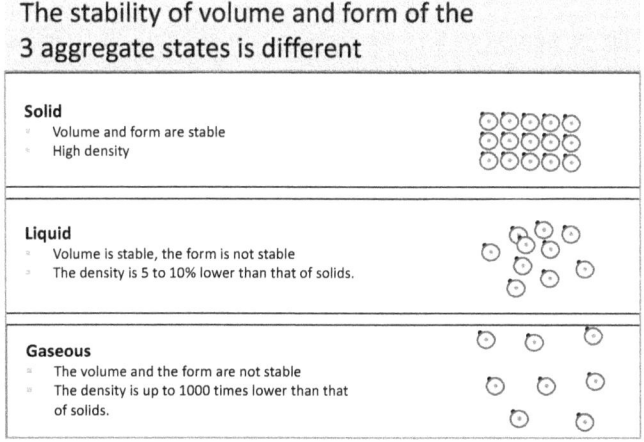

Fig. 4.28 Pictoral representation facilitates understanding

The same applies to videos. It doesn't make any sense to overload the audience with a large number of films because the uniqueness of the individual sequence is lost. There is another aspect to the presentation of film material: long videos - especially if the room is also darkened - often cause the audience to look elsewhere. Videos of more than one minute's duration run the risk of becoming long-winded and boring. Longer film passages should be presented with interruptions for comments and additions by the speaker in order to prevent a "cinema effect" and not to lose contact with the audience.

▶   Remember that images, photos and videos on the Internet are protected in many countries.

4.3.3.4 Structural Images

Scientists who want to explain relationships or clarify the cause and effect of a relationship make use of so-called structural images or pictures for this purpose. This simple form of representation shows the individual aspects of a context in a kind of flow chart by depicting decisive points as boxes. Arrows describe the relationships between these rectangles and the direction of influence. Structural images lend themselves to the illustration of procedures or processes and are suitable for every phase of a presentation. They can be used in scientific talks for the presentation of the method or the experiment. The interrelationships of different variables, factors or characteristics can also be clearly displayed using boxes, numbering and arrows, with the aid of structural images.

This form of visualisation offers advantages for the audience: structural images are clear and can depict complex things in a way that is easy to grasp. They appear logical to the viewer and make it easier to understand multi-layered contexts or extended sequences. It is important to strike a good balance between the necessary depth of detail and simplification to ensure better clarity, so as not to distort information.

The challenge here is to find the right mix of simplification and scientifically correct presentation. A situation may not arise whereby contexts are reduced in favour of clarity to such an extent that their message is distorted. Figure 4.29 shows the structural image in the talk from which the storyline presented in Chapter 3 originates.[16]

The researcher had presented his hypotheses as a "conceptual model" in the form of a structural image before entering the main section.[17] During the talk on "Job satisfaction and fluctuation in the post-merger integration process", the researcher expects that factors such as "integration quality", "uncertainty avoidance", "scope for action" and "income security" will have a positive effect on "job satisfaction" and this in turn will have a negative effect on "fluctuation".

---

[16] Talk by Thomas Zwick, Julius-Maximilians-Universität, Würzburg.
[17] Talk by Thomas Zwick, Julius-Maximilians-Universität, Würzburg.

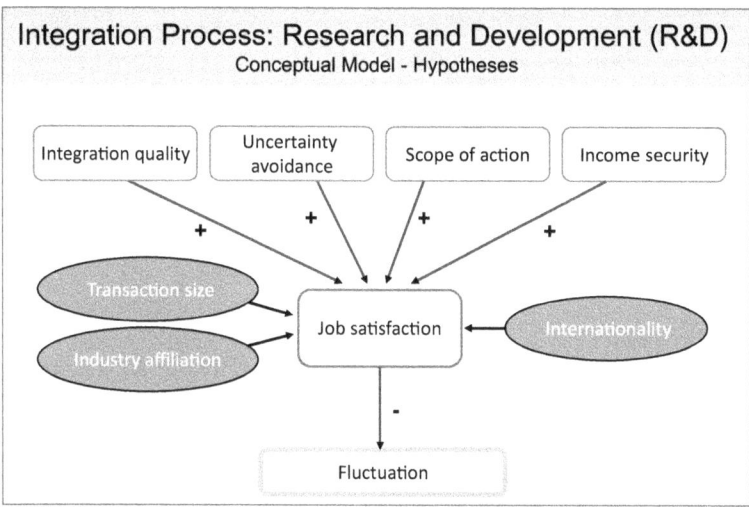

Fig. 4.29 Structural image

4.3.3.5 Maps

Maps offer a special form of pictorial visualisation. One type of map that is often used are the so-called thematic or applied maps. Thematic maps represent one or more specific issues (i.e. the research topic) and depict data, values, observations or results for this purpose. The information is placed in a clear, usually familiar spatial context that the viewer can quickly grasp. Special features, focal points, distributions and changes can be highlighted in colour.

The advantage of thematic maps is that thanks to the high level of abstraction, the information is prepared and shown in an easily recognisable way. In addition, this form of visualisation can show significantly more data at once than would be possible with a chart or table. The possible applications, as well as the depth and breadth of content, are diverse. In addition, numerous design options are open to scientists. How much and what information must or could be shown? Which signs and orientation options help and what is superfluous or even annoying? This decision is not always easy and it sometimes occurs that details are deleted in favour of clarity or the map lists too many details that the viewers can hardly relate to. In the case of maps too, the focus is still upon the target audience. Maps only create added value if the audience is able to read and understand them.

Maps are popular in scientific talks when the audience's attention should be drawn directly to results, implications or problem areas of the study.

They are also good for presenting the results of an investigation or a motivating tool for the topic. They are less suitable for the graphical representation of the methodological approach or the type of data collection.

> **Practical Tip**
> Use maps when they are useful in ensuring a better understanding. For example, if you are presenting the results of a field study, you can use a geographical map to show where the field study took place.

Thematic maps can be broken down into numerous categories. The three variants presented here are frequently used for the cartographic preparation and design of scientific topics.

- **Analytical Maps**

Usually represent only one factual detail (e.g. temperature or population density). This monothematic form of presentation is considered rather simple in terms of content and structure.

- **Complex Maps**

Depict two or more elements of a theme side by side (for instance, a general geographic map) that may be related. Complex maps are also called polythematic. For instance, if a map shows age, population size and density, it is a complex map with three different variables. The individual elements of complex maps are arranged on top of each other. They place higher demands on the audience in terms of their perception and understanding. Researchers should visualise the results shown according to the known design principles as far as possible and explain complex maps in detail.

- **Synthetic Maps**

Show two or more facts that are combined to form one generic term. Complicated individual phenomena are simplified and "merged". The individual variables are no longer shown in their original form. Synthetic maps presuppose a certain amount of prior knowledge on the part of the viewer because the map form condenses a lot of information into one representation.This is why a descriptive legend and a detailed verbal description of which figures and which subjective interpretations of the scientist have been included in the summary are required.

Thematic maps are used in scientific talks involving different characteristics. They can be used in a static or dynamic form. Dynamic maps display the geographical transformation of living beings or objects. Static maps record a state at a specific point in time.

In addition, it is possible to map the results of an investigation quantitatively or qualitatively with the aid of applied maps. Quantitative maps depict how much of a quantity can be found where (e.g. the number of hours of sunshine), while qualitative maps show what is located where (e.g. the nature parks and protected landscape areas).

The combination of maps with diagrams represents a special form of visualization. For this purpose, maps are supplemented with graphics to display distributions of objects of study, for instance in cities, regions or countries. These are displayed as bar or pie charts, which depict the values by means of the height or size.

4.3.3.6 Caricatures, Cartoons and Comics

There is a lot to be said for and against the use of humorous visualisations. They are a double-edged sword and not without risk. There is a fine line between a more relaxed approach and ridiculousness. Humour is only funny and helpful when the whole audience (!) can laugh or smile about it.

Thus, humorous images or parodies can bring a certain lighthearted touch that can provide a welcome change and be a refreshing booster of people's concentration levels. Both make a not inconsiderable contribution towards reducing the cognitive load. They also offer, carefully selected, the audience points of reference and things they can associate with. This helps people to better understand, reinforce and retain what is said.

Experience has shown that most scientists prefer it when colleagues maintain a cultivated, humorous presentation style. This is entertaining and motivating.

The other side of the coin is that this can precisely lead to people having the impression that there is a lack of scientific seriousness and respect for the audience. The price for presenters can be high. They can lose parts or the whole audience in this way. In the worst case, they lose acceptance and reputation—possibly irreversibly. The presenter's experience and reputation in the scientific community play a part here, at least in part.

What are the essential points to consider when using humorous elements in a talk?

It goes without saying that caricatures and cartoons must not hurt people's feelings or values under any circumstances. If such visualisations are at the expense of minorities or expose people, they have the opposite effect of what the presenters wanted to achieve.

Furthermore, the relation of the illustration to the research topic is a basic requirement for the visualisation of comic drawings or parodies. Funny sketches just for effect and without a connection to the scientific question are counterproductive. Critical topics should only be presented in a serious manner and with a level of scientific distance and neutrality. Humorous visualisations may only be shown very selectively, preferably once, and are by no means suitable for regular or permanent use.

Another crucial point concerns copyright. Obtaining permission to use a cartoon or comic strip is imperative.

The drawing shown in Fig. 4.30 is from a presentation on the effect of verbal and non-verbal language in a talk when they are contradictory. It is an example of a humorous visualisation that can be created quickly with a few strokes, even without great artistic talent.

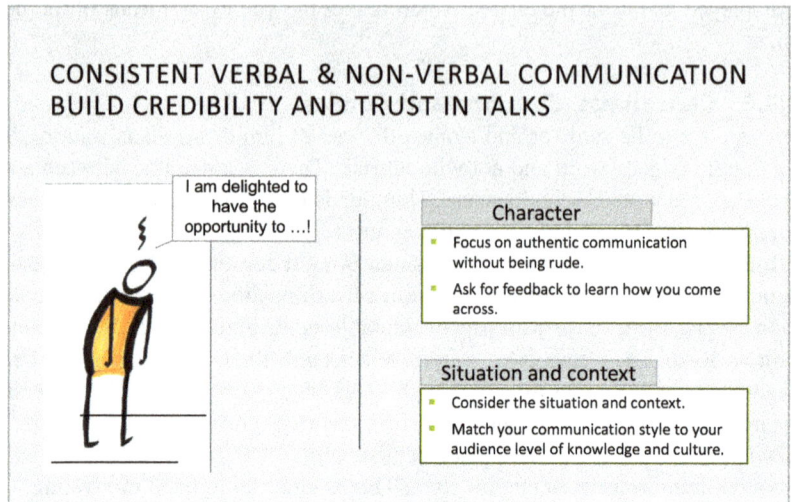

Fig. 4.30 Humorous drawing

4.3.3.7 Infographic—Pictures, Charts, Tables and Text in One Illustration

A special form of visualisation is the infographic. It shows complex scientific content in a compact and easy-to-understand graphic form and has long been used by journalists to attract attention. Infographics present highly condensed (scientific) information as mostly self-explanatory, descriptive graphics that combine familiar symbols and icons with illustrations, numbers and a small amount of text. They can be used as a kind of graphic summary at scientific meetings and conferences, and at the same time they also come to the fore in other fields of scientific communication. The "Research in Germany" portal of the Federal Ministry of Education and Research emphasises that research and science in particular can earn credits in their social media channels with this format and disseminate their information more quickly.[18]

The simplicity and universal visual language make infographics a form of scientific communication that is suitable for heterogeneous and especially non-academic audiences. On the webpage "Information is beautiful"[19] by David McCandless there are numerous examples of scientific infographics.

---

[18] https://www.research-in-germany.org/deutsche-institutionen/wissen/wissenswertes/social-media-grafiken-fuer-wissenschaft-und-forschung.html.
[19] https://informationisbeautiful.net/.

4.3.4 Avoid the Use of Confusing and Unnecessary Elements

The term "Chartjunk" is used by Edward Tufte, statistician and Professor Emeritus of Political Science and Computer Science at Yale University, to describe all visual elements of a visualisation that are unnecessary or irritating, i.e. do not contribute to conveying the information of a graphic in a comprehensible manner. This also comprises any gimmicks that obscure the view of the image. These include purely decorative components, such as gradients or shadows or dark grid lines in a chart. In his classic "The Visual Display of Quantitative Information", he advocates not wasting ink on redundant information in charts that do not tell the viewer anything new:

> The interior decoration of graphics generates a lot of ink that does not tell the viewer anything new. The purpose of decoration varies to make the graphic appear more scientific and precise, to enliven the display, to give the designer an opportunity to exercise artistic skills. Regardless of its cause, it is all non-data-ink or redundant data-ink, and it is often chartjunk."[20]

Chartjunk in the broadest sense of the term also includes elements that make comparisons impossible and make it difficult to understand the slide, for example, through unstable patterns and hatching, a gradient in the background, small pictures in the chart or a superfluous third dimension. "Pimped" charts demand the utmost concentration from the viewer, disturb their perception and can lead to misinterpretations. Even slide transitions break people's concentration on content and also do not contribute to a better understanding of the talk.

Slides without distracting elements are easier to read and understand. The focus is on the core message and the key information required to understand it.

▶ Anything that does not serve the better understanding of the core information of a slide or talk should be deleted and if necessary only said verbally.

4.3.4.1 Marked Contrast Facilitates People's Perception

Elements are never perceived in isolation, they always stand out from their surroundings. This phenomenon is called figure-ground organisation and describes the ability to distinguish the main object from its surroundings or background.[21] Together with other so-called Gestalt laws or principles,[22] it provides valuable information for the creation of slides.

The contrast between background and font, together with the font size and font type, is one of the key aspects in ensuring the good readability of a slide.

---

[20] Edward R. Tufte, "The Visual Display of Quantitative Information", 1991, page 107.
[21] http://www.scholarpedia.org/article/Gestalt_principles#Figure-ground_articulation.
[22] http://www.scholarpedia.org/article/Gestalt_principles.

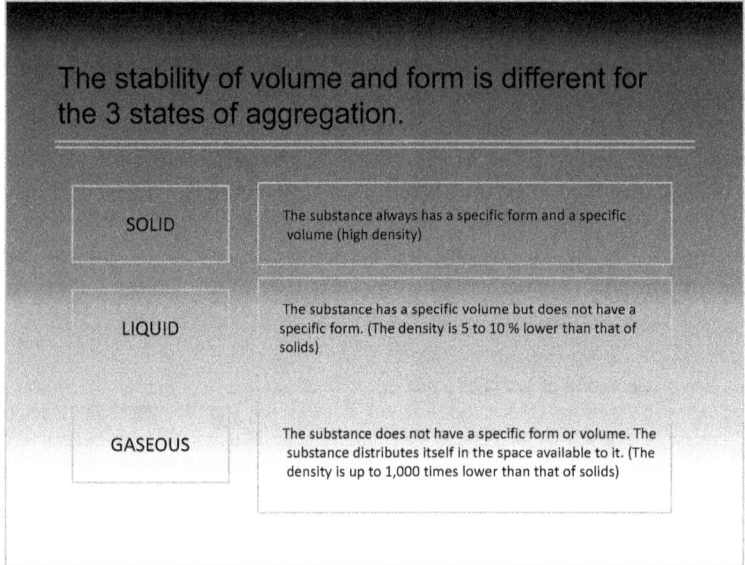

Fig. 4.31 Distracting backgound of slide—Gradient

If the level of contrast between the slide background and the writing is too low, this makes it difficult to grasp the slide or may make it completely impossible. Backgrounds with a colour gradient are an example of this. If there is a strong gradient, the lettering hardly stands out from the background in either the upper or lower part of the slide. If researchers choose a very faint gradient of colour, it may not be noticed at all or it may be irritating. This should be avoided. Figure 4.31 shows an example with a gradient.

Patterns or images in the background also do not enhance the expressiveness of the slide and are distracting. Moreover, in most cases there is no connection between the background and the content presented. For this reason, researchers should avoid distracting backgrounds or gradients in their slide design. This applies to all attempts to decorate or adorn the slide. Certain colour combinations can also lead to an unpleasant, fluctuating image and make prolonged viewing difficult. Caution is also advised because projectors do not always reproduce colours and patterns as they appear on the computer. Simple, two-dimensional diagrams visualise the information on a slide more clearly, are easier on the eye and require less effort to create.

Figure 4.32 shows a negative example with a watermark and its detrimental effect on the impact and readability of a slide.

4.3.4.2 3-D Illustrations Make It Difficult to Read Values

Three-dimensional charts sometimes appear more modern and advanced than two-dimensional charts. From a purely visual point of view, that may be true. In terms

4.3 Five Principles for Effective Slides in Academic Talks   101

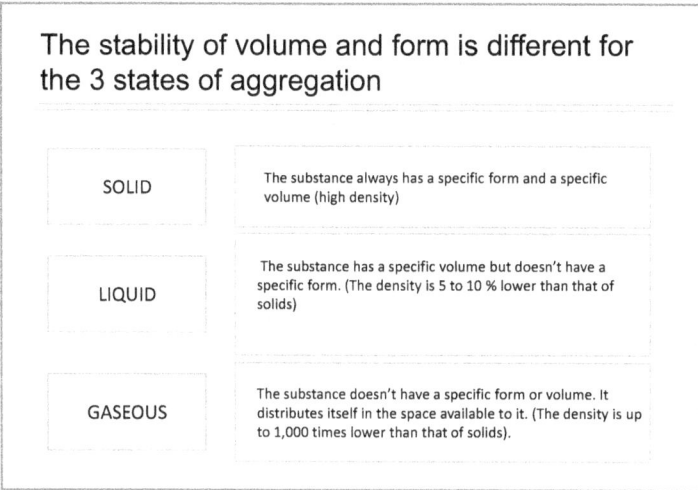

Fig. 4.32 Distracting background of slide—Watermark

of their informative value and readability, 3-D illustrations almost only cause disadvantages. Strictly speaking, the vast majority of three-dimensional charts are difficult and in great need of explanation for scientific presentations due to the distorted representation of values and results. Such charts make it difficult or impossible to read and identify exact values, which makes the graphic inaccurate and, in the worst case, unscientific. If there is no particular reason for the content, researchers should resort to two-dimensional graphics.

The dashed lines in Fig. 4.33 show how a distorted display does not facilitate accurate readings of values.

The addition of the number values would solve the problem and at the same time underline the disadvantages of the 3-D chart and make a bad illustration even fuller. The selected chart illustrates another weakness of three-dimensional representations. If one looks at country E with its low expressions, one could gain the impression that the value of this country is zero or even below without a numerical indication (see white arrow).The outer edge of the bar of country E does not exceed the zero point, although a small deflection can be seen at the bar in question.

The basic problem of 3-D charts can be easily seen in this example. Lack of, or wrong, information will inevitably result and quickly leads to misinterpretations. Even in those instances where the viewer can elicit useful information from the chart with a great deal of effort, three-dimensional representations are almost always a challenge, sometimes an unreasonable demand for the audience.

4.3.4.3 Colours Make It Easier to Grasp a Chart and the Slide

The use of colours is helpful because it makes it easier for the audience to differentiate or summarise information. They aid communication and help the viewer

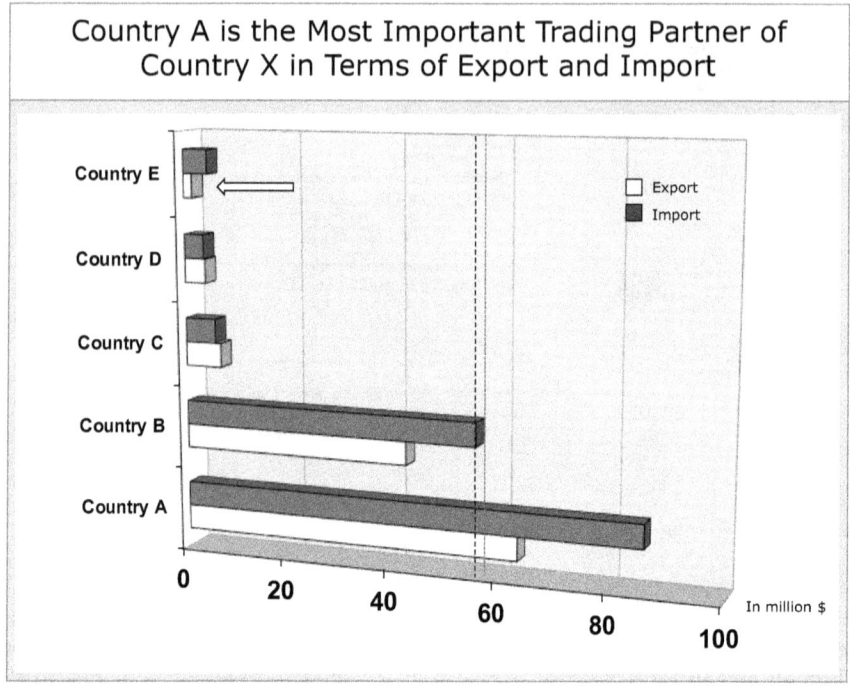

Fig. 4.33 3D bar chart

to orientate him. On the one hand, colours can be used to express the special significance of a particular aspect and, at the same time, identical colours boost the perception of contents that belong together or are formally equivalent. Different colours distinguish what is important from what is less important. Colours provide an additional benefit: They are more easily memorised than patterns or hatchings. Nevertheless, colours must not dominate the presentation, nor should they distract from the actual information.

▶ Limit yourself to a few colours - preferably no more than 3 per slide and use them consistently.

A high contrast between the different colours on a slide is crucial due to the fact it is difficult for the viewer to distinuguish between similar colours. This in turn leads to a laborious assignment or differentiation of individual blocks of information on the slide.

▶ On a slide where (almost) everything is highlighted in colour, it is also true precisely because of this, that nothing is highlighted any more. It is just colourful.

4.3.4.4 Making Special Features, Sequences, Procedures and Processes Visually Recognisable

In the case of slides with a lot of details and elements, it is advisable to present special features, important or difficult things orally and to additionally support them visually. Numbering and alphabetical outlines are simple and effective ways to make a process or sequence more recognisable. In order to highlight an element, a colour marking of the decisive aspect or a text field in the form of an arrow with additional information pointing towards this item is a good idea.

▶ Actively guide your audience's gaze through your language and visual cues.

4.3.5 Make Use of Animations

In scientific talks complex procedures, experiments, processes or machines are often explained. This places large demands upon the audience. Animations constitute professional ways to present the density of information in smaller and more understandable bites. Step-by-step slides help to arouse curiosity, control the concentration of those present and make complex things easier to understand. In addition to the size of objects, strong contrast and signal colours, elements that move[23] are also one of the ways to attract the audience's attention. For this purpose, the standard presentation programmes offer numerous forms of animation that make objects appear and disappear, move them on the slide and change their size or colour. Four variants are available to presenters for this purpose.

▶ Using animations, you focus the audience's attention on one point at a time.

1. Showing and hiding slide contents

Where it is not possible to shorten text or delete elements for content or didactic reasons, speakers can use the slide space more efficiently with the aid of fade-ins and fade-outs. Animations ensure that only the element that is being discussed and presented at the moment is shown. The rest is not or only slightly visible in the background. In this way, scientists can show the individual aspects step by step and at the pace and length that suits the respective audience and the given time window. This rectifies the slide, helps reduce the amount of information at any one time and keeps the cognitive load on the audience smaller.

---

[23] https://www.ncbi.nlm.nih.gov/pmc/articles/PMC9453061/.

▶ Resist the temptation to add sound effects. In almost all cases these are annoying.

2. Highlighting and enlarging a section

In order to analyse a detail, it is useful to pick out a section of an experiment or part of a formula and look at it in isolation without any distractions. If necessary, these elements can also be displayed enlarged. Especially when the complexity should be reduced or a certain section is of particular importance for the achievement of the objective of thje talk, this form of animation is recommended—a tried and tested means of visualising what is important in this slide.

3. Assembling complex things step by step

Animations are very suitable for breaking down processes or experiments into comprehensible blocks and making them easier to understand. The same applies to before-and-after representations in which changes are faded in one after the other and dynamically built up to form a whole. Using selective visual aids, such as arrows or coloured borders, important information can be highlighted and, if necessary, hidden once more.

4. Displaying simple simulations

Elements of the slide are moved using so-called animation paths and make a presentation more dynamic. For instance, the path of an algorithm can be played back "live". When visualising formulas and equations, it is possible to introduce individual elements one after the other or to show how an equation has evolved. Numbers, variables, mathematical symbols or objects are moved to a new place via animation paths and thus catch the viewer's eye directly. This visualises processes in moving images, builds up tension and creates moments of surprise. Such forms of visualisation set the talk apart from other presentations.

Most presentation programmes offer an almost unmanageable number of effects and invite you to use them all. But beware: Bouncing, spinning, flying or sound presentation elements are annoying and usually perceived as gimmicks.

▶ Choose low-motion, low-effect animation styles such as "Appear" and use this variant for the entire talk.

Animations are powerful tools that give presenters the opportunity to direct the audience's gaze in a targeted way. Nevertheless, it is important to use them sparingly and only where they serve to aid comprehension of the slide in question. If too many animations are used, the positive effects quickly wear off and can have the opposite effect and distract people from the content. This also applies to animations that are too small, e.g. when text is faded in word by word. Here, too, the rule applies that animations must serve to aid a better understanding of the slide, otherwise they should be dispensed with.

References

Alley, Michael: No date indicated, Assertion-Evidence talks are comprehended better by audiences and project more confidence from speakers, https://www.assertion-evidence.com/, last retrieved: 29.12.2023.
Alley, Michael: 2022, PowerPoint Templates for Assertion-Evidence Talks, https://www.assertion-evidence.com/templates.html, last retrieved: 29.12.2023.
Defeyter, Margaret Anne et al., 2009, The picture superiority effect in recognition memory: A developmental study using the response signal procedure, https://www.researchgate.net/publication/247213377_The_picture_superiority_effect_in_recognition_memory_A_developmental_study_using_the_response_signal_procedure, last retrieved: 29.12.2023.
Deutscher Akademischer Austauschdienst e.V. (DAAD) No date indicated, Social-Media-Grafiken für Wissenschaft und Forschung, https://www.research-in-germany.org/deutsche-institutionen/wissen/wissenswertes/social-media-grafiken-fuer-wissenschaft-und-forschung.html, last retrieved: 29.12.2023.
Garner, Joanna K. et al., 2013, https://www.researchgate.net/publication/286042632_How_the_Design_of_Presentation_Slides_Affects_Audience_Comprehension_A_Case_for_the_Assertion-Evidence_Approach, last retrieved: 29.12.2023.
Max-Planck-Institut für Plasmaphysik, No date indicated, Plasma, https://www.ipp.mpg.de/15096/plasma, last retrieved: 20.03.2023: , last retrieved: 29.12.2023.
McCandless, David, 2023, Information is beautiful, https://informationisbeautiful.net/, last retrieved: 29.12.2023.
Medina, John: "Brain rules for work", 2021, page 199, Pear Press.
Medina, John: "Brain Rules (Updated and Expanded): 12 Principles for Surviving and Thriving at Work, Home, and School", 2014, S.193 ff, Pear Press.
Praveen C. K. et al., 2022, Psychological Impact and Influence of Animation on Viewer's Visual Attention and Cognition: A Systematic Literature Review, Open Challenges, and Future Research Directions, https://www.ncbi.nlm.nih.gov/pmc/articles/PMC9453061/, last retrieved: 29.12.2023.
Proulx, Michael J., 2010, Size Matters: Large Objects Capture Attention in Visual Search, https://doi.org/journals.plos.org/plosone/article?id=10.1371/journal.pone.0015293, last retrieved: 29.12.2023
Small Business Computing, 2001, Death by powerpoint, https://www.smallbusinesscomputing.com/software/death-by-powerpoint/ last retrieved: 29.12.2023.
Spektrum der Wissenschaft, No date indicated, Bewegungssehen, https://www.spektrum.de/lexikon/neurowissenschaft/bewegungssehen/1436, last retrieved: 29.12.2023.
Spektrum der Wissenschaft, No date indicated, Figur-Grund-Verhältnis, https://www.spektrum.de/lexikon/psychologie/figur-grund-verhaeltnis/4958, last retrieved: 29.12.2023.
Spektrum der Wissenschaft, No date indicated, Gestaltgesetze, https://www.spektrum.de/lexikon/psychologie/gestaltgesetze/5876, last retrieved: 29.12.2023.
Studifix: No date indicated, Aggregatzustand einfach erklärt, https://studyflix.de/chemie/aggregatzustand-einfach-erklart-4087, last retrieved: 29.12.2023.
Sweller John: 2011, Cognitive Load Theory, https://www.sciencedirect.com/science/article/abs/pii/B9780123876911000028, last retrieved: 29.12.2023.
Tufte, Edward R., "The Visual Display of Quantitative Information", 1991, page 107, Graphics Press.

5 Communicating Methods, Results and Knowledge Gains—The Talk and Presentation

Scientific conferences have always been face-to-face meetings where the focus is on the talks and the exchanges with other researchers. A wide range of opportunities are available to speakers here: they can learn about the latest research in their specialist field and also have the opportunity to network with peers, potential employees and future employers. Above all, they present their work to an audience that usually consists of scientists from their own discipline. Speakers receive guidance and feedback on their paper from these experts, contributing to their own development and that of the research field. A carefully prepared and professionally presented talk forms the basis to support and benefit from this exchange. Talks can in this way contribute to a successful career in science. It is therefore worthwhile for researchers to invest in making their presentation skills and techniques more professional.

This chapter presents the criteria to pull off a coherent and convincing performance. The steps for a motivating introduction, a convincing main part and a memorable conclusion are successively presented here. At the beginning, you will come across numerous tips on final organisational and personal preparation to prevent potential problems and pitfalls.

5.1 Final Preparation Activities at Home and in the Conference Room

The talk has been fully prepared. The structure and content have been laid down and the slides have been created. Now some final preparatory activities remain on the list of outstanding items. This includes announcing—repeatedly, if necessary—participation in the conference via social media, as well as taking precautionary measures to be able to master technical and other challenges with confidence.

Finally, the packing list of things that should be definitely and advisably taken along with you must be worked through.

5.1.1 Preparatory Activities from Home

5.1.1.1 Announce Your Participation and Talk via Social Media

Social media have established themselves as an important information channel in connection with scientific conferences. Scientists benefit from disseminating their participation and the topic of their talk through these channels, as they can reach and inform many researchers in this way. This is a good opportunity to motivate people to attend your own talk, to make appointments for individual meetings and to maintain or expand your network.

1. Use social media to draw attention to your (virtual) presentation or poster early on.
2. Use the hashtag of the conference to make contact with interested people, to arrange meetings and to make it easier for other visitors to find you, even before the event takes place. Arrange for individual exchanges and meetings.
3. Send personal invitations for your (poster) presentation, to colleagues, potential cooperation partners or scientists you would like to meet.
4. Inform them through different channels when, where and what you will present. Attach a picture of your poster or an interesting slide as a motivational booster. Send a short reminder briefly before the conference is due to take place. Also share the link to your motivational slide or poster on the conference organiser's homepage.

5.1.1.2 Avoiding Mishaps in Advance

Scientists have been expressing the same concerns in presentation seminars and coaching sessions for many years: Questions from the audience, a blackout and technical problems are considered the biggest causes of stress and anxiety generators. And this is regardless of their nationality and discipline. Good preparation is an important part of the solution here.

There are speakers who not only work on their set of slides the night before the presentation, but even just a few hours before holding it. "Last-minute actions" of this kind not only give rise to careless mistakes, they are also an inevitable source of stress and increasing uncertainty. If you have not put together all the materials until the actual day of the talk, then you deprive yourself of the opportunity to rehearse it once. You also no longer have the time to test the order and content of the slides, as well as transitions, links and animations, which increases the risk of mishaps and the likelihood of feeling very nervous.

▶ Complete your presentation in good time—at the latest one day—before your departure. This calms your nerves, provides you with a sense of assurance and reduces the risk of mishaps.

CHECKLIST FOR THE TALK

- [ ] Send set of slides to the event organiser
- [ ] Business cards or A4 printout of poster with current contact details
- [ ] Set of slides on a USB stick
- [ ] Copies of your own papers or books on related topics
- [ ] Printout of the documents for emergencies
- [ ] Flyers of your own research institution
- [ ] Samples/ prototypes/ examples
- [ ] Notebook and pen for notes, feedback etc
- [ ] Laptop and mains plug, adapter
- [ ] Presenter/ Laser pointer

Fig. 5.1 Checklist for the talk

As a next step, scientists should send their presentation to the organiser in advance so that it will definitely be available on the day of the talk. Experienced speakers send their presentation as a PDF document to ensure that there are no changes to fonts, colours, charts, bullet points or variables in an equation during the presentation. In addition, most researchers take a copy of their file (talk and additional information) in electronic form as a backup. The speaker will also feel more secure if he brings his own laptop with him because he is familiar with how it works. If he has his own computer, he can also check in advance whether animations and links to other files run without errors.

In addition to the obvious items, such as a computer, you should take helpful devices, such as a small notebook for writing notes that is always to hand, with you. Even something that might seem unusual, such as a printout of the set of slides, can become very important in rather rare situations and provide a valid fallback option, for instance, in the event of a loss or malfunction of the computer.

The checklist in Fig. 5.1 shows what is necessary for the talk.[1]

5.1.1.3 What to Wear at Scientific Conferences

Personal preparation also includes the selection of the right clothing for the talk. While the dress code at events outside of the science fields—for example, at fundraising organisations, companies or interviews—usually includes business attire, a casual form of dress predominates in the scientific community. This varies from discipline to discipline and from country to country. While the dress code for the humanities includes suits and costumes here and there, depending on the occasion, this is considered a waste of time for most natural scientists. In some

---

[1] Sybille May, „Das Checklistenbuch", 2. Edition, 2014, Gabler Verlag.

disciplines, it is therefore even frowned upon to appear dressed in this way, as it suggests setting the wrong priorities. The American molecular biologist and columnist for the online edition of "Science" Adam Ruben describes it as follows: "Dressing well for an interview makes sense. But for many scientists, dressing well is not just something that fails to interest us. It's something we actively shun because it might broadcast the wrong priority".[2] By contrast, the online platform for economists "Inomics" advises: "It's always better to dress up than down" and "... it's better to be the only guy with a tie than the only one without".[3]

In general, researchers should bear in mind that there are also occasions in science, such as laudations, where an official dress code is desired or even explicitly required. Scientists should seek information on this from the organiser or experienced colleagues. It is also important that the clothes fit the person and that the person feels comfortable in them.

▶   Pack a spare shirt or blouse for events with a business dress code or similar. You will then be prepared if you can no longer use your original garment because of stains or damage.

A certain degree of caution is nevertheless advisable. Even at informal meetings, a certain level of professionalism in terms of dress is recommended. For example, flip-flops or sandals may produce unpleasant noises while walking during the presentation and may be considered inappropriate depending on the culture. With regard to clothing and accessories, presenters should also bear in mind that necklaces or bracelets may create distracting noises when presenting with a microphone at large events. Some dress fabrics can have a similar effect when the lapel microphone transmits rustling sounds that are audible to everyone. Especially at virtual events, this can be very irritating for the audience, as the sound is usually transmitted directly to people's ears via headphones (see Chapter 7).

▶   Put jewellery and accessories away before your presentation to eliminate distracting background noise. If possible, test the microphone before you start your talk.

5.1.1.4 Personal Preparation (Just) Before the Date of Departure

Shortly before your departure, it is advisable to check whether the crucial things for the trip and yourself have been packed. This can be a reason for not being able to travel, especially with regard to a visa that may be required or necessary vaccinations, but also in the case of expired identity cards or passports. Less critical,

---

[2] Adam Ruben in http://www.sciencemag.org/careers/2014/04/dress-profess-what-should-scientists-wear.

[3] INOMICS Team in https://inomics.com/insight/dress-code-for-academic-conferences-what-to-wear-and-what-to-avoid-48004.

5.1 Final Preparation Activities at Home and in the Conference Room

CHECKLIST FOR THE TRIP

- ☐ Clarify and book means of travel (flight, train, car) and accommodation
- ☐ Save tickets, booking numbers, seat reservations and take them with you
- ☐ Charged mobile phone, charging cable and powerbank and take them with you in your hand luggage.
- ☐ Carry credit card and foreign currency with you abroad outside the euro region
- ☐ Carry your laptop and mains plug, adapter in your hand luggage
- ☐ Take a valid identity card or passport with you
- ☐ Take your visa and vaccination certificates with you
- ☐ Inform important persons
- ☐ Initiate representation scheme
- ☐ Activate e-mail out of office function

Fig. 5.2 Checklist for the trip

but nevertheless an important form of professional conduct, is the activation of the e-mail absence function and informing other persons affected by the trip, such as a deputy. Figure 5.2 displays a checklist of the key points for the trip.[4]

5.1.2 Preparatory Work in the Conference Room

It goes without saying and is in the researchers' best interests that they arrive rested and on time on the day of the talk. On time means being at the venue early enough to ensure that, without running into any time constraints, they can take care of organisational matters such as registration, greeting the host, registering or checking in at the hotel or checking the technology. If a conference starts very early and you have to travel a long way to get there, it is advisable to arrive the evening before. This ensures that no traffic jams or train or flight delays jeopardise your participation. It also helps to be more relaxed going into the talk and attending pre-conference meetings.

5.1.2.1 Room Check, Getting in the Mood for the Talk and Networking

An early appearance offers another significant advantage: The opportunity to take an early look at the lecture room and "acclimatize". People often underestimate how important and reassuring this is. The room check helps people to get used to the technical, organisational and spatial conditions.

---

[4] Sybille May, „Das Checklistenbuch", 2. Edition, 2014, Gabler Verlag.

▶ Gain an impression of the situation in the conference room, get used to the atmosphere and familiarise yourself with the conditions. This reduces feelings of nerves and the likelihood of mishaps.

If you know the specifics of the room, its design and technology (podium, lectern, height of the screen, steps, trip hazards, etc.), you can adjust or make changes if necessary and possible. Even if the conference is already underway, a visual "site inspection" is still worthwhile. It makes your arrival easier and helps you to get used to the circumstances.

▶ Check in advance where you want to stand and whether you still need to move anything so that everyone can see well and there are no more trip hazards. If at all possible do not leave anything to chance.

Arriving early in many cases also opens up the opportunity of having a few words with the organiser, other speakers or conference participants before the presentation. This first small talk helps you to make contacts and meet friendly colleagues. This is fun, makes a big contribution towards cultivating relationships and is of great importance for one's own network—one of the most valuable resources for researchers. Especially with regard to content-related or methodological support, career opportunities and, last but not least, dealing with challenging professional situations, the network plays an extremely important role.

▶ Use the opportunity at all conferences to actively establish contacts and consolidate existing ones. Face-to-face meetings are valuable ways to cultivate your network.

5.1.2.2 Technology Check on Site

Probably everyone can remember presentations where the first impression was one of technical glitches or mishaps—presentations that started with the wrong set of slides, for instance, where smileys replaced all the currency symbols, or where no image appeared on the screen at all. Such a start is problematic for the speakers concerned in two respects. From a purely pragmatic point of view, valuable minutes of the scarce time allocated are lost for the "repair job". From a psychological point of view, there is much to suggest that anxiety levels will increase.

▶ Check your presentation material and technology in advance and once more on site. Test everything in front of the audience as well. If you try to be quick here and save time, you may stumble over it later in the talk.

5.1 Final Preparation Activities at Home and in the Conference Room

To prevent such unpleasant situations, it is advisable to test the technology and media. This includes making sure that everything that is needed is in the right place and works—such as a projector and laser pointer or paper and pen. In addition to checking that the computer is working properly, also check that the correct file has been called up and that the resolution has been set to ensure a correct display. This also includes checking microphones, loudspeakers, playback devices and—if necessary—whether the internet access is stable. Depending on the design of the talk, it helps to check before the presentation whether media such as whiteboards or flipcharts are at the designated place and pens or chalk are ready and usable.

In the case of smaller and informal events, researchers should also ask how the lighting is switched on/off and how the room can be darkened if necessary. It is also important to know whether replacement units or replacement lamps are available and who will take care of the repair or replacement in the event of a breakdown. In principle, it is helpful to ask for a permanent contact person in the event of any questions or difficulties that may arise regarding the technology. If the person cannot stay in the room during the talk, the speaker should ask how the person in question can be reached in an emergency.

The following questions will help you prevent you forgetting any important checks shortly before the presentation:

5. What needs to be changed so that all members of the audience can see the presentation well?
6. Where are there any tripping hazards for me (cables, steps, lids of floor tanks, etc.)?
7. What else do I still need for the talk (presenter, additional table, etc.)?
8. Do the projector, laptop, microphone, speakers, internet access, wireless presenter work?
9. How can the room be darkened and the lighting switched on?
10. How is the technology controlled?
11. Who can I contact in an emergency and how?
12. Have I switched off my mobile?

▶ Take a notebook or a piece of paper and a pen to the podium to write down questions, ideas, criticism and comments. This shows your interest, can help you improve your work and helps with a mere glance if you have lost the thread.

5.1.2.3 The Last Minutes Before the Starting Signal

At many conferences, meetings and workshops, a chairman or chairwoman leads the event. They announce speakers and in most cases also take over their introductions. Depending on the brevity of the presentation, this may be limited to the name of the speakers, their research organisations and the presentation titles. In the case of longer talks, short remarks on the academic qualifications and scientific achievements of the speakers are also added. In addition to the professional qualifications, chairpersons also tell a short story about the speakers from time to time, depending on the event. On special occasions, such as award ceremonies or laudations, personal details of the speaker's background, family or hobbies may also be mentioned. If required, such information will be requested together with the talk notes.

▶ Be sure to look at the screen to check that the correct set of slides is displayed and in the presentation mode.

At a classical conference, presenters wait for the introduction by the chairperson and then quietly walk forward. There they quietly set themselves up by positioning things needed for the talk—such as manuscript, pointing aids—according to their needs. They then briefly check the technical equipment and make sure that the correct title slide is displayed. Now they look into the audience in a friendly manner, wait a few more seconds until as many people as possible are looking at them and the room slowly becomes quieter. After that they start with the prepared introduction to the talk. At less formal events, researchers should start more quickly, as the scientists present usually already know each other.

5.2 Introduction—First Impression, Lead-Up to the Topic and Increasing People's Attention

Getting started on a talk is something very few researchers actually enjoy doing. It is seen by many as a necessary evil that causes them to lose time for the actual presentation and has nothing to do with the content. The importance of the introduction for the success of a scientific talk is therefore often not known or underestimated. It is the first contact between the speaker and the audience and has a lasting influence on the rest of the talk.

This is where the first impression is made, a psychological phenomenon that strongly shapes the audience's attitude towards the researcher, the topic and the rest of the presentation. It is known from psychology that the first impression of a person is formed within a few seconds, is relatively long-lasting and influences the overall perception of the person and the situation. In the absence of other possibilities, people rely on this first impression to form an initial picture of the competence as well as trustworthiness of the counterpart. The individual usually unconsciously draws initial conclusions from this as to whether interesting facts and a benefit can be anticipated from this presentation.[5]

▶ Do not jump the gun. You do not get a second chance to make a first impression.

---

[5] https://www.psychologicalscience.org/observer/studying-first-impressions-what-to-consider.

5.2.1 Three Elements Form the Basis for a Classic Introduction

The introduction has a significant impact on the attitude and attention of the audience and thus on the success of the presentation. On the one hand, it should bear the individual handwriting and imprint of the speaker and at the same time be adapted to the respective audience. It is important that researchers set the course accordingly right at the start of the talk. This can be achieved if, firstly, they do not simply present to themselves, but establish a connection with the audience, secondly, show them that something interesting and relevant will follow and, thirdly, inform them when what will happen in the talk. It is about contact, motivation and guidance. A suitable introduction is necessary and important even if parts of it have already been presented by the chairperson or party who invited the speaker.

5.2.1.1 Contact: Welcome Speech and Introduction

In the contact phase, speakers establish a connection and relationship with the audience. It is like the process of getting to know other people in person, where they greet, introduce and look at each other. Content does not play a part at this point. This is where the first impression is formed and therefore scientists should take this part seriously and consider it an important element of their presentation. If you routinely reel this off, you waste an opportunity to win the audience over for yourself, your research, the talk and possibly even for your own network.

The following five tips will help you establish the first contact and leave a good impression.

1. Stand up straight.
2. Look at your audience in a friendly way.
3. Wait briefly until the room is quiet.
4. Thank them for having been given the opportunity to speak and welcome your audience briefly and sincerely.
5. Speak in such a way that you can be easily understood.

It is always useful to have concise and preferably memorable information ready for your own introduction, that has been adapted to the event in question. This applies especially to meetings where no chairperson or party who has issued an invitation is present.

The most commonly used structure for presenting oneself at conferences includes the points listed below:

1. Introduce yourself with your first and last name. Pronounce both clearly and slowly so that the audience can understand it well and know how to pronounce your name correctly. You can support this with the title slide. One aspect is particularly important here. As with any greeting, eye contact with the other person plays a decisive part in how you are perceived.

2. Some speakers completely refrain from introducing themselves because they do not want to repeat what is already known. This needs to be carefully considered. After all, this means that a familiar and culturally expected part of the personal establishment of contact is lost.
3. State your position, rank or function and the name of your research institution. Tell the audience what you do and have done. Demonstrate your scientific experience and credibility without appearing boastful. Underline why you are the right person for this talk.
4. Outline your research. Focus here on the relation to the presentation topic.

Quite a few speakers make use of the opportunity to provide advice on how to get in touch and on networking opportunities and point out their activities in social media. It helps many speakers to learn these by heart. This provides a sense of security and ensures that nothing is forgotten.

In this context, it is important to bear in mind that neither an artificial, friendly greeting nor a "Welcome to my talk." spoken in a monotone voice is motivating. A short and authentic "Good afternoon, ladies and gentlemen and welcome" is just as appropriate as a simple and friendly "Hello everyone" at an informal event. A frankly expressed appreciation for the time and effort the audience has put into coming is expected, especially in an international context.

Many also thank the respective chairpersons for their words of welcome and the organisers for the opportunity to hold a talk. If you feel good, you can express that: "I'm delighted to be here today and to see so many familiar faces". In some countries, words of praise for the conference venue are also welcome: "This is my first time in ... and I am deeply impressed".

▶ Bear in mind that in some cultures they appreciate it if you say something personal or humorous about yourself.

All forms of excuses for incomplete material, insufficient preparation time, lack of expertise in the topic of the talk, omissions by colleagues or project staff are inappropriate and psychologically counterproductive. This makes things unnecessarily difficult for the speaker and the audience. The audience usually has no interest in the circumstances under which the presentation was created and how challenging the conditions were. They expect a professional presentation with interesting results. If you draw the attention of your audience to negative things, it is difficult to expect people to be motivated and enthusiastic about your presentation and thus influence the attitude of the audience to your disadvantage.

Remarks such as: "I know this is a dry topic, but I hope you still enjoy it to some extent" or "Unfortunately, I didn't manage to prepare all the slides for my talk on the train journey here. The last two are a bit chaotic" are counterproductive and motivational own goals. They put mistakes, weaknesses and problems in the centre of people's attention and do not help to make the audience lenient and benevolent towards the speaker. It is very likely that parts of the audience will concern themselves with something else following such statements.

How must an audience member who has come to hear this talk feel when he learns that the presenter has not taken the time to prepare appropriately or is not even convinced of his topic himself? The reputational damage that can result from such a performance is difficult to repair.

From a psychological point of view, it is wiser to focus on the positive. The following example amply demonstrates this. One scientist planned to present the five aspects of his current research paper at a conference. The time he had until the event was due to start was not sufficient for him to prepare a complete presentation. In his introduction he said: "Regrettably, I did not manage to prepare all five aspects of my intended talk. Unfortunately, I can only show you three today!" Presented in this way, it can lead to disappointment and dissatisfaction on the part of the audience due to the fact something has been withheld and the presentation is incomplete. By simply rephrasing this, the scientist could have made the effect on the audience more positive with the following sentence: "I am pleased to present to you today, fully up-to-date, the first three aspects of my paper!".

▶ To start your talk, don't say what you can't show, but name what you will present.

Those who still need time to conduct their research or to prepare a professional presentation should first present their paper at internal exchange formats of their own research institution or ask experienced colleagues for help in preparing their presentation.

Speakers only refer to critical aspects in exceptional cases, for instance, if the presentation cannot be shown on a slide because of a defective projector.

▶ Negativity does not belong in the introduction and makes it harder for the audience to develop an interest in the presentation and keep their attention levels high.

5.2.1.2 Motivation: Research Topic and Its Relevance

The second part of the introduction focuses on the topic of the talk and its relevance for the science field and the audience. Even if the title of the presentation and initial information are likely to be known to the audience from abstracts in invitations and programmes, practised presenters refer to both explicitly at the beginning of their talk. The point here is to show why it is worth following this talk. The goal is to arouse the interest of the audience, to get them tuned in and to motivate them. Speakers lay the foundations for a successful presentation here. To do this, it is advisable to outline the following points—preferably from the storyline.

– Briefly describe the current status of your topic.
– State the challenge or problem.

- Briefly formulate the goal of the talk or the research question(s).
- Highlight—without going into detail—the knowledge gains arising from, as well as the new and special aspects, of your work.

In this way, researchers answer why exactly there is a need for research or action at this point and why they are dealing with the topic. This is particularly memorable if specific comparisons and examples are used.

▶ It should be one of the goals of your talk that the audience say afterwards: that was a good talk, I would like to delve into the topic in more depth and then ask for the article or paper.

5.2.1.3 Guidance: Sequence and Agenda

The last element of the introduction is concerned more with organisational aspects than matters of content. It is not only polite but also important that the audience is informed about the agenda and organisational aspects, if any, in the introduction. This includes the content of the talk, but also any breaks, demonstrations, change of location (for example for laboratory visits) and, if applicable, information on how to spend the evening.

If you do not want to provide a detailed description of the individual items due to time constraints or if you only have two topics on your agenda, you should briefly present the sequence to your audience orally, without any slides and in-depth information.

If not specified by the organiser, information on the duration of the talk and on opportunities to ask questions will follow at this point. It goes without saying that this should be formulated as diplomatically as possible so as not to offend the audience. Indirect references to it such as "My *talk will last 30 min. Afterwards we will have enough time to discuss open points and answer your questions.*"

Presenters who feel confident and know how to navigate difficult question situations can invite their audience to do so by saying "p*lease feel free to interrupt me whenever you have a question*".

Especially at the beginning, when they feel a bit more nervous, many scientists tend to speak at a fast pace in order to save time on the one hand and to get to the main part, which is more interesting and enjoyable for them, as quickly as possible on the other. This is understandable and yet it is important not to quickly rush through the introduction, but to use it wisely for the preparation and to get the audience in the mood.

Figure 5.3[6] shows the elements of the introduction, motivation and guidance

---

[6] Own research and own representation.

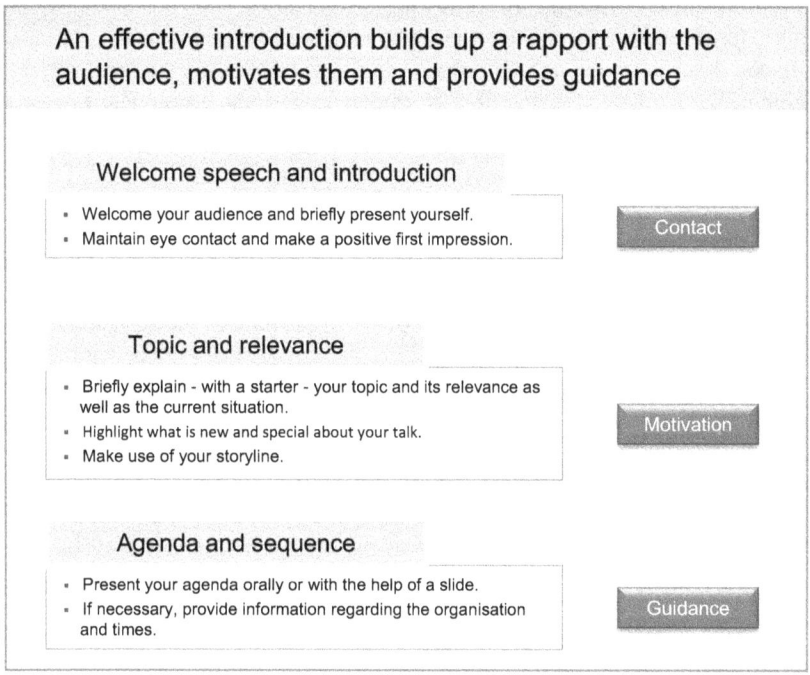

Fig. 5.3 An effective introduction builds up a rapport with the audience, motivates them and provides guidance

▶ Think about the introduction beforehand. Pre-formulate the first one or two sentences and learn them off by heart if necessary. This will calm you down and reduce the number of errors you make.

One could argue that the vast majority of introductions follow this structure. That is true, and is at the same time the reason why the audience hardly pay any attention to them. They know what is coming and that usually nothing new and interesting follows. The audience has become accustomed to this and usually pays little attention to the introductions—a wasted opportunity for presenters. Current brain research provides some clues as to how this happens and what researchers can do about it.

Researcher Carmen Simon works in the field of cognitive neuroscience and says that this process of accustomisation "can destroy presentations".[7] She advises using different stimuli and changes to make it more difficult for people to grow accustomed to this process and, similarly to frequent cuts in TV films, to ensure that viewers stick with it.

---

[7] https://www.youtube.com/watch?v=UzrWcEIedH4.

Neuroscientist Friederike Fabrizius also emphasises that presentations should begin with something that is new, stimulating or surprising.[8]

If you don't offer enough stimulation in the presentation and especially at the beginning, you make it easier for the audience to look away. The prospect of something new, special and relevant and a touch of uncertainty motivate people and keep their attention levels high. The human brain is designed for this and rewards with dopamine. It is less important what is changed. What counts instead is the frequency of change.

John Medina therefore recommends using "hooks" that appeal to emotions such as curiosity or joy.[9] These should, indeed must, be as relevant as possible for the audience and have to do with the topic of the presentation. Hooks are sometimes also called "starters".

In order to establish contact with the audience and motivate them to take an interest in the presentation, speakers use the findings from the audience analysis (level of knowledge, interests and attitudes) that was conducted as part of the preparation for the talk. It is also important to take your time and not to barge in with the door.

Careful planning and preparation form the basis for a motivating start and at the same time help to reduce early nerves.

▶ As a rule of thumb, approximately 5% of the total time of the talk should be allocated to the introduction.

5.2.2 Tailor the Introduction with "Hooks"

Hooks or starters are special stylistic devices to make the introduction more individual and interesting. In the scientific field, these inputs are called "Emotional Competence Stimuli" (ECS). Emotions provide the organisational prioritisation that leads to people paying attention to some items in a presentation and not others. The more emotional a stimulus is, the more likely we are to pay attention to it and recall it.[10]

ECS help on the one hand to get the audience in the mood for the topic, to arouse their interest and on the other hand to increase their levels of attention. They enable scientists to stand out from other speakers, display their own enthusiasm for the topic and stay in people's memory for longer. Precisely because most talks are often presented in a very sober manner, it is a pleasant change for the audience when researchers make a departure from familiar and frequently used structures. Starters make it easier for the audience to understand what is being presented

---

[8] Friederike Fabrizius, Hans W. Hagemann: "The Leading Brain", 2018, page 191.
[9] https://mannerofspeaking.org/2015/07/03/a-brain-hack-for-your-next-presentation/.
[10] John Medina: "Brain Rules for Work", 2021, page 186.

5.2 Introduction—First Impression, Lead-Up to the Topic and Increasing ...

because there is a more concrete, often pictorial, point of connection. Another aspect that should not be neglected is the increase in a speaker's popularity that is often associated with this.

▶ The simplest way to make the introduction to the talk tailored to the interests of the audience and different, is to make statements with reference to a previous speaker, the audience or the time of the talk.

All hooks are elements that influence the dramaturgy of a talk and should only be used in a planned way if possible. It makes sense to choose the positioning in the introduction in such a way that the starter achieves the most lasting effect. This can, for instance, be a quotation that is mentioned together with the topic or a short anecdote that is told before the welcoming address. The prerequisite for all starters is that they are highly relevant to the topic, fit the style of the speaker and that the audience can easily understand them and place them in the context of the talk. Appropriately selected and carefully placed hooks can be real icebreakers and motivation boosters. If used incorrectly, they achieve no effect or the opposite effect to what was intended. It is therefore essential to rehearse hooks.

Starters break a pattern familiar to the scientific auditorium. On the one hand, this is the great strength of these instruments; on the other hand, it can lead in some cases to irritation among listeners when familiar structures are changed. In these cases it makes sense to prepare the audience and announce the starter. This can be done verbally ("Let me start with an interesting story") or non-verbally by taking a short pause before and/or after the starter and letting this short moment of silence sink in. Speakers achieve a similar effect when they deliberately reduce the pace of their speech or combine both techniques. This makes it clear to the audience that something special is about to happen.

The most frequently used starters are listed in Fig. 5.4.[11]

1. Reference to conversations with other conference participants

An obvious, quite spontaneous way to use a starter for the talk lies in the exchange with other conference participants on the evening before or the day of the event itself. This source often allows for an unexpected, humorous and unique view of one's own topic and quickly leads to appropriately individual hooks that are also highly relevant to the current conference. Anyone who can refer to a conversation with a colleague present in the room at the start is very likely to have everyone's eyes on them. For all its positive aspects there are also some drawbacks here. Starters of this kind cannot be planned and must be incorporated into an existing

---

[11] Own research and own representation.

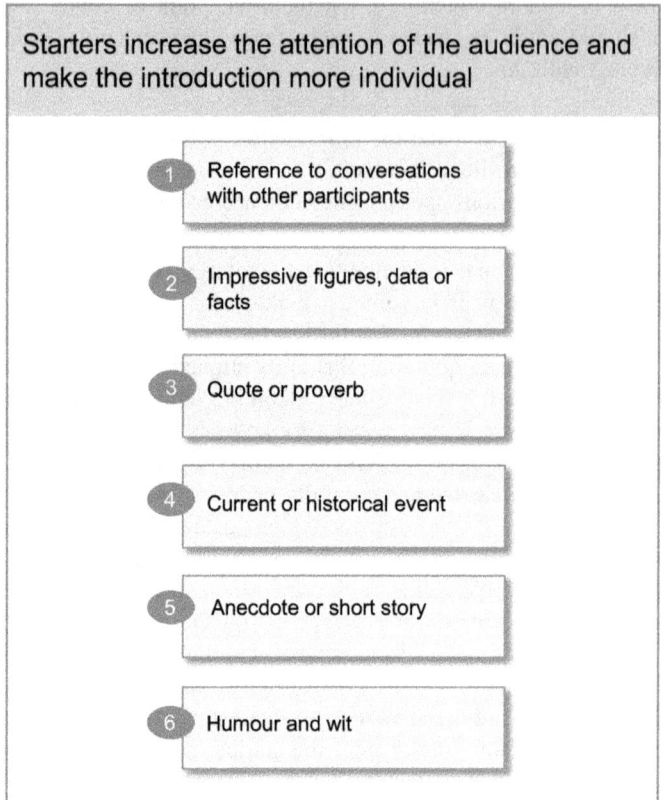

Fig. 5.4 Starter make the introduction more individual

concept. Of course, no confidential statements or comments that might be embarrassing to those involved may be quoted or their names mentioned without their permission. It is safest to use only approved quotes.

Scientists often find the starting point for their talk in casual or accidental conversations, as the following example shows:

Example

"Before I start my talk, I would like to tell you about an interesting conversation I had. Some colleagues and I just realised at the welcome coffee that today's session topic is exceptionally multi-faceted because…! That fits in perfectly with my talk today". ◄

2. Impressive figures, data or facts

Impressive facts can be found for any scientific presentation. The audience is provided with interesting figures, data and facts right from the start. These "did you know" questions arouse people's curiosity because they convey something astonishing. That motivates and binds people. They want to know how you arrived at these facts. For this purpose, unusual and unexpected information or events that have provided the impetus for this research project or research results or their implication, which are then justified and substantiated in the course of the presentation, are suitable. Depending on the setting and duration of the talk, the audience can be activated with estimation questions. This works very well with smaller audience groups, where speakers ask for the audience to directly assess things. In the case of a large plenary, there is the possibility for people to contribute by a show of hands. Those who do not want to keep their audience in the dark any longer state the impressive figure directly and then move on to the main part. If you want to keep the tension high, you resolve the question later in the talk when presenting your results. Speakers must allow up to two minutes of time for this variant, depending on the design.

▶ Impressive figures, data and facts can be combined very well using assessment questions to the audience to create interactive starters.

Impressive facts can also be supported visually, although experience has shown that they have a stronger impact when speakers present them orally and with the slides hidden. This usually quickly creates a connection with the audience and a good first impression. Many presenters choose such an introduction, because it often creates sit-up-and-take-notice-effects and increased interest thanks to the high connection to the actual presentation. The fact this is not always the case can be seen from the following situation. After the welcome address, a natural scientist fades in a picture that displayed him and a famous politician. The audience members looked at each other slightly bemused. Employing the sentence: "That was impressive" he clicked on the first slide and began his talk.

The example below shows a simple way of using impressive facts to start a talk.

Example

"Ladies and gentlemen, welcome to my presentation on the impact of X. Some of you may now wonder why we have focused on women in our research". (Pause) "Well, the question is quickly answered when you realise that more than 95 per cent of the people who apply for X are female".◄

3. Quotation or proverb

Quotations and proverbs are not uncommon in scientific talks. They are time-saving starters that can be used without much effort at the beginning of a presentation. For a quotation or proverb to have an impact, it is crucial that it fits the topic of the talk on the one hand and is (relatively) unknown on the other. "Hackneyed" proverbs or quotes are boring and achieve no effect or have a negative impact on the audience. Quotations are best received when they refer to something topical—this makes them seem less outdated—and are presented embedded in two short pauses in speech. Quotations require some research in terms of the preparation, but do not require a significant amount of time for the presentation. A well-sorted collection of materials can also prove useful here.

Following the completion of a comprehensive annual report, the chair of the expert group presents the most important results to a general audience and starts with the following words:

> **Example**
>
> "Voltaire reputedly once said: 'Forgive me for writing you a long letter, I had no time for a short one.' We have taken the time for you and today present the most important findings from X's annual report". ◄

4. Current or historical event

Speakers often start their presentation with a reference to a current or historical event when they want to point out a particularly positive or negative development. Such events are striking if the listeners associate something with them or have even experienced them themselves. This connectedness appeals intellectually and emotionally and almost always brings increased interest from the audience. Anyone who uses a current serious political event or a new, scientific achievement as a starter should therefore either be sure that the audience is aware of the events or must briefly describe them and their impacts.

After the welcome address and the short introduction to the presentation topic "Post-merger integration of research and development", the speaker provides the following example of a current event.

> **Example**
>
> "An example of a different integration process was provided in 2012 by Company X, which featured in the press every day at the time. The merger of A, B and C into X demonstrated, on the one hand, how cultural and national differences negatively influence the post-merger integration process and, on the other hand, how a relatively smooth integration was achieved in the area of research

and development, as indicated by the development of the successful products 1 and 2.

My presentation today deals with the special integration situation to be expected in an R&D sector as well as the question of which integration measures are actually relevant for success". ◄

5. Anecdote or short story

Narratives have always connected people and—as neuroscience proves—also their brains. So much so that it synchronises the brain activity of the narrator and the listener. Uri Hasson, professor of psychology and neuroscience at Princeton University, has demonstrated in experiments that brain responses when listening to a story become increasingly similar to that of the presenter. And what's more: The stronger the coupling, the better people's understanding is of what is being said.[12] So a good and short narration not only helps to build a relationship with the audience, it also makes it easier to understand and remember the content presented. It can be used in a variety of ways and, moreover, can be taken up again and again in the talk like a common thread. Stories in many cases contribute towards the success of the introduction and the presentation.

▶ Anecdotes and short stories are like a kind of Swiss army knife for presentations. They can be used for different purposes and many people carry them with them in their thoughts.

Depending on the type of story, this kind of starter is the most individual, personal and often most appealing way to begin a talk. The use of anecdotes is especially useful for longer presentations because you need more time for the narration than with other hooks.

Stories must not be too long and must be delivered fluently and without mistakes, otherwise they lose their positive effect. The tension falls as soon as speakers get bogged down or have to correct themselves. Some intensive preparation is necessary to make the best use of stories for the introduction and presentation. A certain narrative talent is also not a disadvantage. Those who do not want to or cannot spend this time are better off using other starters.

From experience, short stories during the introduction should not last longer than 90s and should not be told spontaneously.

---

[12] https://www.brainfacts.org/neuroscience-in-society/the-arts-and-the-brain/2021/why-the-brain-loves-stories-030421.

> **Example**
>
> "A few years ago, the scientific director of our research institute invited me to accompany him during his inaugural talk at an association of high-ranking scientists and science managers. He said he didn't want to go alone and that it would give me the opportunity to briefly present my current paper. That sounded somehow strange to my ears, for me as a young scientist, to present my paper in such a setting. I was about to turn the opportunity down when the thought occurred to me that it might be interesting for me to see how such an old hands club works. So I agreed to do it. My talk went well and at dinner I sat next to an older gentleman who asked me a few questions about my paper, then introduced himself as a board member of a renowned science publisher and asked abruptly: "Would you have the confidence to write a book on your topic." That sounded somehow really strange to my ears again. I had never written a book before. While I was looking for a polite way of wording my rejection, a thought popped into my head out of nowhere: I have no idea how to write a book, but that's what I'm going to try and do now. I accepted the offer and had my first book published two years later. Others have since followed.
>
> Today I would like to introduce you to why it is important to be courageous and self-confident even in spite of doubts and what science has found out on this subject". ◄

6. Wit and humour

Wit and humour are the most difficult and risky ways to introduce a talk. The reasons for this are simple: Humour is a phenomenon that can be understood in different ways. The violent joke, a joke that not everyone can laugh at or that offends parts of the audience, is an embarrassing opener. In this respect, caution is advised, especially when using humorous starters. It is easier if scientists know their audience and a more informal style is chosen overall. It is obvious that it would be completely inappropriate to start the talk with a joke on your lips in case of results that are negative for the audience.

All forms of irony are risky and unsuitable for talks because they are misleading.

At a talk in front of an audience of some 2000 people, the speaker starts by announcing interesting and unexpected results and the tongue-in-cheek remark:

> **Example**
>
> "The results are not yet intended for publication. But, we are among ourselves!". ◄

Starters complement the classic entry and can be used at the beginning, in the middle and at the end. Hooks are useful tools especially when academics want to start the presentation with more content and not with their own introduction. For example, if you start with an impressive fact, you put your research first and not yourself.

The use of these hooks serves to build up and maintain the relationship between the speaker and the audience and to arouse their interest. Starters must not become an end in themselves. They must (!) suit the speaker, the audience, the occasion and above all the topic. If these basic requirements are not met, a scientist should consider whether there is another way to start the presentation and refrain from using a starter.

▶   If in doubt, speakers should rather choose a good classical starter than an inappropriate one.

5.2.3 Starting With and Without Visualisation

Most researchers start their talk with a cover sheet or title slide. This serves as visual support for the introduction, which is shown "silently" in the background without explanations and provides the audience with initial information. Cover slides contribute to the first impression and have a certain influence on the motivation of the audience. As with all other slides, the basics for good slide design apply here as well—as described in Chapter 4.

There are several reasons for starting with a title slide: First, there is the standard of the talk expected by the audience. Many members of the audience want a title slide right at the beginning of the presentation with the name of the presenter and, if applicable, the co-authors, the institution and, of course, the presentation topic. This visualisation helps the audience, especially at conferences involving a large number of talks, to orientate themselves better. Title slides are particularly useful and supportive when, for example, the title of the talk is long or many co-authors should be named.

Title slides make do with a few items of well-structured information and will be shown without footers and animations if possible. The following information on a title slide is usually sufficient:

- Title of the talk
- Occasion of the talk (project title, name of conference, etc.)
- Name of the scientist and his co-authors
- Institution of the scientist with logo
- If applicable, cooperation partner, sponsor, client
- Date and location of the event

Some scientists prefer to speak to their audience without any visual support during the introduction in order to have their undivided attention. Here it is advisable to control the focus of the audience by a planned fading in and out of the title slide.

The slide is visible to begin with. Just before the speaker begins to speak, he fades out the slide. This is particularly useful when starters are used and a slide in the background would be distracting, because light always attracts people's attention for evolutionary reasons. Now the introduction follows with or without a starter. Then the agenda is faded in and the main part begins.

5.3 Main Part—The Actual Presentation

The main part forms the core of the talk. It shows the path from the research question or hypothesis through the methodological procedure to the results. The focus is on gaining knowledge and providing benefits for the audience. Therefore, prior knowledge, interests and composition of the audience play an important part in ensuring the success of the talk, in addition to one's own objectives. Thus, presentations that go into great depth and show many details are interesting for experts. In the case of mixed audiences, it is advisable to present the topic more broadly and to focus more on the outcome and implications than on the methodological approach and contribution towards literature. Different structures lend themselves to the design of a target group-oriented main section.

▶ Resist the temptation of wanting to say and display everything!

5.3.1 Classic Structure

This structure of the main section has become standard at conferences and presents the individual blocks of information in chronological order. In this way, no necessary elements of scientific work are forgotten. It works like a kind of funnel, with the core message of the talk at the end.

At the beginning, the current situation and the current state of research are outlined. The categorisation of the work in the previous literature then follows. In the process, it is made clear what contribution one's own research has made towards this and where the gain in knowledge lies. This is followed by the formation of hypotheses and the formulation of the problem. The procedure, i.e. method, model or experimental set-up, is then explained. At the end of the main section, scientists present their findings, interpret them and explain how they relate to those of other researchers and the research question. It is crucial that they clearly show what the viewer can and cannot discern from the data or the experiment.

Figure 5.5[13] reveals an overview of the classic structure of the main part.

---

[13] Own representation.

5.3 Main Part—The Actual Presentation

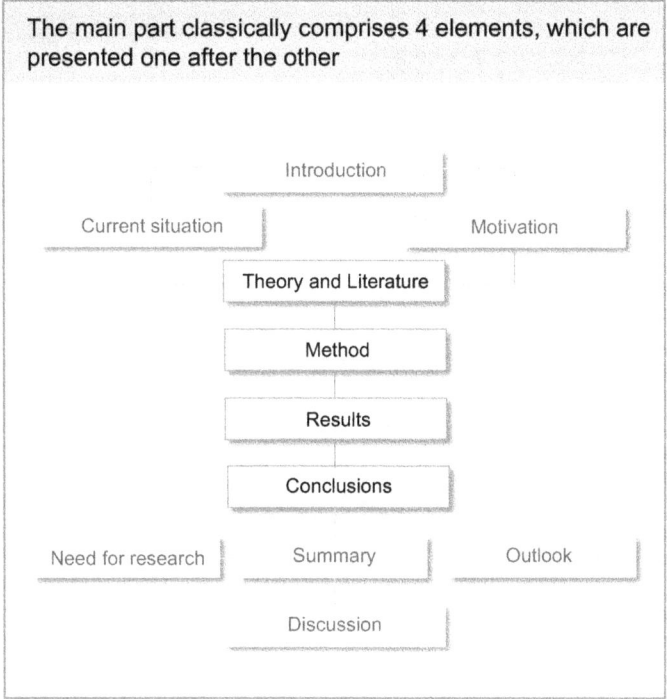

Fig. 5.5 Classical main part

▶ In the case of scientists who know more than you, only what is new counts. Don't present any old chestnuts. Where students are concerned, the backgrounds are more important.

5.3.2 A Results-First Structure

Compared to the classical, sequential structure, this structure is arranged in a more parallel form. It begins with the result and implications of the paper and places their significance in the thematic context. Following this an explanation is provided of why and how this question was examined. If necessary, secondary results, the contribution towards the literature, theory and further research needs can still be presented. This form of structuring often has a refreshing effect because it differs from the standard and begins with the new, the interesting. It also ensures that the audience definitely hears the most important part of a talk and that it does not fall victim to time problems. However, with this structure, speakers run the risk of losing audiences with little knowledge of the topic more quickly.

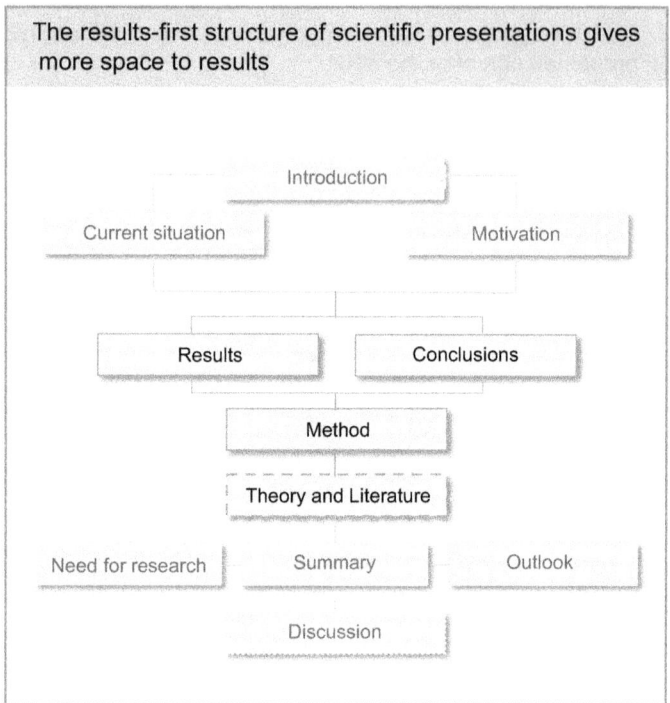

Fig. 5.6 Results first struture

Figure 5.6[14] displays the structure.

▶ Every change ensures that the audience's attention stays high or at least falls away more slowly. Those who start with the results ensure there is a bang right at the start of the talk.

5.3.3 Hourglass Structure

This information sequence is ideal for a heterogeneous audience. Scientists begin presenting on a broad, generally comprehensible level. In the course of the talk, they condense the contents into a specialised area of knowledge of interest to experts. The results and implications are again presented in such a way that the whole audience understands them. In the case of longer talks a tried and tested method has proven to be dividing up the main part into several blocks and to present each of them according to the hourglass principle. This provides advantages. This is because: Especially where the main part is concerned, scientific

---

[14] Own research and own representation.

talk run the risk of losing the audience or overrunning the allocated time slot. In the case of longer presentations, it is therefore helpful to fall back on the hourglass principle and show a slide with the agenda before each chapter for better orientation and to summarise the key statements of the section at the end of the section.

5.3.4 Keeping the Audience's Level of Attention High

Scientists have numerous possibilities at their disposal to positively influence the attention and concentration of the audience.

▶ Keep the audience's attention high by ideally changing something in the talk regularly to counteract the brain's tendency to switch off when it sees uniformity.[15]

Thus, concisely formulated transitions help the audience to better understand what is presented. The change in speaking tempo and volume has a direct effect on the audience. Short pauses in speech are among the most powerful tools to keep the audience engaged. For instance, if you briefly interrupt your talk in the middle of a sentence, you can observe how the audience changes their body language and raises their heads. The same thing occurs when speakers change their position in the room. The audience follows them with their eyes and in this way changes their perspective on the speakers and their talk.

A simple and at the same time effective means is the rhetorical question, which is interspersed into the talk from time to time and answer to which follows after a short pause in speech. Speakers can also incorporate changes into their presentation by showing an example or changing the visualisation format. This could be a sketch on the whiteboard or the presentation of an experiment with a video.

Speakers who want to use special and unusual techniques to attract and hold the audience's attention will now and then fade out their slide and continue speaking without visualisation, or they will invite the audience to participate in interactive estimates and votes. This can be achieved by a show of hands or—in the case of large audiences—also via smartphone.

Speakers who do not simply present their results but link them to their own impressions ("We were quite surprised that …" or "Then we discovered something unusual".) address the audience more personally and intensively.

It helps to develop a sense of when the audience can no longer follow—for example, when more and more audience members leave the room, stop looking ahead or become preoccupied with something else.

---

[15] John Medina „Brain rules for work", 2021, S. 186.

5.4 Conclusion—Anchoring Core Theses and Knowledge Gain

This final section of the presentation is the last chance to give the audience what they need to take away from the talk and remember in a concise way. Using sentences like "So, that's it from my side!" or "If you don't have any more questions, thank you for your attention!" speakers throw away the last opportunity to anchor their core message with the audience. Instead of activating the audience once again for the finale, such statements usually leave the auditorium unsettled and drain them of any remaining energy. For this reason, it is important to carefully prepare and make use of this part of the talk as well. Researchers plan 5 to 10% of the available time for this—analogous to the introduction—and do not impart any new information at this point. The main part is finished and if something has been forgotten, it can be woven into the discussion.

▶ The conclusion to the talk is the final impression that the audience takes away with them. Use this opportunity to place your key message and motivate the audience to ask questions.

Experienced scientists do not abbreviate the conclusion by simply ceasing to talk and moving on to the discussion. On the contrary, they use the scheduled time and explicitly announce the conclusion of their talk. With classic key phrases such as:

- "I am now coming to the conclusion of my talk".
- "Let me briefly summarise the most important statements again".
- "In essence, the following can be concluded".

they are indicating that the main part is finished and the end of the presentation is approaching. Usually, after this announcement, the audience is visibly stirred and knows that now the most important information will be summarised.

▶ Announce you are coming to a conclusion. This increases the audience's attention levels for a short time.

Figure 5.7[16] shows the elements for a professional conclusion.

5.4.1 Summary and Visualisation of the Important Contents of the Talk

In the first part of the conclusion, the presenter summarises the most important (!) statements, results and information and visualises them—usually with slides—in

---

[16] Own research and own representation.

5.4 Conclusion—Anchoring Core Theses and Knowledge Gain

Fig. 5.7 Closing and last impression

order to "anchor" them better. Here the core messages are presented in a concise, low-detail form (telegram style). It is useful to emphasise one to a maximum of three key messages of the work, because the audience is then more likely to retain them.

Some researchers when speaking before smaller groups sometimes use whiteboards or flipcharts for the summary. On the one hand, because the core statements are thus also present in the Q&A session, so that individual presentation slides do not have to be faded in when answering questions. On the other hand, the use of such spontaneous media produces a positive effect on the audience. It leaves the impression that something special will now follow, which is not part of the computer-based talk and was created individually, only for this audience. This makes people curious and increases their attention levels.

▸ Summarising does not mean repeating the talk or parts of it.

5.4.2 Conclusions and Future Research

From the summary, scientists can now derive the conclusions and implications. This includes the key results and findings, whether or not the hypothesis was supported, the significance of the study, and future research.

It is important for scientists to describe what is new and the knowledge gained by the audience from this talk. This is a very good way of connecting to the aim of the talk or the research question. Subsequently, the gaps in the present study and the need for further research are identified.

▶ You should not completely ignore problems of your own approach. A little self-criticism—that is preferably productive in the sense that you want to consider adding this or that element in the future—often has a positive effect.

5.4.3 Closing Point and Transition to the Q&A Session

The last part of the talk is about formulating the concluding (powerful) sentence. This is particularly effective if it makes reference to the aim of the talk, the research question or the starter. Where the conclusion is concerned, a slide with the summary or with contact details as well as other own publications is also suitable for the occasion of each talk. It is good practice in scientific presentations for speakers to thank the audience at the end and then invite them to ask questions or share comments, thus leading to a discussion session.

A smooth and clearly structured transition between the talk and the discussion part prevents feelings of uncertainty and irritation on the part of the audience. The following structure has proved useful for the transition to the discussion:

1. Thank the audience.
2. Invite them to ask questions, share comments or impressions.
3. Look at the audience in a friendly and silent (!) manner.
4. Give the floor to people who wish to ask questions.

A bad habit is the use of "thank-you-for-your-attention slides" or "any-questions slides". Both are impersonal and distant. Thanks to people are conveyed via a slide, although the presenter is present. Speakers thus hand over the opportunity to convince with their personality and enthusiasm for their work and to leave a corresponding final impression on the audience. Scientists who close their talk with such visualisations should consequently also show a "welcome-to-my-talk slide". The welcoming speech and thanks should be mentioned personally without any visualisation.

▶ Formulate your thanks to the audience verbally and refrain from using "thank-you-for-your-attention slides".

5.5 Question and Answer Session and Discussion

The discussion after a talk is just as important, in some situations even more important than the talk itself. In the best case, an exchange develops that is useful for all parties. Researchers are given the opportunity to critically exchange ideas with colleagues about their own research topic, to identify gaps or weaknesses in their work and to develop new ideas. The audience can deepen their understanding of the topic through discussion. For the Q&A session, it is a good idea to show the slide (or other visualisation) with the summary of the most important results and, if necessary, to fade in other or additional slides of the presentation.

▶ As long as you speak, no one can ask a question. Give your audience time to think and formulate questions. Let the silence take effect.

5.5.1 Chairperson—Moderator and Timekeeper

The discussion leader at large scientific conferences is also referred to as the chairperson, session chairperson, moderator or chairman or chairwoman (in short: Chair). In principle, it is the responsibility of this person to provide a framework for the conference in general and the talk in particular, to ensure the orderly running of the entire event and to support the speakers as well as the participants. Chairpersons usually find out about the speakers and their topics in advance and discuss with them how organisational matters, such as time constraints and opportunities to ask questions, are handled. Chairs have a role as moderators and should be as neutral as possible. They relieve the speakers of their administrative tasks and steer the discussion. They ensure that everyone can ask questions and participate in the discussion on an equal footing and make sure that the time limits are adhered to and that there is no deviation from the topic.

Before and during the talk, it is one of the tasks of chairpersons, …

1. … to thank opening speakers and welcome the audience. In some situations special thanks go out to the participants who have travelled a long way to attend the conference.
2. … to announce the first speaker. Sometimes chairpersons also use this welcome speech to make the situation more relaxed with a little starter.
3. …to introduce the speaker and his background at the beginning of the talk and provide a brief overview of the topic of the talk. Chairs of the sessions may use their own short slide presentation or structural picture on the topic.

4. ... to point out time limits and inform the audience that they should ask their questions at the end of the presentation.
5. ... to give the floor to the presenter and, during the course of the presentation, to point out, if necessary with signs, that time has been exceeded. During the presentation, he ensures that rambling discussions are contained and shifted to the discussion round. However, he permits questions on the topic.
6. ... to register questions from the floor and close the list of requests to speak. The chair of the session notes down questions that arise during or after the talk and gives the floor to interested persons in the correct order after the presentation. If possible, he addresses the respective scientists by name.

After the talk, it is one of the tasks of chairpersons, ...

1. ... to ask speakers if they would like to make a final comment, thanking them and asking for a round of applause for them.
2. ... to open the discussion.
   Chairpersons usually briefly underline the significance and explain their own classification of what they have heard before giving the floor to the first person to ask a question. If there is no request to speak at the beginning of the Q&A session, the Chair asks the first question to stimulate the discussion.
3. ... to give the floor to interested persons in the correct order and to address if possible the respective scientists by name.
4. ... to steer and support the discussion.
   Here it is important to avoid irrelevancies and, if possible, not to take sides or to oppose a single position too strongly. The chairperson shall ensure that the order in which speakers take the floor is correct and that interrupted points of discussion do not fall by the wayside and, if necessary, are taken up again later. In large lecture rooms and/or in the event of poor acoustics, the chair repeats the questions so everyone can understand.
5. ... closes the discussion by thanking the audience and the speakers once the end of the discussion time is reached or there are no further requests to speak on the talk.

The tasks of chairpersons are diverse and require experience and assertiveness. The focus is to manage the discussion without leading it.

5.5.2 Discussant—Critic and Promoter of Understanding

Discussants are co-presenters of the talk who know the paper presented and have familiarised themselves with it. They usually show their own slide presentation of 10 to 15 min in length. They fulfil the role of the "institutionalised critic" and thus help to show other perspectives on the presented topic, to name any professional errors, to arouse the interest of the audience for the presented work and to stimulate a discussion or a scientific exchange.

For this purpose, co-examiners first summarise the contents of a talk and, if necessary, classify them in the literature. Their comments may include constructive criticism regarding the research questions, the theoretical foundations and/or the methods used. Furthermore, discussants deal with the results and the resulting conclusions. They show where problems of understanding have occurred and indicate what might cause problems.

5.6 Follow-Up After a Scientific Presentation

For many reasons, it is recommended that speakers take the time to follow up after the event. In addition to their own analysis and reflection, feedback from conference participants is a valuable source for their further development. Possible questions that speakers can ask in such a conversation with a view to academic and presentational development are:

Scientific:

- What was particularly valuable and interesting for you?
- Which parts were difficult to understand?
- Which part of my talk was less important for you?
- What was lacking?

Presentational:

- What impression did I make on you?
- What feedback would you give me on the time management, structure and content?
- What could I do better from your point of view?

The coffee break and the meetings after the talks—such as the conference dinner or an official get-together—present excellent opportunities to discuss scientific aspects with a wide range of participants. This can include ideas and suggestions from people you would not otherwise meet, or expert opinions (e.g. from respected professors).

▶ After the talk, take notes on questions of understanding and criticisms of the content. This way you can adjust your paper and be better prepared for the talk next time.

Presenters are most likely to receive more open and detailed feedback, especially with advice on how to improve their presentation technique, from colleagues who attend the same conference and may even have been involved in the preparation of the talk.

Each talk offers you the opportunity to learn for your own scientific work as well as upcoming presentations. It is worth noting the questions and comments from the discussion and reflecting on them. They help to improve the content and approach and to develop new ideas for your own research.

▶ Also note down your own impressions from the talk and discussion.

References

Alston, James Matthew, 2020, Dress Code for Economic Conferences: What to Wear and What to Avoid, https://inomics.com/insight/dress-code-for-academic-conferences-what-to-wear-and-what-to-avoid-48004, last retrieved: 29.12.2023

Fabrizius, Friederike und Hagemann, Hans W., The Leading Brain, 2018, TarcherPerigee

May, Sybille, "Das Checklistenbuch", 2nd edition, 2014, Gabler Verlag

McMurray, Calli, 2021, Why the Brain Loves Stories, https://www.brainfacts.org/neuroscience-in-society/the-arts-and-the-brain/2021/why-the-brain-loves-stories-030421, last retrieved: 29.12.2023

Medina, John, "Brain Rules for Work - The Science of Thinking Smarter in the Office and at Home, 2021, Pear Press

Okten, Irmak Olcaysoy, 2018, Studying First Impressions: What to Consider?, https://www.psychologicalscience.org/observer/studying-first-impressions-what-to-consider, last retrieved: 29.12.2023

Ruben, Adam, 2014, Dress to Profess: What Should Scientists Wear, http://www.sciencemag.org/careers/2014/04/dress-profess-what-should-scientists-wear, last retrieved: 29.12.2023

Simon, Carmen, 2017, Using Neuroscience to Create Presentations with Lasting Impact, https://www.youtube.com/watch?v=UzrWcEIedH4, last retrieved: 29.12.2023

Zimmer, John, 2015, A Brain Hack for Your Next Presentation, https://mannerofspeaking.org/2015/07/03/a-brain-hack-for-your-next-presentation/, last retrieved: 29.12.2023

Remarkable and Useful Things—A Toolbox for Scientific Talks

The penultimate chapter of this book contains a small toolbox. It gives scientists additional instruments to ensure they are professionally prepared for different situations before, during and after a talk. Researchers will find communication psychology tools in it, with advice on the impact of communication, free speech and how they can lead discussions successfully. The toolbox also contains tips on how to deal with feelings of nerves and shows how speakers can reduce their stress levels before and during the performance using neuroscientifically proven techniques. It also offers helpful guidance on how presenters can direct their audience's gaze and skilfully use hyperlinks to focus the audience's attention specifically and respond flexibly to the talk.

Figure 6.1[1] shows how the toolbox is arranged.

6.1 Communication and Its Impact at Talks

Each talk is a form of communication, in which at least two persons are involved. These persons always (!) communicate—whether intentionally or unintentionally—with each other. This is due to the fact that all participants, whether they speak, remain silent or look away, transmit verbal and/or non-verbal signals to the other person. The Austrian communication scientist Paul Watzlawick describes this phenomenon with the statement: One cannot not communicate".[2]

---

[1] A figures in this chapter are own representations.
[2] Paul Watzlawick et al., „Menschliche Kommunikation", 2003, pages 50–53.

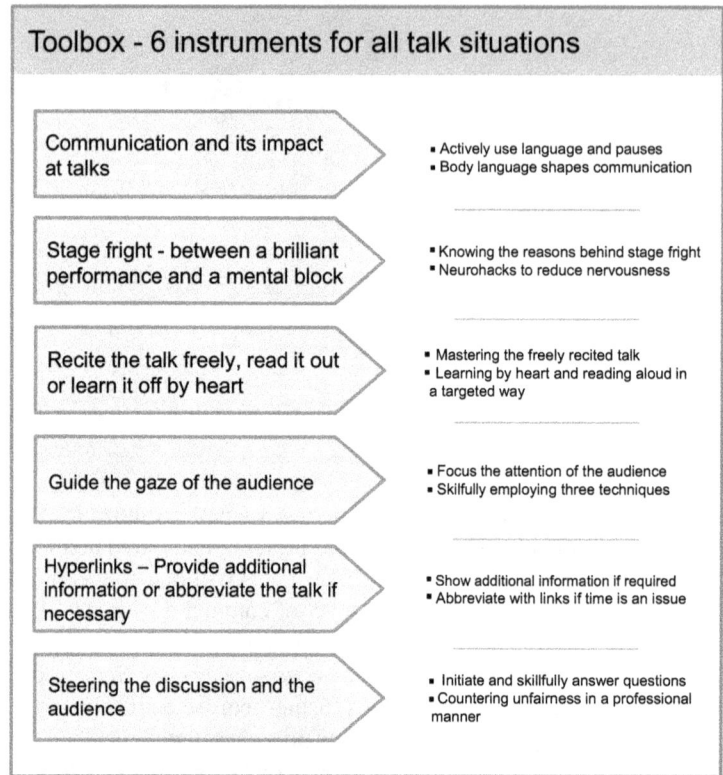

Fig. 6.1 A toolbox for scientific talks

▶ Speakers and the audience communicate with each other, even when they are not speaking!

Body language has a special role to play here. Even though research has not yet been completed on the exact influence of body language signals on communication, it is nevertheless clear that non-verbal communication is closely linked to spoken language. What is interesting in this context is that the same areas of the brain are active when performing and observing an activity. This makes it easier for people to infer other people's intentions based on their body language. Body language facilitates communication in this way. It provides additional information, makes it clear how something is meant and can prevent misunderstandings. Gestures and facial expressions contribute to better understanding and communicating one's own concerns.[3]

---

[3] https://www.spektrum.de/magazin/nonverbale-kommunikation-was-der-koerper-verraet/1313420, Anna Gojowsky and Anna Gielas pages 42–45.

Contrary to the widespread assumption that in communication the transmitter sends his message and the receiver receives it, communication is not simply a one-way process, but circular. Paul Watzlawick describes communication as circular. Every (form of communicative) behaviour is both a cause and effect in communication.[4]

▶ Regardless of who is speaking and who is listening, both sides influence communication simultaneously.

6.1.1 Body Language in Lectures—Eye Gaze Behaviour, Facial Expressions, Gestures and Posture

Body language influences the impact of the speakers upon their audience and vice versa. Scientists who appear uncertain or disinterested therefore usually elicit different reactions from the audience than those who leave a motivated and convinced impression. By contrast with verbal language, non-verbal communication is predominantly controlled subconsciously. For this reason, it is also often perceived as more "honest" than verbal signals, which people can control and use in a more targeted way. In most cases, body language that is used deliberately comes across as contrived. It is also ambiguous and depends on the person as well as the situation. Many presenters find the use of body language in a presentation challenging. That is why the questions frequently asked in seminars and coaching sessions very often include those relating to non-verbal communication. The most interesting aspects here are:

- Where do I look during the talk?
- Should I smile?
- What do I do with my hands?
- Where should I stand?
- Can I move around?

6.1.1.1 Eye Contact and Avoiding Eye Contact—Where Do I Look During the Talk?

Eye contact with the interlocutor is a crucial body language element in most cultures. It is part of socialisation that people who speak to each other look at each other when this is possible in the given context. Eye contact builds an important connection between the people involved and often signals attention, interest and openness. This shows the importance of this means of expression for communication in general and for presentations in particular.

---

[4] Paul Watzlawick among others, „Menschliche Kommunikation", 2003, pages 50–53.

Even in scientific talks, an axis of communication is established between the speaker and the audience through eye contact. At the same time, scientists often avoid looking at the audience because it can increase the tension felt by the speaker. Eye contact can be perceived not only positively but also negatively, depending on its duration, intensity and frequency. This usually happens when speakers perceive the body language reactions of the audience as stressful and indicating rejection, for instance when they feel like they are being stared at or ignored. Here, the intention for the behaviour does not play any part in this. The effect it has on the speaker concerned determines what happens next in the situation.

Some people therefore feel more comfortable with their gaze directed at the screen or their own computer.

▶ Look at your audience as frequently as possible. If it affects your concentration and presentation performance, reduce or briefly interrupt eye contact with the audience.

What can scientists do to help themselves when reactions and signals from the audience unsettle them or make them nervous? There are several techniques that can be employed here:

1. Look at friendly faces
   At the beginning of a talk, when your stage fright is at its highest, find one or two friendly looking participants as a kind of "visual anchor" and look at them. Eye contact with an approvingly nodding or smiling audience provides you with a feeling of self-assurance and makes it easier to get going. Invite colleagues to your talk and ask them to sit at the front of the audience. As soon as you have overcome your initial feelings of uncertainty and are securely progressing with your talk, you will also "take care" of the people in the audience who look back with less encouragement. Caution: Please take care not to look at any one single person for too long.
2. Look into the audience at certain points
   In large auditoriums it is impossible to look at all the members of the audience. In these cases, look out for individual points at different places in the audience in whose direction you are facing. If possible, give all members of the audience the feeling that they are being addressed directly.
3. Briefly break off your eye contact to concentrate
   To be able to think and concentrate, break off eye contact for a moment. Look briefly for a few seconds at the projection screen, the floor or the computer screen or let your gaze wander. Focus, then look back at the audience and continue your talk.

▶ Look at as many different people in the audience as possible. No member of the audience enjoys being stared at.

6.1.1.2 Facial Expressions—Should I Smile?

Facial expressions mainly include the movements of the facial muscles around the mouth, nose, eyebrows and forehead. It displays the speaker's attitude towards the topic and the interlocutor. As with all body language elements, naturalness and authenticity are paramount in facial expressions. It is therefore easiest and most sensible to present your talk using your natural facial expression. This ensures that they match the rest of your behaviour and appear authentic. Inauthentic mimics—for example in the form of an artificial smile—take energy away from you that is lacking elsewhere and are quickly exposed. Those who smile a lot by nature can of course make extensive use of this gift.

6.1.1.3 Gestures—What Am I Doing with My Hands?

Anyone who observes themselves and others will notice that people use gestures to support their words. We have a natural repertoire of gestures that suits us. Scientists should also make use of them in their talks. What is meant is not an exaggerated "waving around with your hands" that does not fit the occasion and the talk you are giving, but the natural support of the spoken word with hands and arms, which makes the talk more lively and enhances it.

People usually conduct their gestures between the chin and the belly button, the so-called "neutral area". It goes without saying that all hand movements made in front of the face make eye contact difficult and confusing. Gestures that are shown at the level of the hip appear small and restricted.

Gestures should not be copied or practised. Members of the audience notice—at least subconsciously—when something is played out for them. In contrast, natural gestures appear genuine and convincing because they are in keeping with the speaker's personality and the situation. This influences the credibility and authenticity of speakers. The use of coherent gestures is independent of the frequency, intensity and manner in which they are displayed. It is dependent on the personality of the speaker. Calmer contemporaries usually cope with fewer gestures than more extroverted presenters who "work" more with their hands.

▶ Nervousness can lead to unusual gestures in the presentation, which serve to reduce the stress level—this is a normal and usually uncritical reaction.

It happens that people who hold a talk sometimes use gestures in the talk that they would not normally display. Many inappropriate and uncharacteristic gestures are the result of nervousness that occurs under special circumstances. The talk is about such a situation. Speakers are left to their own devices and speak in front of a sometimes critical audience. In this situation, it is normal to look for something that supports. If there is nothing—such as a lectern—for presenters to hold on to, they sometimes have little other choice but to hold themselves. This is done, for instance, by scientists putting their hands together, folding them or clasping them behind their backs. This usually happens subconsciously, is hardly noticeable and should not be overestimated. If these gestures give the speakers security for the moment, then that is perfectly fine. Such behaviour helps to keep speakers keep their nerves under control and stay fit for work.

Gestures become problematic when hands and arms develop a life of their own that is difficult to control and mutate from an endearing quirk to an annoying one that eventually annoys the audience. Depending on the gesture, the audience's judgement can range from "one of amusement" to "finding it unpleasant". Researchers who run their fingers through their hair every second or stroke their cheeks after every statement are examples of such tics. Most unfortunately, it is usually the speakers who fail to notice this.

Scientists should therefore ask trusted colleagues to provide them with honest feedback following presentations. "Honesty" is the keyword in this context. Researchers get much more out of receiving constructive advice on their foibles than from verbal pats on the back. As a rule, no one will provide this feedback of their own accord. Speakers thus have to address selected colleagues. An ideal and very instructive option involves having a video recording made of one's talk. The knowledge of one's own gestures of embarrassment often already helps speakers not to show them (so often).

▶ A laser pointer or presenter in one's hand works wonders in the "fight" against nervousness-induced displacement activities.

A special form of gesture that is often seen in talks is where the speaker has his "hands-in-his-pockets" or loosely hooks his thumb into the waistband of his trousers. Both are supposed to signal a healthy amount of self-confidence and make the speaker appear relaxed and casual.

Which impression is actually created depends on the age, scientific reputation and gender of the speaker. For instance, if an inexperienced scientist speaks with his hands in his pockets in front of an audience of renowned colleagues, it can come across as arrogant and inappropriate and elicit a corresponding response.

If the speaker sinks both his hands into his pockets, he deprives himself of his natural gestures and the opportunity to back up the spoken word. This quickly comes across as being arrogant. Academics can do permanent damage to their reputations in this way. This also often results in strange-looking balancing movements of the shoulders. Experience shows that gestures are experienced as more appealing with two hands. There is much to be said for taking at least one hand out of your pocket. The following tip underlines this:

▶ Consider what the effect of putting your hands in your pockets might be: One hand is confidence—two hands that's arrogance!

6.1.1.4 Posture—How Should I Stand?
The posture of speakers provides information about basic physical and emotional moods, such as the level of attention or interest, but also discomfort or fatigue.

Together with gaze behaviour and gestures, posture is a decisive factor in how presenters are perceived.

They should stand upright and distribute the body weight evenly on both feet, as this puts less strain on their backs and facilitates improved breathing and supply of oxygen. It also prevents fatigue because one leg is not overstressed.

People who have the choice should hold the talk while standing so that they can notice the reactions of the audience more quickly. They are more visible and present to their audience than seated colleagues, which makes it easier for the audience to follow the talk. In general, standing presenters produce a more dynamic talk.

In the event of there being just a few participants, scientists should opt for a seated presentation. A table presentation is in these cases more appropriate than a beamer-supported screen projection in a standing position. Here it is important for speakers not to hide. Talks presented while sitting quickly seduce people into adopting a passive and slouching posture. Sitting upright in a slightly bent-over posture, making eye contact with everyone present and using gestures ensure that the talk is presented with more energy. Ideally, speakers sit on the front part of the chair and have the computer positioned to the side to ensure there is no visual barrier between themselves and their audience.

▶ If you are presenting the talk while sitting down, do not hide your hands under the table, but use them to support the presentation with gestures.

6.1.1.5 Using Positions in the Room—Am I Allowed to Move?

Changing positions during the presentation offer many advantages. They provide a change of perspective for the audience and thus influence the dynamics of the talk. By means of a little movement, whether it is in order to explain a slide or to allow eye contact with other audience members, scientists avoid an unnaturally rigid and stiff posture. Even if this is only possible to a limited extent, it is advisable to switch your positions for three reasons:

1. Increasing the dynamism of the talk
   A major reason for changing position during a talk is that it allows you to consciously set highlights. Used selectively, it helps you to increase the attention levels of your audience. If, for example, you move towards the audience during the presentation to describe the methodical procedure, this is a clear signal that something new or special is about to follow. This enlivens your presentation and arouses the curiosity of the audience.
2. Change of perspective
   If you move to a different location in the room, you make the audience get a different perspective. The spectators follow your movements and in this way, also change their own perspective in terms of what is happening.
3. Calming your nerves

Moving around uses up energy and causes a reduction in your stress level and any lingering feelings of nervousness. The short burst of physical activity favours a more balanced style of talk.

> When presenting with a lectern, take advantage of the small range of motion available to you. Stand next to the lectern (adjust microphone) for the welcoming address and the conclusion. If using wireless microphones, you can also move freely around the room from time to time.

What is important in this context is the fact that changing positions does not mean that speakers are constantly on the move. This comes across as restless and exhausting for your audience and yourself. What is meant is an intentional and controlled switch from one speaking position to another. Exaggerated, continuous or hectic actions annoy the audience and distract them from the actual content of the talk. Walking backwards and forwards along a strip—like a tiger in a cage—will be received very negatively by the audience.

Speakers have various options at their disposal in terms of where to position themselves during a talk. Three locations are predestined for different phases of the talk:

- A position "Close to the audience"—for the start and conclusion of the talk

  By adopting this position, you consciously reduce the geographical distance to the audience. Stand at a clear distance from the screen and not too close to the audience. If possible, speak freely and without standing behind a lectern or table. This signals interest, authority and openness. You are the centre of attention for this brief moment, and you have the undivided attention of the audience. Enhance this effect by fading out the slide transmission and ensuring that no light distracts the audience. Make use of this moment where you are the focus of people's interest for a few key parts of your talk. Select this exposed location close to the audience, especially at the beginning and end of the talk or to announce important segments. For the audience, the transition from the introduction to the main part or from the main part to the conclusion is thus clearly recognisable. You thus ensure a change and provide the talk with a structure.

  You should not stay in this position for a longer period or permanently as you would be standing in the way of the picture and covering parts of the slide with your body.

▶ The position "Close to the audience" should not be used for more than one or two minutes, as it can become uncomfortable for everyone involved in the long run.

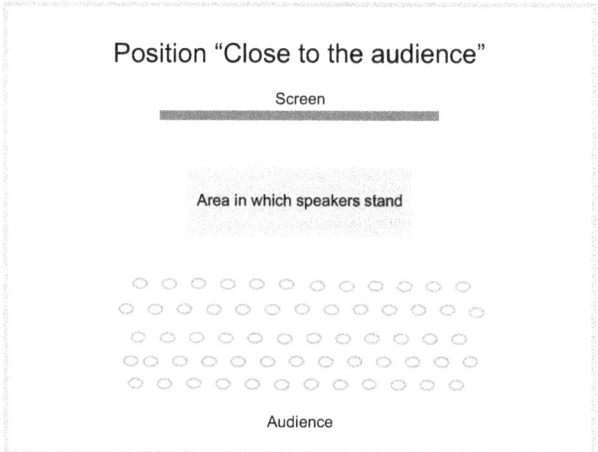

Fig. 6.2 Position close to the audience

The dotted area in Fig. 6.2 shows where you can position yourself at the beginning or end of your talk.

- Position "Next to the screen"—for the main part of the talk
  The second position is suitable for the main part of the talk. Allow the audience an unrestricted view of your slides or other medium. To do this, stand to the side of the screen. From here, guide the audience's gaze to the key points of your talk. If you assume this position, the audience can see you and your visual representation on the screen at the same time.

  Move around every now and then when it suits you to provide a different dynamic and some variety. A short change of position in the direction of the audience, or the other side of the screen, are tried and tested means of this. Do not move too far away from the screen. You run the risk of disappearing out of your audience's radius of perception at some point. This means that contact with the audience is lost, which can lead to a drop in people's attention.

Figure 6.3 shows where you should be, especially during the main part of the talk.

- Position "next to the audience"—for special situations
  The position next to the audience is very suitable if you want to provide a completely unobstructed view of the screen and focus all your audience's attention on a particular slide. Announce this unusual change of location so as not to irritate the audience (*"Let's take a look at this approach together now"*). Then stand at the edge next to the audience as if you were part of it and watch the presentation together with the audience. Present the slide from this position. In this way, you draw attention to the visualised contents. The position next to the audience is inappropriate in the long run because you lose touch with the

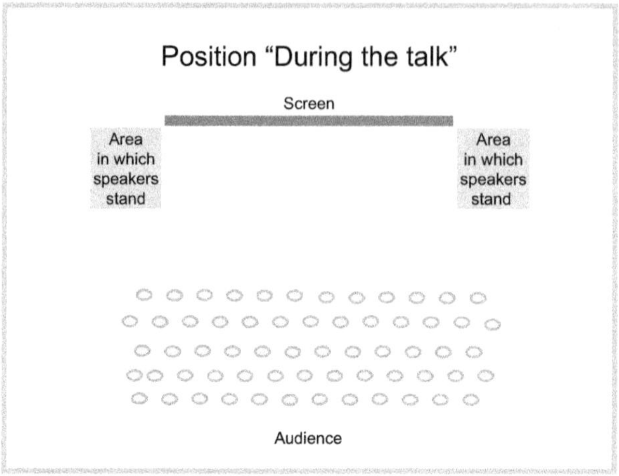

Fig. 6.3 Position during the talk

audience, and it is difficult to maintain eye contact with them. Therefore, return to the audience's field of vision after two to three minutes. If you stand with your audience, you set special accents in this way. You should take up such positions specifically and only once in the talk. The example in Fig. 6.4 shows where you can position yourself briefly for special situations.

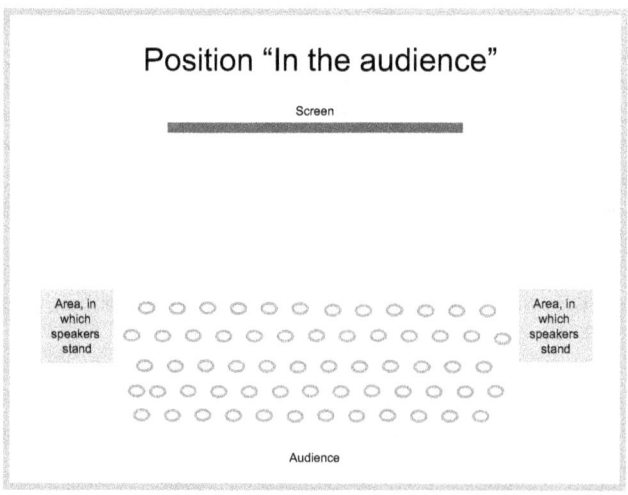

Fig. 6.4 Position in the audience—for special situations

6.1 Communication and Its Impact at Talks

Modern presentation remote controls enable position changes and increase the freedom of movement of speakers. These so-called presenters enable wireless control of slide-based presentations. They relieve speakers of the constraint of having to be near the computer to click on the slides. On the contrary, you can move around the lecture room without any hindrance.

Such presenters usually integrate several key functions and provide the scientist with many helpful and necessary control elements. This includes, first and foremost, the possibility to scroll forwards and backwards in the slide set and to hide the inserted slide if necessary. In addition to the buttons for the slide management, such a remote control usually has a laser pointer, a time display and a programmable gentle vibrating alarm that announces the end of the time of the talk to the speaker without the audience noticing.

▶ You should practise using the presenter, on the one hand, to learn which movements enable good visual guidance. On the other hand, as you become more familiar with the unit, you will be able to press the necessary buttons "without looking". This makes you appear calmer and more confident.

6.1.1.6 Paraverbal Language

Paraverbal communication describes the way in which a person talks. For a motivational linguistic presentation, the tempo of speech, voice pitch and volume should be used in a variety of ways, but above all authentically. Using paraverbal communication elements, scientists can set accents and highlights in the lecture and present it in a more varied way. This is important because a monotonous way of speaking can become tiring and boring. In addition, listeners have difficulty recognising when a sentence is finished and which statements are of greater importance.

If the power of their own voice is not sufficient to reach the people in the last rows, speakers should use a microphone. This ensures that they are always heard, regardless of whether they are speaking to the screen, for example.

> **Practical Tip**
> Use a microphone especially in unfavourable rooms and acoustic conditions for groups of 30 or more. This is easy on your voice and the audience can hear you better.

Driven by the concern of not using a limited amount of time efficiently enough, or driven by the desire to get "it" over with as quickly as possible, quite a few speakers rush through their presentation without pauses or taking breaths. This is also because they believe that short pauses to speak will be interpreted as a sign of weakness. Not only does non-stop talking increase the danger of losing the thread or getting muddled (time must then be invested again for correction), but there is also hardly any time for the audience to understand what is being said and to reflect on it. Speech pauses are essential communication tools. They belong in every talk, no matter how tightly scheduled they are. They structure the presentation and increase the concentration levels of those present. The brief interruption of the constant flow of speech acts like a wake-up call. The previous pattern of the talk is interrupted. Such "disturbances" are felt to be pleasant and arouse people's curiosity. Especially where complex presentations and explanations are concerned, it also helps the audience to be able to recapitulate what has been said before new information pours down on them. The talk becomes easier to understand.

It is important to note in this context that the perception of time is different between the speaker and the audience. What seems like an eternity to the speaker, is perceived by the listeners as just the right amount of time.

Pauses in speech are not only valuable from the audience's point of view, but they also offer advantages to presenters. They can use these short pauses to formulate the next sentence or the coming transition or simply to refocus.

> **Practical Tip**
> The least noticed communication tool in talks is the pause in speech. Use pauses in speech deliberately to make your talk more interesting and to embed highlights effectively.

6.2 Stage Fright—A Human Survival Programme Between Brilliant Performance and a Mental Block

Nervousness is a natural state that causes a series of physiological reactions that run autonomously. It results from an innate survival programme that is activated in situations experienced as dangerous or unsafe. In principle, it is an evolutionary response to the life-threatening encounters of our ancestors with natural hazards or wild animals. In such situations, the human body had to be quickly prepared for fight or flight. To this end and controlled by the brain, the stress hormones adrenaline and noradrenaline were released via the adrenal cortex. As a result, the heartbeat increased, and the muscles were supplied with more blood and oxygen. In terms of self-preservation, the body was put into a state of alert and now had an increased level of energy available by means of which it could better defend itself physically or run away more quickly.

Anyone who holds a talk exposes themselves to the judgement of others and naturally wants to look good and be perceived as positively as possible by the audience. Precisely because a lot is riding on a talk, most presenters feel a high level of stress and thus stage fright before holding the presentation—a completely natural reaction. On the one hand, stage fright manifests itself in reactions that are only noticeable to those affected. This can range from simply feeling unwell to feeling your heart pounding up to your neck. While the hands become moist with sweat, the mouth dries out and the knees tremble. On the other hand, there are symptoms of stage fright, that the audience can also see and hear, such as red spots on the face, shaky voice, avoidance of people's gazes and no or hectic movements.

6.2.1 Negative and Positive Effects of Nervousness

Researchers in presentation seminars and coaching sessions named the following causes of your nervousness during presentations:

1. Fear of not meeting people's expectations, of failing and thus embarrassing oneself
2. Concern about forgetting something important
3. Uncertainty of making mistakes in this exposed position in front of the (scientific) public
4. The feeling of being defenceless in front of an unpredictable audience
5. Bad experiences and memories from previous talks.

In just the same way as nervousness can cause speakers to make mistakes or have mental blocks, it can also enhance their concentration and focus, block out the inessential and drive people to achieve peak levels of performance. For their everyday levels of performance, people need a normal energy level, for extraordinary levels of performance, they consequently require a significantly higher one. Thus, the increased adrenaline level in the blood provides an energy level that can lead to people surpassing themselves and producing extraordinary levels of performance. Theatre actors and athletes repeatedly report on the positive effects of nervousness. A certain amount of stage fright is consequently desirable and prevents presenters from reeling off their presentation without any passion.

▶ It is a good sign if you feel an uncomfortable sensation and experience stress. This is because Most people perform at their best when they feel slightly overwhelmed because that's when the brain releases just the right amount of norepinephrine (adrenaline) to get them in top form.[5]

---

[5] Friederike Fabrizius, Hans W. Hagemann The Leading Brain, 2018, page 6.

6.2.2 Classic Techniques to Reduce Nervousness

Scientists can use different techniques or tools to help calm their nerves before a presentation and to benefit from the positive effects of stage fright

- Deliver talks regularly

    This technique only bears fruit over time. The more talks presenters deliver, the higher the likelihood that the stress level will be lower in upcoming events. They know what to expect and can look back on several successful presentations. In the case of researchers with little experience in delivering talks, it is therefore advisable to take advantage of every opportunity to deliver a talk. For example, small initial performances within a (protected) circle of colleagues, presentations to a learning group or short reports on the results in the scientific project team have proven to be helpful ways of getting started and practising. Stage fright is generally not as marked as the group is smaller and known to the speaker. In the next step, it is worthwhile to deliver talks at larger events. Presentations at large conferences also become easier with increasing levels of routine and self-confidence.
- Carefully prepare and practise the talk

    The better researchers prepare and practise the talk, the more familiar they will become with their presentation, transitions, media and timing. This provides them with a sense of security and consequently they will not get as agitated. For instance, talk slides can be organised and structured in such a way that speakers can quickly orient themselves in an emergency and retrieve the lost thread—for example, by means of the assertion evidence approach presented in Chapter 4. Those who feel a high level of stress at challenging points such as the introduction can learn one or two sentences by heart. One key thing to remember: Meticulous does not mean pedantic.
- Predicting and answering questions

    Most scientists are aware of the weaknesses and criticisms of their research. This is exactly what they can take advantage of in their preparation by considering what questions
    - they would ask themselves if they were a member of the audience;
    - colleagues have asked in this context;
    - are raised in the literature;
    - came up during the rehearsal of the talk;
    - lay people (friends) have asked about the topic.

        Anticipating questions makes it possible to prepare answers, to better adapt texts on slides to the objective of the talk and to formulate misleading passages more clearly. Furthermore, it opens up the opportunity to frame critical points more diplomatically.
- Professional support

    In addition to the aforementioned suggestions, training or coaching on how to deliver talks can make people feel more self-assured. Courses are especially recommended that are specifically aimed at scientists, are conducted in small groups and offer individual video analysis. Researchers thus receive objective information from the video in addition to their own impression (self-image) and the feedback of others (external image). Scientists who see themselves on a video report that they do not seem as nervous as they felt.

> **Practical Tip**
> Deliver speeches as often as possible. You learn over time that a certain amount of nervousness is positive and what questions are typically asked.

6.2.3 Techniques to Reduce Nervousness Just Before the Talk

One part of the human brain—the limbic system—controls emotions.[6] One of its functions is to protect humans from physical, emotional and social dangers through fight, flight or freezing. It reacts instinctively, unconsciously and very quickly to everything it perceives as a potential threat, regardless of whether it is an objectively dangerous situation or not. Affected people experience reactions such as a rapid heartbeat, trembling hands, heavy sweating and goose bumps. When this process is triggered, it overrides the prefrontal cortex—the area of the brain that controls conscious activities such as thinking, moving, planning and making decisions. This can lead to situations in which people display unwanted and unusual, sometimes irrational behaviour.[7] In the worst case, those affected experience a blackout.

How can this surplus energy be put to use and reduced? A few minutes before the presentation, speakers require techniques that take hardly any time to use and reduce their nervousness and anxiety quickly, almost in real time. Andrew Huberman, professor of neurobiology and ophthalmology at Stanford University, describes two innate levers that people can use to actively reduce their own stress levels: About the mind and about the body.[8] The following are mental and physiological techniques that presenters can use just before and during a talk.

6.2.3.1 Mental Techniques to Reduce Stress

- Reframing physical reactions
  Interestingly, the physiological patterns associated with anxiety and positive excitement are identical. Researchers can take advantage of this before they

---

[6] https://www.simplypsychology.org/limbic-system.html.
[7] Friederike Fabrizius, Hans W. Hagemann The Leading Brain, 2018, page 30.
[8] https://www.gsb.stanford.edu/insights/hacking-your-speaking-anxiety-how-lessons-neuroscience-can-help-you-communicate.

are due to speak by reinterpreting or reframing the feeling and looking at it differently. Thus, it is a matter of how the bodily reactions are perceived and reinterpreted.

The time that elapses between the reaction of the limbic system and the interpretation of this reaction by the executive functions is short, but it holds great potential for emotional regulation.[9]

▶ For instance, just before the presentation, make it clear to yourself that it is a good thing that your pulse rises a little with excitement and that your body sweats a little because this is normal and increases your own level of performance. Turn anxiety into positive excitement or anticipation, for example, because a presentation is a great opportunity to share your work with others.

- Name stress and fears

Many people try to suppress their nervousness, feelings of insecurity or fear in the hope that they will be able to control them. The opposite is the case, as this causes emotions to build up and intensify.

Psychologist Matthew D. Lieberman shows in his article "Putting Feelings Into Words",[10] that people can reduce emerging stress with a fairly simple method. By perceiving and naming their feeling ("Name it to tame it!"), they ensure that the activity of the involved areas of the limbic system is reduced.

▶ Do not fight your emotions. In situations of great inner tension, put your emotions into words verbally or in writing. You thus defuse the situation—at least temporarily—and regain control over yourself.[11]

Reduction of mental stress can be trained—mostly through positive experiences from similar situations. If the stress level is too high, people are no longer able to reinterpret or name their emotions. Speakers should then resort to physiological techniques. Andrew Huberman describes this in the following sentence:

▶ Trying to control the mind with the mind is like trying to grab fog.[12]

6.2.3.2 Physiological Techniques to Reduce Stress
- Facial feedback hypothesis

---

[9] Friederike Fabrizius, Hans W. Hagemann The Leading Brain, 2018, page 70.
[10] https://journals.sagepub.com/doi/abs/10.1111/j.1467-9280.2007.01916.x.
[11] Friederike Fabrizius, Hans W. Hagemann The Leading Brain, 2018, page 68.
[12] https://lewishowes.com/podcast/unlocking-the-power-of-your-mind-with-neuroscientist-dr-andrew-huberman/.

When people are happy, they smile. Smiling lowers stress levels and has a positive influence on well-being.[13] This shows how thoughts and feelings affect physical functions via the so-called body-mind connection. This is not a one-way street, because conversely, a person can also influence the mental state of the body, and this can be used very well to reduce the perceived stress level before presentations.

One example of this is the facial feedback hypothesis. It says that facial expressions can arouse the feeling that corresponds to the activated facial muscles, i.e. that emotions can be influenced at least in part by facial expressions.[14]

▶ Facial feedback: To reduce nervousness, deliberately create a smile and hold the facial expression for a few seconds. Repeat this exercise if necessary.

- Lateral eye movement

  This technique was developed by the American psychologist Francine Shapiro as part of the psychotherapy method EMDR (Eye Movement Desensitization and Reprocessing) and leads to people relieving themselves of anxiety and stress. It is suitable for use before a presentation as it creates a reduced state of stress and enables people to approach a task with (a little) more ease.[15]

  In fact, lateral movements of the eyes suppress the activity of the amygdala, the "fear organ" in the human brain. This movement of the eyes occurs automatically when people physically move towards something, which subsequently makes them calmer and more relaxed. Speakers can achieve this before a presentation through activities such as walking or moving their eyes sideways.[16]

▶ Lateral eye movements: Move your eyes from side to side for about 30 s to calm down and reduce nervousness.

- Breathing technique "Physiological Sigh"

  The recommendation to take deep breaths when stressed and excited is widespread—but is not a good tip, as it transpires. This is because in such situations, the reduction of the carbon dioxide level in the blood through exhalation is more important than the oxygen intake through breathing. At the same time, the heart rate is slowed down. Both lead to the activation of the parasympathetic nervous system, the part of the autonomic nervous system that ensures

---

[13] https://journals.plos.org/plosone/article?id=10.1371/journal.pone.0235851.
[14] https://pubmed.ncbi.nlm.nih.gov/30973236/.
[15] https://www.ncbi.nlm.nih.gov/pmc/articles/PMC6596227.
[16] https://www.youtube.com/watch?v=8TGaxpasdmw.

relaxation. A breathing pattern that was discovered in 1930 and that can help to reduce stress levels in this context is the "physiological sigh".[17]

Humans and animals access it subconsciously and when they are in confined situations or when they are asleep when the carbon dioxide concentration in the blood is too high. The physiological sigh is composed of inhaling twice and exhaling once. This ensures that all the alveoli are filled. This allows oxygen to be absorbed and, above all, more carbon dioxide to be released. In this way, stress levels quickly drop and speakers become calmer.[18]

▶ The Physiological Sigh:

- 1 longer inhalation
- 1 shorter inhalation
- 1 very long, extended exhalation.

Repeat this pattern two to three times. Ideally inhale through your nose and exhale through your mouth.

6.2.3.3 Personal Tips from Other Researchers

Well-versed presenters have a great deal of experience and have developed their own techniques to reduce their levels of nervousness. Their tips are presented here.

▶
- Find a quiet room, the toilet, if necessary, where you can relax without being spoken to and rehearse your first sentences again.
- Run cold water over your forearms just before the talk. This cools and refreshes. Or go out for some fresh air.
- Put aside your fear of making mistakes. The audience does not know your talk and your process and therefore does not notice any changes. Sometimes the small deviation is even fruitful. Simply continue with your talk.
- Remember that the audience does not perceive your nervousness as intensely as you do, if at all. No one will hold it against you if you are excited because it also demonstrates your commitment.
- Ask a colleague who is a friend to accompany you. It helps most people to know that there is at least one member of the audience who is on their side. Especially at the start of the talk, it is good to be able to look at someone's friendly face.

---

[17] https://www.youtube.com/watch?v=kSZKIupBUuc.
[18] https://www.youtube.com/watch?v=rBdhqBGqiMc.

6.2.4 Techniques to Reduce Nervousness During the Talk

Even during the presentation, there are several ways to release excess energy and reduce tension.

6.2.4.1 Movement
Switching positions is a professional way of reducing tension through physical activity and is suitable for any talk that does not take place from a fixed position, such as behind a lectern. Use positional changes in as controlled and well-dosed manner as possible.

6.2.4.2 Presenter, Pointer and Cue Cards
The remote control is a professional device for controlling slide-based presentations. With such a remote control, presenters have a prop at hand that is a perfect way of conveying stability. It is something that speakers can "hold on to" and that gives the hands something to do. Cue cards achieve a similar effect. Moreover, they are good cue cards that the speakers can look at when needed. They fit well in the hand and help people to calm their nerves. However, they do not offer as many advantages as presenters. Caution: Those who use cards and a wireless clicker no longer have a free hand. Presenters should choose one variant.

▶   Give your hands something to hold onto and keep them busy in a meaningful way.

6.2.5 Slips of the Tongue, Forgotten Points and Losing the Thread

6.2.5.1 Slips of the Tongue
Due to nervousness, simpler mistakes often occur in the form of slips of the tongue. This happens, for instance, when in the heat of the talk a double negation is used instead of a single one. The two negations cancel each other out, the speaker has expressed the opposite of what he actually wanted to say.

Simple linguistic mishaps can be ignored or briefly corrected. If a presenter is guilty of a technical slip of the tongue, it is best to correct the statement without much apology and resume the thread of the talk.

Slips of the tongue are natural and not detrimental to the success of the talk—unless a technically incorrect statement is not corrected. On the contrary: most of the time, slips of the tongue make the speaker seem more human and likeable. They demonstrate that he is not simply reeling off a routine talk.

6.2.5.2 Forgotten Points
Forgotten points can be added by means of a brief transition.

In this context, I would like to add the following point or

At this juncture I would like to briefly come back to the following point .....

It is unnecessary to apologise profusely for omitting or forgetting a point and thus draw the audience's attention to the mistake all the more. The audience frequently does not even notice that information is missing.

> **Practical Tip**
> Don't be afraid of any slips of the tongue. They can have quite a positive effect. Your presentation will then not sound too perfect, the audience will be able to follow better and sometimes slips of the tongue will make the audience smile.

6.2.5.3 Losing the Thread

Despite careful preparation, it can occur that you suddenly lose track of the thread and your mind becomes a complete blank. Everything that researchers knew before is suddenly no longer to hand. Control over the presentation is lost or only partially present in front of everyone's eyes. Too high a stress level leads to a mental block and even a blackout. This is hard to bear for those affected.

The goal must now be to be able to resume the talk as calmly and quickly as possible. For this to happen, the brain must realise that the "danger" has passed or has diminished in order to reactivate the silenced synapses. The seven reactions below have proved successful:

1. Breaking eye contact
   Simple mental blocks can be solved by simply breaking off eye contact.
   Stop looking into the audience so that you are no longer aware of the stressful signals from the audience and you can collect yourself.
2. Show and view the last slide again
   In some cases, it helps to show the last slide again and to orient yourself using it.
   Go back to the point after which the mental block occurred and resume the thread at that point.
   Make use of your Talking Headlines to get back on track.
3. Summarise what has been said so far
   Relatively inconspicuous and obvious options are summaries or repetitions of what has been said so far because they seem like planned action.
   Release smaller mental blocks to thinking with one sentence to get back to work.
4. Look at the slides, the manuscript or the cue card
   If you do not succeed in overcoming the blackout, a look at the documents will help.

Take the time to look at your manuscript or notes. You will find hints and keywords for the continuation of your talk and you will give yourself a breathing space. This is often sufficient to calm your nerves and regain the thread.
5. Drink something
A special and simple option is to interrupt the talk to have a drink. This is an inconspicuous reaction to dealing with a mental block. Especially during long lectures, drinking helps on the one hand against some of the body's physiological reactions to stage fright, such as a dry mouth or feeling unwell. The intake of fluid also cools the body. It also provides those affected with a short break. All of these things reduce the stress factors.
6. Admit that you have lost the thread and ask the audience for help if necessary.
If nothing else works, the only thing that really helps is to address the unpleasant situation offensively. The audience are happy to help in these exceptional situations.
Ask them to help you with the following sentences.

"Now I really have lost the thread. Where did we get to?"

"I have now just forgotten what I wanted to say. I'm sure one of you can help me. What was the last thing we were discussing?"

6.3 Recite the Talk Freely, Read It Out or Learn It off by Heart

Scientists can draw on three forms of academic talks. Depending on the situation, personality and research discipline, free speech, reading aloud, memorisation or a mixture are suitable for the presentation.

6.3.1 Reciting Freely

For the vast majority of situations, it is advisable to speak freely. A presentation recited freely comes across as more natural, pleasant and professional than those that are read out or memorised. The freely recited talk strengthens the contact with the auditorium. It thrives on the coherent choice of words, modulation and body language, is more authentic and is therefore more appealing to the audience. When reciting the talk freely, it is easier to make eye contact with the audience, which demonstrates confidence and underlines the competence of speakers. Another advantage of this method is the flexibility to adapt to changing situations in the talk, such as questions from the audience, technical problems or unexpected time constraints. Depending on the time available, scientists control the presentation accordingly by only briefly discussing a topic, describing it in more detail or presenting interesting additional information.

Well-designed slides, the comment function of the presentation programme or index cards can be used as cues and reminders.

6.3.2 Reading Aloud in a Talk

The talk that is read out aloud offers great protection from a blackout, prevents points from being forgotten and consists of polished and correctly worded phrases. In some research disciplines, this is an advantage and in certain cases an obligation. However, just reading out aloud also brings with it some challenges and disadvantages. In the talk, there are hardly any possibilities for adaptation. There is little eye contact and this limits the connection with the audience. The modulation of the voice changes and often seems more monotonous and less authentic. The written language of the talk also deprives it of its liveliness. This is exhausting in the long run even for hardy and interested members of the audience.

Talks and parts of the talk should only be read out in exceptional cases. This includes all texts where there must be no deviation in the wording, such as original quotations, formulae, definitions, paragraphs or detailed legal texts. Texts in these categories may be partially abridged if this does not distort their meaning. Changes, on the other hand, are not permitted. For this reason, scientists should read out these passages. In this way, they avoid inaccuracies and citation errors. Those who wish to emphasise the importance of the original passage can explicitly announce when they are going to cite a section:

> "I do not want to leave anything to doubt at this point and I will read the text of the paragraph out to you."
>
> "Walter states in this regard, and I quote verbatim …"

6.3.3 Reciting from Memory

What speaks in favour of this method, as with the case of reading the talk out loud, is that formulations can be selected in advance and placed precisely. This provides the speaker with a sense of reassurance and reduces nervousness. On the other hand, talks that are presented mainly or entirely from the mind carry some risks with them.

The presentation of a talk that is recited from memory requires a lot of preparation in terms of the formulation and writing down of the text of the talk and also in terms of the learning of the text. This technique forces presenters into a rather rigid corset and makes it almost impossible to adapt the presentation to changing circumstances over time. It is difficult to get back into the talk after a question or other interruption. In addition, speakers should bear in mind that most people's body language and voice modulation change when they deliver a presentation from their head. Eye contact is frequently lost in the process.

Apart from the introduction, there are only a few parts of the talk where learning things by heart is useful. These include difficult transitions from one slide to the next and the conclusion of the talk.

> Practise your introductory sentences on the drive to the venue. Go through them again in your head shortly before the performance. If the opportunity arises, you can use them away from the public to warm yourself up for the talk.

6.4 Guiding the Audience's Gaze—Using Laser Pointers, Animations and Your Hands

Complex and detailed slides, which are shown without hints and aids, usually lead to the audience wavering between reading and listening and their attention being on different parts of the slide. Leading the audience's gaze is a simple and effective technique to control the audience's focus and direct it to a point on the slide.

Researchers have laser pointers, their own hands and animations at their disposal.

> **Practical Tip**
> Synchronise speech and visualisation by employing active eye guidance. This makes it easier for your audience to follow the talk and grasp complex issues.

6.4.1 Guiding the Audience's Gaze Using the Laser Pointer

Very few talks can do without the laser pointer. It is small, easy to handle and can be used from all positions in the lecture room and is predestined, to explain detailed presentations. Its use takes a little practice, as the human eye finds it difficult or impossible to follow the light spot when there is rapid movement on the screen. Laser pointers should be used in doses, slowly and preferably while making use of circular movements. Speakers must bear in mind that the light mark always has an unsettling effect on the viewer. This is because regular contractions take place in a person's muscles, which ensure a weak level of tension even when at rest. Therefore, a person can never hold his arm completely still. Nervousness further amplifies the effect of the muscle tone. The resulting tremor is amplified by the laser pointer and projected onto the screen in this potentised form. For this reason, the laser pointer should not be used permanently.

When using a light pointer, it is unfavourable that speakers have to turn their backs to the audience and speak towards the screen during longer demonstrations.

It is therefore important to make sure that eye contact with the audience is not interrupted for too long.

Modern laser pointers have a brighter green light that is easier on the eyes. This facilitates perception and helps people with colour vision deficiencies in particular.

6.4.2 Guiding the Audience's Gaze Using Animations

Modern presentation programmes offer possibilities to guide the attention of the audience with animations. They are—if used professionally—an excellent way to convey the core messages, processes and interesting details more clearly on individual slides and to set accents in the presentation. The focus of the audience can thus be precisely controlled. Used selectively and in a targeted manner, they are a perfect tool for guiding the audience's gaze.

However: Animations seduce presenters quickly. Often animations that are too many in number, too fast and inappropriate are used—when, for example, each word is faded individually or in a bouncing manner. Chapter four presents animations and their effective use in detail.

6.4.3 Guiding the Audience's Gaze with Your Hands

This most natural form of gaze guidance occurs directly on the projection surface. It shows the relation of the presenter to his content, can always be used and works independently of batteries or technology.

This method entails that speakers sometimes stand in the way of the picture when directing the audience's gaze. This becomes difficult for the audience in cases where they spend a longer time in the light of the projector. If you need more time to present something on the slide, you should therefore opt for other ways of directing the audience's gaze. This also applies to events where a large projection surface is used or the screen hangs too high. This is where this kind of guidance aid reaches its limits. To be on the safe side, researchers should prepare for such situations by taking a laser pointer with them.

Where eye guidance is concerned using your hand, the touch-turn-talk technique[19] is ideal, which structures the presentation of slides in an audience-friendly way with three simple, easy-to-implement steps. For this, presenters stand to the left of the projection screen (usual reading direction) or, if necessary, to the right if it is important that they start there. Then they tell the audience what they are going to present and show the slide. After this they point to the element with the hand that is near the screen, look at the audience again and begin to speak.

---

[19] It was not possible to find the author or developer of this method.

▶ **Touch Turn Talk technique:**

1. Point to the element (touch).
2. Look at the audience (turn).
3. Explain the element (talk).

6.5 Hyperlinks—Provide Additional Information or Abbreviate the Talk if Necessary

Links to websites, documents or other slides of the lecture, are a useful tool. They open up the possibility for scientists to act flexibly and in an audience-oriented manner in talks and at the same time to be able to meet tight deadlines professionally.

6.5.1 Provide Additional In-Depth Information

Sometimes presenters do not know the exact composition of the audience or their level of knowledge on the topic. This makes it harder to determine the right content and the appropriate level of detail of the information. A heterogeneous audience, in particular, can pose a challenge to researchers in preparing a lecture because they have to reckon with different levels of knowledge and interests. It is also not easy to find out to what extent the audience or parts of it are familiar with the topic, the literature and the methodological approach. Hyperlinks can help here and provide additional information if needed. At points in the talk where more detailed information might be helpful, researchers create a link to use as needed. In this way, they design their presentation in a target group-oriented way and can respond to different expectations and levels of knowledge, especially in the case of mixed audiences.

Such links leave all available options with the researcher delivering the talk. Not only do they significantly increase the scientist's flexibility and professionalise the presentation, but they also have a psychological effect: The member of the audience receives something extra. Namely, information that is inserted specifically for this audience and is not part of the main set of slides.

6.5.2 Dealing with Time Constraints

Hyperlinks are simple and efficient problem solvers when scientists run into time problems. If, for instance, there is less time available because previous speakers have overrun, a technical problem has occurred in their own presentation or an important person (supervisor, decision-maker or the person who invited the speakers) has to leave the event early, presenters can defuse the situation by using links. Instead of clicking past individual slides and explaining themselves with sentences like "That's not so important" or "Too bad, we don't have time for that now", researchers now simply activate the prepared link.

▶ Make sure you do not make your audience feel like they have missed out on something. Use hyperlinks to skip slides. This prevents you from having to "click past" slides at the end of the talk and the audience from seeing what was not presented to them.

Due to the fact no one knows when this will be needed, a hyperlink should be placed on each slide in order to be able to go directly to the last or most important slide in the event of time constraints. For this purpose, a corresponding link is placed in a fixed position on each slide—for instance, in the logo of one's own research organisation. This is easy to remember and to recall even under stress.

▶ Remember that in order to activate a link, you will generally need to have access to the presentation computers. Only a few wireless presenters have access to a function with which to activate links.

6.6 Steering the Discussion and the Audience

Launching the discussion or question and answer session (Q&A) is like entering unknown territory. It is full of surprises: Nobody knows how it will go, whether questions will be asked and what the atmosphere will be like. This makes it difficult to plan and for this reason, in the perception of many scientists, it ranges from the "best part of the event" to "an extremely unpleasant experience". Viewed objectively, this is a unique opportunity to receive feedback from experts and thus to further develop one's own paper and make it more valuable. Subjectively, researchers look forward to and fear questions from the audience in equal measure. In terms of their effect on the presenter, they range from polite to condescending and from persistent to hostile or scathing, and ideally, they prove helpful. Questions are like the salt in the soup: Too much of it makes the meal too well seasoned and inedible. If there is not enough salt, it is bland and does not taste good. Therefore, it helps academics to know and be able to use appropriate ways of reacting and intervening to steer the discussion and deal with difficult situations and conference participants.

> **Practical Tip**
> Do not force a discussion upon the audience after your presentation and do not ask any intrusive questions. Keep two basic elements in mind: Politeness and diplomacy!

6.6.1 Answering Constructive Questions and Responding to Factual Statements

In many cases, members of the audience ask helpful questions or share interesting information that leads to an enriching discussion. However, it can also occur that contributions have no relation to the topic of the talk or that questions cannot be answered by the speaker. Five reactions or interventions come into question here.

6.6.1.1 Repeat a Question in Your Own Words
If a member of the audience asks a question, the speaker should maintain eye contact with the person asking the question and, if possible, let them finish. It makes sense for him to repeat the question for everyone to hear or reproduce it in his own words. With this form of "active listening", the scientist ensures that all listeners and he himself have understood the question correctly. In addition, he wins time to think about a possible answer.

> "If I understood you correctly, you are asking how …?"
>
> "In other words, you would like to know, why …?"

Short questions formulated in a way that everyone can understand should be answered immediately and without any repetition.

▶ If you did not understand the question, ask the person asking it to repeat it and—if necessary—for the person to formulate it differently.

6.6.1.2 Interrupt Politely if the Question Is Not Related to the Topic or No Question Was Asked
It is basically a matter of courtesy to let the person asking the question finish the sentence. At academic events in particular, participants tend to formulate things in a complex manner. Some exploit this courteous behaviour in order to expansively lecture on their own point of view or to express their personal experiences at epic length. There are people who ask questions that repeat the talk, present themselves and "adulate" or simply relate something that had no relevance to the talk. Such people should be interrupted by the speaker for several reasons. On the one hand, these contributions provide no benefit to anyone and, on the other hand, they deprive other members of the audience of the opportunity to ask questions or make comments. Pauses the member of the audience takes to breathe are ideal opportunities into which the speaker can interject. If he knows the individual asking the question personally, he should be addressed by name.

> "Please excuse me for interrupting you for a moment, Dr Schmitz, just to make sure I have understood your question correctly, …"

> "I am pleased that you share my interest in this topic. Thank you very much! I hope you won't be angry with me if I now give other colleagues the opportunity to ask me a few questions."

Now the speaker can take control once more by answering the question and then giving the floor to the next member of the audience. After the answer, the speaker should deliberately break off any eye contact and no further attention should be paid to the person who asked this question. Otherwise, the person in question might feel encouraged to make further contributions.

At more informal events with scientists who are more the speaker's peers or with audiences that the speaker knows well, more relaxed statements can also be effective.

> "Sarah, sorry to interrupt you. What exactly was your question?"

The more senior the questioner and the more formal the conference, the more difficult it is to interrupt a participant's torrent of speech. In these situations, speakers need to be more patient. They may have no choice but to wait until the person has finished speaking.

> **Practical Tip**
> Cultivate a confident approach to answering questions and value them as an indication of interest. However: Take questions from members of the audience seriously and don't brush them aside (*"No, that's not true!"*).

6.6.1.3 Honestly Admit It When the Question Cannot Be Answered

Scientists have to do their homework and ideally should know everything about their research. Nevertheless, no one can expect them to know the answer to all questions asked. This will not always be possible, especially where future-oriented questions are concerned. If the scientists cannot answer a question, they have only one option: honestly admit the fact that they do not know the answer to the question. At such moments, it is crucial not to pretend and to resume the discussion as quickly as possible. If it is information that is not available in the situation, it can be submitted subsequently.

> "Interesting notion, I hadn't thought about that yet. I don't know the answer to the question at the moment."
>
> "Currently, we do not have sufficient data on this. I can't answer your question (yet)?"

> **Practical Tip**
> If you don't know the answer, don't delegate a question to people who aren't there (*"That's my co-author's job!"*). And don't beat around the bush; it's better to admit openly if you don't know, or haven't considered (or forgotten), something. If desired and possible, provide answers by mail.

6.6.1.4 Say if You Need Time to Answer the Question

It can easily occur that a question from the audience cannot be answered immediately and the researcher needs some time to formulate his answer. That is not a sign of weakness but of professionalism. It is important that he lets the audience know this. Otherwise, it is irritating for the audience if speakers stand in front of them in silence for a longer period of time. The longer this unannounced period of reflection lasts, the more unpleasant it becomes for everyone involved.

> "This not an easy question to answer. Please give me a moment."

> "Interesting question. Let me briefly reflect on this one."

6.6.1.5 Deferring or Ruling Out Questions

Some questions are asked without reference to the topic or go far beyond it and necessitate a detailed answer that exceeds the time frame. Both forms should be politely dismissed or deferred.

> "I am afraid that this question exceeds the parameters of today's topic. Perhaps we'll have time to go into that in more detail after my talk."

> "Exciting way of viewing things. Unfortunately, it exceeds the scope of today's talk. Shall we talk about this after the conference? I could give you a call."

> **Practical Tip**
> Avoid a lengthy bilateral discussion with one person from the audience (the rest often cannot and will not be able to follow). Put off difficult but good questions to a personal conversation with the person posing the question after the event. If possible, invite others present to participate in the discussion so that no one feels excluded.

6.6.2 Dealing with Unfair Criticism, Killer Arguments and Deadlocked Situations

Discussions can end in endless, unfair debates coupled with personal attacks. It can become heated and people can feel insulted. Speakers must not only be prepared for very heated discussions but also arm themselves against unfair questions and personal attacks. The range of such "methods" includes exaggerations or simplifications of problems as well as the disputing of facts, scientific results or the competence of the presenter. It is possible that the member of the audience will question everything or, as a "continuous interrupter", will need to have every statement explained to him in detail.

Therefore, researchers should have intervention strategies at their disposal for critical situations in which members of the audience interrupt and disrupt the lecture or discussion with malicious questions or comments.

6.6.2.1 Ignoring or Briefly Paying Attention to Them

Presentation professionals advise speakers not to react to everything that is thrown at them in the context of unfair behaviour in the talk. A lot of statements are not worth commenting on. Scientists should simply ignore them. A thought that is suitable for this as a first reaction is: allow rubbish to float by. In some cases, people posing questions want to make feel important or simply want to test how the (young) colleague will respond to such a remark. In some situations, it also helps to pay some attention to this member of the audience. It is normally sufficient just to briefly look at them.

6.6.2.2 Exposing Killer and Suggestive Phrases

If non-verbal reactions from the presenter are not enough, it is important to respond as early and as calmly as possible. It helps here if the speaker demonstrates that he has seen through this behaviour.

> **Example**
>
> Statement: *"I am sure you will agree with me that it would have been better …"*
> Possible answer: *"That's a leading question and no, I don't agree with you. The advantage of our method lies in …"*◄

Open questions in particular are excellent ways of countering unfair behaviour. They have a rather neutral character and play the ball back into the court of the person posing the question.

> **Example**
>
> Statement: *"This point was refuted by Smith years ago, wasn't it?"*
> Possible answer: *"I have a different recollection of that. What exactly do you have in mind?"*◄

6.6 Steering the Discussion and the Audience

Another helpful technique is to question the meaningfulness of the behaviour and demonstrate that you are an advocate for everyone by using the personal pronouns "we" and "us". The speaker goes on the (factual) offensive by means of such reactions and asks the member of the audience to clarify his assertions, which are presented as generally valid. It is often difficult for the people posing the questions to substantiate their claim.

Example

Statement: *"I believe I can speak on behalf of everyone here. What you are presenting here cannot be right!"*

Possible answer: *"It is not clear to me what you are trying to achieve by making such a blanket statement. I don't see how that gets us anywhere in the discussion at hand. Please substantiate your statement."* ◄

All attacks are unpleasant that are aimed at the person and not at the content of the presentation, and whose aim is to disparage the speaker. These make no constructive contribution towards the discussion and make further debate almost impossible.

The absolute certainty with which these "killer arguments" are presented, their supposed generality and their sometimes hurtful character often tempt scientists to react more emotionally than intended.

6.6.3 Interrupt Deadlocked Discussions with Metacommunication

Many researchers remember lectures and Q&A sessions that were characterised by never-ending debates—often between two people—and deadlocked situations. The same arguments and accusations are repeated again and again without any conclusion being reached. From a psychological point of view, the scientists involved are in a communicative vicious circle that both parties keep alive through their conduct. In such cases, it is the task of the presenter to interrupt the rather ineffective vicious circle and to continue offering other members of the audience the opportunity to ask questions. To do this, he adopts a metacommunicative level, i.e. the focus of attention is not what was said, but how the participants interact with each other.

> "At the moment, I have the impression that this debate is not getting us anywhere. I would like to revisit this issue later and for now give others the opportunity to ask their questions."

> "You two have been discussing this issue for some time now. Somehow the situation seems to me to be deadlocked and not very useful for any of us. I think it makes sense to continue with other questions and if there is time, come back to the issue."

> "Well, it looks like we won't be able to reach an agreement on this issue. Maybe we should just simply 'agree to disagree'."

Metacommunication also helps in situations where the speaker conditionally agrees with the critic.

> "I can understand your line of argument on the first point, here I also see a need for modification. I do not concur with your statements on point two. Let's hear what other members of the audience have to say on this."

By adopting this approach, researchers minimise the amount of time wasted and ensure that endless discussions are broken off. Presenters should be careful not to "bully" anyone or display inappropriate attempts at domination. No one expects that at the end of a lecture or a discussion all those present will be of the same opinion and have agreed on one view of things. In this respect, it can be a smart move to end a prolonged dispute without an outcome and without a loss of face for any of the parties involved.

6.6.3.1 Use Open Questions to Defuse Difficult Situations

The more tempers flare in a question and answer session, the more difficult it is for the participants to return to an objective discussion. Open questions are valuable tools in such situations. Making use of words such as what, where and how in your questions aids a positive talk and discussion climate as closed questions, as they stimulate reflection, evaluation and new questions. Especially in the context of audience criticism, an open questioning technique can be rewarding. Speakers use these methods in order to understand audience questions better and to be able to draw as many clues as possible from criticism and comments for their own research work. In doing so, they ask the person posing the question to describe and elaborate on their comments for a better understanding of all:

> "What exactly do you have in mind there?"
>
> "What do you base that on?"
>
> "What do you conclude from that?"
>
> "So how exactly did you go about your investigation?"
>
> "What do you think should belong in it and what shouldn't?"
>
> "How do you arrive at the conclusion?"
>
> "What's the difference there for you?"

6.6.4 4 Strategies for Different Situations in the Discussion

6.6.4.1 Make Strategic Use of the Microphone

A stationary microphone can be used for medium-sized groups and has several advantages over mobile devices. Firstly, this creates a certain dynamic in the audience and secondly, the speaker can see how many people are in the queue. This facilitates good time planning and if necessary, there is the possibility to limit the number of people who pose questions. Unlike mobile microphones, which are passed around in the audience, the speaker keeps track of the order of the people who are asking questions, can intervene if there are any time problems and also never misses a request to speak. Moreover, the discussion can be recorded using a fixed camera without any effort. This method helps to activate the audience and at the same time requires some courage on their part. In the case of larger groups, comprising more than 50 people, several stationary microphones should be used. Depending on the seating arrangements—for instance, long rows or an unsuitable room layout—mobile microphones handed out by the organiser's staff may be the better choice.

6.6.4.2 Using a Throwing Microphone

Throwing microphones represents a quick, energising and fun way to pass the microphone around the audience. By contrast with conventional microphones, there is no need for the occasionally awkward passing of the microphone. The device, wrapped in a foam cube, is thrown from one questioner to the next in the auditorium. This makes the discussion more lively and interesting. Presenters should not lose sight of the fact that the audience´s passivity is broken up, as throwers, catchers and "intermediate stations"—while overcoming greater distances between the participants—stand up to throw and catch the microphone. Especially at more informal events, throwing microphones ensures more relaxed discussions.

6.6.4.3 Summarise Things After the Discussion

Scientists who want to prevent their last impression from being spoiled by a shallow discussion have the option of changing the classical structure of scientific talks by not presenting summaries at the end of the lecture, but only following the discussion. This ensures that—especially if few or no questions have been asked—the key messages of the talk are prominently placed and the presentation does not end in awkward silences. In addition, this method can also be used to include interesting points from the discussion in the presenter's summary.

6.6.4.4 Discussing Things Before the Actual Discussion

Applying this unusual method avoids the awkward silence at the beginning of the Q&A session and enables everyone to participate more easily. The audience is invited to have a short exchange with the person(s) sitting next to them before the actual discussion. The presenter asks the audience one or two discussion questions and visualises them. It usually only takes a few seconds for the groups to form. They then have two to three minutes to exchange views on the questions mentioned until the presenter starts the actual discussion.

This energising of the audience initially causes some astonishment and raises the energy levels in the room. This increases the likelihood that interesting questions will be asked in the following plenary discussion. What's more: the opportunity to network emerges at the same time.

▶ **Examples of Questions:**

- What was your first thought during (or after) the talk?
- What impressed you most?
- What do you assess critically?

References

Coles, Nicholas A et al., 2019, A Meta-Analysis of the Facial Feedback Literature: Effects of Facial Feedback on Emotional Experience Are Small and Variable, https://pubmed.ncbi.nlm.nih.gov/30973236/, last retrieved: 27.12.2023

De Voogd Lycia et al., 2018, Eye-Movement Intervention Enhances Extinction via Amygdala Deactivation, https://www.ncbi.nlm.nih.gov/pmc/articles/PMC6596227/last retrieved 27.12.2023

Fabrizius, Friederike and Hagemann, Hans W., 2018, "The Leading Brain", TarcherPerigee

Ferriss, Tim and Huberman, Andrew, 2021, Breathing Techniques to Reduce Stress and Anxiety | Dr. Andrew Huberman on the Physiological Sigh, https://www.youtube.com/watch?v=kSZKIupBUuc, last retrieved: 27.12.2023

Gojowsky, Anna und Gielas, Anna, 2014, Was der Körper verrät, https://www.spektrum.de/magazin/nonverbale-kommunikation-was-der-koerper-verraet/1313420, last retrieved: 27.12.2023

Guy-Evans, Olivia, 2023, Limbic System: Definition, Parts, Functions, and Location, https://www.simplypsychology.org/limbic-system.html, last retrieved: 27.12.2023

Howes, Lewis and Andrew Huberman Andrew, 2021, Unlock Your Mind, https://lewishowes.com/podcast/unlocking-the-power-of-your-mind-with-neuroscientist-dr-andrew-huberman/, last retrieved: 27.12.2023

Huberman, Andrew, 2021, Hacking Your Speaking Anxiety: How Lessons from Neuroscience Can Help You Communicate Confidently, https://www.gsb.stanford.edu/insights/hacking-your-speaking-anxiety-how-lessons-neuroscience-can-help-you-communicate, last retrieved: 27.12.2023

Huberman, Andrew, 2021, Reduce Anxiety & Stress with the Physiological Sigh | Huberman Lab Quantal Clip, https://www.youtube.com/watch?v=rBdhqBGqiMc, last retrieved: 27.12.2023

Huberman, Andrew, 2022, Eye Movements, https://www.youtube.com/watch?v=8TGaxpasdmw, last retrieved: 27.12.2023

Lieberman, Matthew D et al., 2007, Putting Feelings into Words, https://journals.sagepub.com/doi/pdf/10.1177/1754073917742706, last retrieved: 27.12.2023

Watzlawick, Paul et al., 2003, "Menschliche Kommunikation", Hogrefe AG

Zander-Schellenberg, Thea et al., 2020, Does Laughing Have a Stress-Buffering Effect in Daily Life, https://journals.plos.org/plosone/article?id=10.1371/journal.pone.0235851, last retrieved: 27.12.2023

Mastering Virtual Presentations 7

Virtual presentations share common features with face-to-face events and at the same time they are very different from each other at certain points. What both forms have in common is that scientists reveal a part of their research in a given time window, supported by slides, which is then discussed. The big difference in virtual events is the spatial separation between the presenter and the audience. Speakers as well as each individual member of the audience sit alone in a room. In the case of international virtual conferences, they are not only in different locations, but often also in different time zones.

The audience is visible either as a collection of many small videos or, if the cameras are deactivated, via profile pictures or as many dark rectangles. Where there are large groups of participants, not everyone is usually visible on the screen at the same time. It is easy for speakers to gain the impression that they are talking to a wall or into a black hole. There is a lack of chance encounters over a coffee, the opportunities for personal exchanges are more limited and, last but not least, technical problems can mean that no contact at all is possible between speakers and audience members. Overall, the conference situation is much more distanced and anonymous than in face-to-face events.

On the other hand, virtual conferences offer new possibilities and speed up many things. They enable researchers to take part in significantly more events, receive information on their own research more quickly and establish and maintain contacts with colleagues more easily from their desks or kitchen tables. This saves a lot of time and money for everyone involved. The technical possibilities, such as chats or electronic whiteboards, encourage interaction and exchange, and are sometimes more interesting and lively than was previously the case in most face-to-face events. At the same time, these innovations can also be reasons for problems and breakdowns. It is therefore important to know the possibilities, limitations and special features of virtual lectures.

© The Author(s), under exclusive license to Springer Fachmedien Wiesbaden GmbH, part of Springer Nature 2024
B. Hey, *Mastering Scientific Presentations*,
https://doi.org/10.1007/978-3-658-44184-5_7

This chapter shows which similarities there are with face-to-face events, where adjustments are necessary and what is new with regard to the preparation, implementation and control of virtual presentations.

7.1 Preparation

7.1.1 What Remains the Same

- Knowing the size and composition of the group
- Identifying the level of knowledge and interests of the audience
- Formulating the benefits and knowledge gain of the audience
- Define your own goal
- Know and take into account the time frame; plan for buffers
- Write a storyline
- Designing visualisations and slides according to principles of perception psychology
- Set the link to the most important slide
- Set up animations for the guidance of the audience's gaze
- Provide information about conference participation and the topic in social media and arrange with other participants if necessary
- Practise and record the talk aloud, record the presentation time with a stopwatch
- Perform video analysis and make adjustments if necessary

7.1.2 What is Different

The preparation often takes longer than it would for face-to-face events. At virtual events, academics should take the fact into account that participants dial in with laptops, tablets or mobile phones, which means they have to follow the talk via smaller screens. Accordingly, it is important to make text, figures and illustrations (even) larger and clearer.

▶ Virtual talks are demanding for the audience and the speaker. Think carefully about when you will present what in your virtual talk and how you will go about presenting it.

Too many, cluttered and text-heavy slides lead more quickly to a high cognitive burden in online talks and to viewers switching off and occupying themselves with something else. Meaningful illustrations, carefully placed animations, little as well as well-structured text and clear eye guidance become even more important here because they help to control the audience's attention and keep them engaged for longer. In addition to animations, virtual pointing aids, pens, pointers and the mouse pointer can be used for this purpose.

▶ Practise using virtual pointers and pens and ensure that the respective stroke width is appropriate.

The presentation becomes even clearer if speakers also use words to direct the audience's focus ("At the top left of the illustration you can see …") and prepare good transitions to the next slide. This visual and acoustic aid helps people to understand the slide and provides the audience with a good orientation.

Because of the higher likelihood of malfunctions—such as problems with dialing in or with network stability—it makes sense to plan for a larger time buffer than at classic events and to place links strategically so that they can be used as a shortcut to the most important slide or to present additional information.

▶ Be sure to familiarise yourself with the videoconferencing technology used - regardless of whether you use activating elements or not. Test all the functions that you want to use.

7.1.3 What Additional Elements Are There

By contrast with physical meetings, scientists often sit in front of a screen for hours during video conferences. This has an impact on the presenter and his audience in several ways. Body language, the phenomenon of digital fatigue, the didactic preparation of the lecture, the conscious use of language as well as the activation and participation of the audience play a decisive role here.

7.1.3.1 Too Much or not Enough Body Language

Body language in virtual meetings can range on a scale from "no non-verbal signals at all" to "an overwhelmingly large number of non-verbal signals". Both entail disadvantages that are sometimes very serious. Thus, little or no visible body language can lead to misinterpretations because large (or all) elements of non-verbal communication remain concealed. In addition, the modulation, i.e. volume, variability of the voice and its pitch, change for speakers who present in a seated position. This often makes the performance seem less energetic and more monotonous. This is reinforced by the fact that pauses in speech are (even) less commonly used in the digital setting. Experience demonstrates that the following three forms of behaviour prevent this and make presenters appear more natural and imposing:

1. Presenting standing:
   This ensures the speaker has a more active, upright posture with higher levels of body tension and better oxygen supply.
2. Use your hands and arms naturally:
   This aids a more authentic modulation and appears more dynamic. To a certain extent, it makes it possible to compensate for a lack of body language.

3. Make use of brief pauses in speech between sentences and paragraphs:
   This helps the audience to better absorb what is said, gives the speaker the opportunity to collect himself briefly and ensures a more varied style of speaking.

7.1.3.2 Digital Fatigue

A second influential aspect of digital events concerns the brain. Non-stop online meetings—for all their advantages—are a real energy drain that put a lot of strain on the brain and can lead to fatigue and exhaustion. The terms "ZOOM or online fatigue" have become established for this phenomenon of digital fatigue.[1]

Jeremy Bailenson, of the Stanford Virtual Human Interaction Lab, cites four causes of online fatigue[2]:

1. Excessive and intense eye contact

   The amount of eye contact and the relative closeness and size of people's faces are unnatural and unusual. The number of eye contacts is increased and can give rise to the feeling that you are being stared at. Whereas in face-to-face talks, both the audience and the speaker can allow their gazes to wander to relieve themselves, in the virtual space this looks like disinterest. Speakers should therefore resize audience videos to a size they are comfortable with and avert their eyes from the screen if the stress becomes too much. Large screens with their own camera as well as an external keyboard convey a greater distance to the audience.

2. Seeing your own video permanently in real time

   Seeing oneself constantly during the talk is a new phenomenon that does not occur in face-to-face formats. Speakers unintentionally receive permanent feedback. This may be helpful in cases where speakers inadvertently move out of range of the camera. In all other situations, it irritates, distracts and disturbs. Those who see themselves on a permanent basis usually also judge themselves more critically, which has an influence on the presentation performance and impact of it.

   Here it is advisable to switch off the self-view on your own screen after you have checked that the position in front of the camera is OK.

3. Restriction of habitual movements during talks

   Speakers normally move around during face-to-face talks. They take up different positions in the room for this. Even if a lectern restricts the range of movement, presenters move behind it with small steps and use gestures when pointing towards the screen, for instance. This is not the case at virtual conferences, where the camera severely restricts physical activities in an unnatural way.

---

[1] https://papers.ssrn.com/sol3/papers.cfm?abstract_id=3786329
[2] https://tmb.apaopen.org/pub/nonverbal-overload/release/2.

Presenters who want to get some exercise during the talk should—as mentioned above—present standing up. Whoever deactivates the camera before their own presentation, loosens up physically and activates themselves moderately, is able to better bridge the phase of the presentation where they are physically inactive.

4. Higher cognitive burden

In online presentations, the participants have to make more of an effort in terms of their verbal and non-verbal communication than in the face-to-face format. The speakers now need to reflect on self-evident, natural and internalised ways of communicating. Speakers deliberately position themselves in front of the camera. If they want to know whether the sound and image transmission are working, they ask the audience to nod or give a thumbs-up. Gestures can also have different meanings in a videoconferencing context or not be fully captured by the camera. All of this constitutes an additional cognitive burden and can be irritating.

For scientific meetings that have longer sections for exchange in addition to presentations, "audio-only phases" are therefore a good idea.

▶ If the situation allows, deactivate your video to give yourself a break from the multitude of visual signals. Inform the other participants about this, especially if the group is smaller in size.

7.1.3.3 Didactic Preparation and Presentation Duration of Individual Elements of the Talk

The risk that members of the audience might be distracted during online talks is significantly higher than during face-to-face events. Some advisors assume a 10- to 15-min attention limit of the audience and recommend adjusting the presentation duration of the individual blocks of a talk accordingly. It's not quite that simple, as Neil A. Bradbury from Chicago's Rosalind Franklin University of Medicine and Science demonstrates.[3]

According to this, the available primary data do not corroborate the concept of a 10- to 15-min attention limit. Instead, the duration of the students' concentration depended on the way in which the speakers presented the content, had it developed and adapted to the needs of the group. Interesting information and data presented in a monotonous and uninspired manner in a short time slot only helped to hold the viewers' attention to a lesser extent afterwards.

First and foremost, didactic aspects play a decisive role when it comes to the audience's attention, followed by the presentation duration of individual lecture elements and content-related aspects Transferred to (virtual) scientific presentations, this means that—even significant—content should be shown in an appealing

---

[3] https://journals.physiology.org/doi/pdf/10.1152/advan.00109.2016

and methodically varied way so that viewers are able to recall it better and remain attentive.

7.1.3.4 Distractions and Multitasking

At virtual events, it is tempting to do other tasks on the side. Even more so when presentations are not very interesting, long-winded or predictable. Members of the audience then often quickly turn to other things.

A calculation by Robert M. Ewers of Imperial College London shows what can happen when researchers deliver a talk unprepared, in an uninspired manner and out of touch with the audience.

▶ "For every 70 seconds a speaker talked to himself, the likelihood that his talk was boring doubled."[4]

Energising elements, variety and surprise therefore have an important part to play if presenters want to keep the audience onside and make it as difficult as possible for them to drift away. Different tools and techniques can be used depending on the occasion and the size of the group.

1. Use language and modulation in a targeted way:
   In the virtual setting, speakers are more dependent on the impact of their verbal language than in face-to-face events. In addition to the what, the how of what is said also has an influence on the audience and should therefore be used in a well-considered and planned way. Short sentences and active formulations make the language more interesting and seem less distant, as the following example shows.

Example

Passive tense: The presence of x was determined by y.
Active tense: We determined the presence of x with y. ◄

Changes in modulation—such as deliberately changing the tempo of speech or using a short pause in speech to increase tension—show the audience that something special is coming. Speech pauses in particular provide two decisive advantages. They allow the audience to better process what has been said so far and they focus attention on what is about to follow.

---

[4] https://www.nature.com/articles/d41586-018-06817-z

Example

The fact that x would break under the influence of y was predictable. What surprised us, however, was the following result: (brief pause and fade in the result).◄

2. Incorporate changes into the talk:
    Using purposefully placed unusual or unexpected lecture elements, scientists succeed more easily in offering the audience variety. Anything that arouses the curiosity of the audience, surprises them, gets them involved and fits the topic is a good choice. Practical examples of these are:
    - Stop slide sharing and briefly present an example without visualisation or weave in an interesting incident
    - Show pictures or short videos
    - Highlight special features on a slide, document or image live with the virtual marker or add to it with the pen
    - Jointly present the talk with the co-author

▶ You can move interesting photos, graphics or documents from a second screen to the first. This will make the change clearer than if you show these photos as part of your slide set.

3. Plan energising and participation opportunities:
    Certainly the most effective tool to keep the audience's attention and motivation high during virtual presentations is audience engagement. Participation offers a unifying element and creates a new dynamic in the lecture. Those who are actively involved are less likely to be distracted. Presenters can choose a format that suits them from the following six frequently used energising methods. These can be used individually and partly also in combination:

- Inform conference participants about the agenda of the talk and any open questions before the event.
    In the case of small groups, change the dynamics of the meeting by sending your detailed agenda to the audience shortly before the event with the questions they would like to discuss- Alternatively, in the case of larger conferences, you could spread this via social media with conference hashtags

▶ Please note: Provide information in the announcement about what you are planning so that interested people can prepare themselves if necessary. Allow a sufficient amount of time for this additional part.

- Offer question rounds throughout

    Inform your audience at the beginning of the talk that you will be offering the option of additional discussions in the talk where people can share their thoughts. Invite the use of the chat to collect the questions already during your talk. Sometimes it helps if friendly colleagues break the ice and make initial contributions in the chat.

▶ Please note: stop the presentation and the screen sharing for a short interim question and answer session at the scheduled point.

- Conduct a short survey by means of a physical (smaller group) or virtual show of hands (medium and larger-sized groups)

    Stop the presentation and screen sharing at an appropriate (planned) point in the talk and let your audience know that you are asking for a (virtual) show of hands on a question, such as: how many of you have had similar experiences?

▶ Please note: Formulate a question that is as closed as possible in order to prevent excessively lengthy responses. Say something about the results and thank the audience.

- Conduct an online survey (large groups)

    Stop the presentation and screen sharing at an appropriate (planned) point in the talk, share the link to the voting tool in the chat and ask viewers for real-time feedback via their mobile phones. Visualise and comment on the result by sharing it via your screen.

    Assessment questions are good ways of getting the audience involved. For instance: Which of the above 5 parameters do you think has the strongest influence on X and should be investigated further?

▶ Please note: Choose a provider that allows your viewers to participate anonymously without registering. Test the functionality of the link and the voting tool in advance with the help of colleagues or friends. If necessary, ask a colleague to share the link for you in the chat. This could also help individual participants in the event of any difficulties. This allows you to concentrate fully on the result and the commentary.

- Showing the live visualisation

    Inform those present at a suitable (planned) point that you will now show something interesting live. Click in the prepared (if necessary also blank) slide. For example, sketch an experimental setup or process in front of the audience. Or make a manual addition to a representation to highlight specifics. Describe what you are doing here and what can be seen and ask for their opinion of what is shown.

▶ Please note: Practise this visualisation several times, preferably also in front of colleagues. To be on the safe side, keep a printout of the finished sketch and your additions next to you to ensure you don't make any mistakes and can look up where you are if you lose your train of thought.

- Collaborating on a virtual whiteboard
  For small and medium-sized groups, let the audience know right at the beginning that you have planned an interactive part. Share your virtual whiteboard or the link to it in due course. As with the voting tools, careful testing with colleagues and confident use of the chosen tools is recommended. If possible, ask a colleague to assist you so that you can concentrate fully on moderating and leading the discussion. Briefly discuss and comment on the result.

▶ Please note: prepare the basic structure of the whiteboard to prevent any irritation and confusion. If you want to ask the participants for their ideas or assessments on four aspects, prepare four fields and, if necessary, the matching coloured virtual sticky notes.

It is important to remember that interactive elements cannot be fully planned. It may occur that only a few spectators participate in the activation phase. Speakers should accept this and then quickly resume the presentation. Conversely, they have to take into account that many people will become involved.

Depending on the size of the audience, presenters should allow a generous amount of time for interactive elements and have additional input to hand in case the active phase is shorter than planned.

Figure 7.1 shows an overview of the six frequently used activation techniques.[5]

7.2 Shortly Before Starting the Presentation

7.2.1 What Remains the Same

- Send a set of slides to the organiser in advance
- Have a printout of slides and notes ready to refer to in the event of any problems—e.g. a blackout
- Wear comfortable clothes that suit the occasion
- Deactivate all background programmes on your computer and mute the phone(s).
- Be in the virtual room early/on time

---

[5] Own research and own representation.

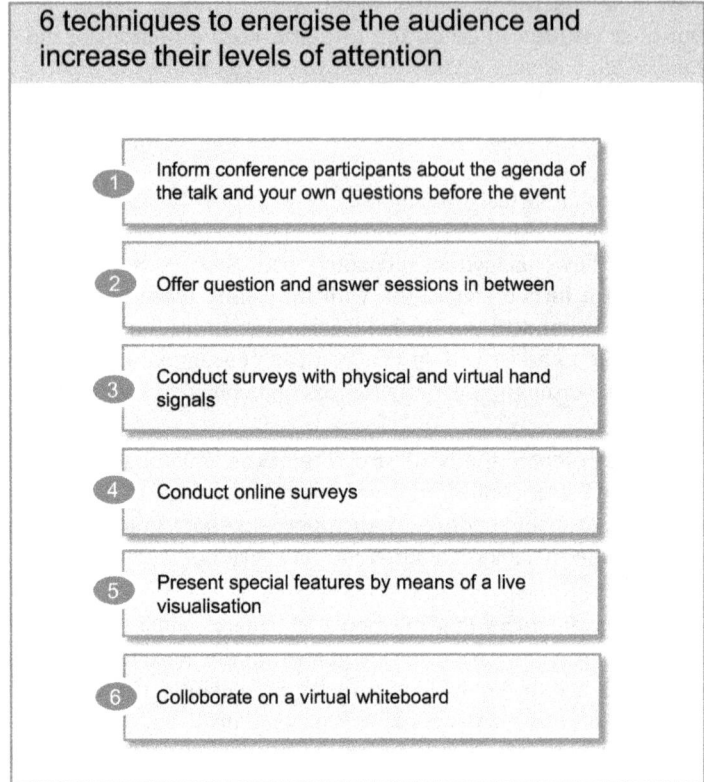

Fig. 7.1 Overview of the six frequently used activation techniques

7.2.2 What is Different

The dependence on technology and thus the risk of breakdowns is higher in the case of virtual presentations than with comparable presence formats. A technical check of all equipment and the programmes used well before the start of the event is a must.

A printout of the timeline helps presenters to adapt the presentation if necessary, for instance to display additional information or to get to the most important slide via a link and thus shorten the presentation.

When checking the microphone and the loudspeakers, researchers should also make sure that neither any clothing jewellery or accessories, nor a microphone positioned too close to the mouth, produce unpleasant noises. It is best to test everything in advance in the virtual room with the help of colleagues who have also dialled in.

7.2.3 What Additional Elements Are There

7.2.3.1 Organisational Activities a Few days Before the Event

- Make sure that you have the invitation link.
- If necessary, download and test the conference software.
- Charge your computer and your substitute computer.
- If necessary find an assistant. If the organiser does not provide someone to do this, ask a colleague to inform you in case of technical problems and keep an eye on the chat.

7.2.3.2 Set up the Workplace on the day (Before) the Event

- Connect your computer to the mains and provide the charged substitute computer. If there is a power failure, you continue to be able to work. Connect a second monitor—if possible—in case you want to show additional information in the lecture or you need space to see more of your participants. Ensure you have a stable internet connection—ideally using a cable.
- Make sure your workplace is tidy. Remove everything you don't need so that you can move freely and concentrate on your talk. Use a (wireless) mouse and have a writing pad and pens ready. Keep yourself hydrated and make sure the audience cannot see anything unwanted, that might distract people or be disruptive in the background. Clean up your desktop. Ideally, only the documents you need for the lecture are actually on it. Open them for the subsequent screen sharing.
- Make sure the lighting is good. The light—ideally daylight—is best projected from the front. Light sources behind you dazzle the audience. But also make sure that the light does not blind you.
- Test the camera position. If possible, use an external webcam instead of the laptop camera, as it surpasses the quality of the integrated cameras and is more flexible, especially if you are working with a second screen.
- Make sure you have a quiet workplace. A (wireless) headset ensures that external noise is suppressed, the sound is better than with the integrated microphone, that you are well understood and can hear well. The microphone should be as close to your mouth as possible, but without producing any unpleasant noises. Exclude interferences. Inform people in your household or office. If necessary, hang a sign on the door and also lock it if required.
- Select the correct camera, loudspeaker and microphone in the settings of the video conferencing software and test everything. Mute your mobile phone and dial in early (at least 10 min before your talk) so that you can get used to the atmosphere.

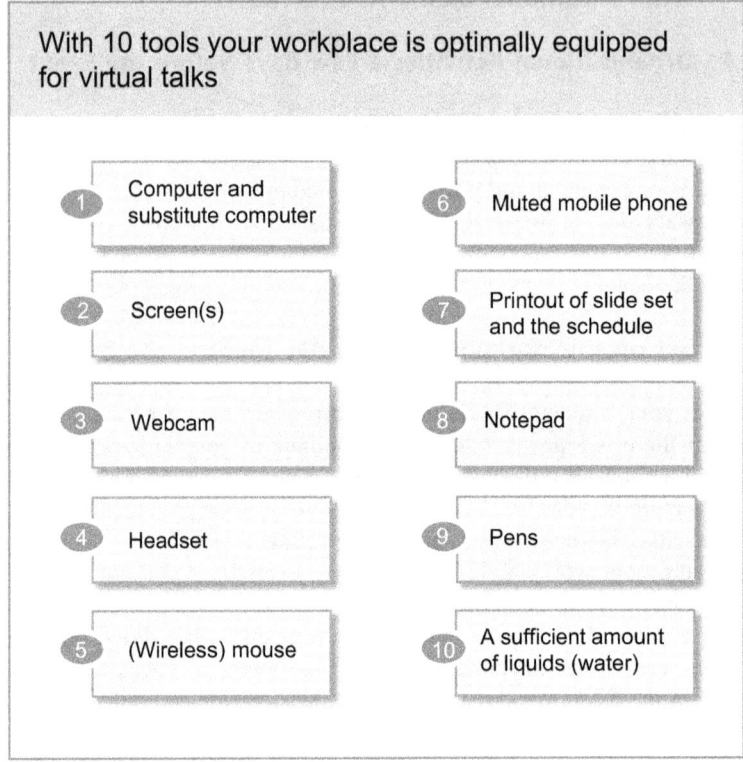

Fig. 7.2 Ten tools for the optimal workspace for virtual presentations

Figure 7.2 shows the ten tools for the optimal workspace for virtual presentations.[6]

7.3 Introduction

7.3.1 What Remains the Same

- In general use the classic structure of academic talks
- Consider the impact of the first impression
- Allow up to 5% of the time for the start of the talk
- Use "hooks" and starters
- Learn the first sentences off by heart if necessary

---

[6] Own research and own representation.

7.3.2 What is Different

7.3.2.1 Verbal Communication
The voice, as described in the "Preparation" part of this chapter, is the dominant medium of communication.

7.3.2.2 The Three Classic Elements of the Introduction
Welcome and introduction, research topic and relevance as well as the sequence and agenda are basically also suitable for online presentations. However, the following minor adjustments are useful:

1. Welcoming speech and presentation—the phase in which you establish contact with the audience:

    Ask at the beginning if the audience can hear you and, if necessary, see you. Ask for a brief visual cue: "I assume that you can all hear and see me! It would be nice if you could give me a quick 'thumbs-up' to confirm that." Hold your own thumb up to the camera as you do this, it motivates people to do the same and everyone knows what you want. This way, firstly, you find out that everything works technically, secondly, you have established a first contact with your audience and thirdly, you have been able to persuade many members of the audience to take part in an activity.

    If this form of introduction is not appropriate, ask a colleague in advance to give you feedback regarding the technology.
2. Research topic and relevance—the phase in which you motivate the audience:

    Introduce your topic, objective and the relevance of your topic in general and for the audience in particular. Underline the novel aspects of your research. Keep it short and use your storyline, but don't rush through this part. This is where you lay the foundations in motivating and attracting the attention of your audience. To achieve this, people have to be able to understand you well and follow you. This in turn determines for you whether and how many questions will be asked in the discussion.
3. Sequence and agenda—the phase in which you inform the audience and provide it with some guidance:

    This part is especially important in the virtual setting because it is more anonymous and the audience feels more uplifted if they know what is happening when and why. You should therefore present a short (!) agenda, which can also be shown again during the main part, in a slide-based manner. Also inform the audience if there are other virtual exchanges and activities planned after the talk.

    For events where there are no guidelines, state the most important rules at this point, e.g. regarding camera use, muting or the chat.

▶ In the virtual setting, it is best to use only short starters to break the ice and establish contact between yourself and your audience.

7.3.3 What Additional Elements Are There

- Bear in mind that your body language can only be seen to a limited extent or not at all. It is best to present in a standing position, as you would in a face-to-face event, in order to at least partially compensate for this limitation. This comes across more naturally because it ensures you have more energy in your body. It also helps you to concentrate better and to produce a more convincing performance. If you want or need to present sitting down, position yourself further forward on the chair and adopt an upright posture.
- Make use of body language, display your natural gestures and do not hide your hands. Even if the audience cannot see your movement or can only see part of it, they will experience you in a more active way.
- Do not be discouraged and remain active, even if you cannot see the audience's reactions. Take into account that your slide on the split screen dominates your viewers' screen and you are not visible at all or only in a very small image.
- Consider whether you can do without any visualisations (e.g. a title slide) at the introduction or display them only briefly so that people can see you well at least once.

7.4 Main Part

7.4.1 What Remains the Same

The different basic structures of the main part of the talk (classic, results-first, hourglass) are all suitable for virtual presentations.

7.4.2 What is Different

- Bear in mind that the audience cannot see you at the same time or only as a small video and that your slides will take up most of your audience's screens. On the one hand, this has the advantage that the attention of the viewer is focused on this. On the other hand, this makes it more strenuous for the audience and can lead to them suffering from fatigue sooner.
- Make sure there are changes and, during online lectures, interrupt your screen sharing every now and then and continue speaking for a moment without any slides. This is useful for transitions and whenever you want to keep or regain the audience's attention.
- Also use activating elements—as described in the "Preparation" part—to prevent members of the audience from drifting off.

7.4.3 What Additional Elements Are There

Use elements of online or e-moderation to steer the main part of your talk. Accompany your audience in such a way that it makes it easy for them to follow you—almost as if you were taking them by the hand. The following techniques are particularly recommended:

7.4.3.1 Guide the Audience's Gaze
Animations, virtual pointers and the mouse pointer can be used for this purpose. Combined with strong verbal guidance, this assists in orienting the audience well. Make sure that everyone focuses on the same part of your slide if possible and that your visualisation and what you are saying are (mostly) in sync.

7.4.3.2 Tell the Audience What You Are Doing
Avoid long periods of silence. This leads to feelings of insecurity and tempts people to occupy themselves with something else. Briefly mention what you are doing. (*"Now let me show you a short video to illustrate the specifics of our experimental setup. Just a moment please!"* or *"I'll quickly check that I haven't forgotten anything!"*).

▶ Don't say what you don't do—the brain is not as good at dealing with negations. Say what you do!

7.4.3.3 Formulate Clear Assignments and Questions
Let your audience know when you want them to do something, for example when you have an activity planned. Issue clear instructions to avoid irritating and annoying the audience. ("I am curious as to how you assess the situation. Please take your mobile phone now and use the link in the chat to participate in the survey!"). It may take a few seconds before the audience becomes active. Grant the audience this time.

Avoid the use of subjunctives and softeners in your wording. These usually irritate the audience and are likely to lead to misunderstandings (*"I imagine we might get to your questions soon"*). Refrain from letting the audience make decisions. Questions such as ("*Would you mind if I deactivate my video?*") are difficult to answer and could cause you problems if a unanimous decision is not reached.

7.4.3.4 Conclude Topics Recognisably and Move on to the Next Slide
Avoid clicking on the next slide if you are still speaking about the previous one. You confuse the audience because they don't know whether they should still be listening to you or already reading the slide. Close topics and slides in a recognisable way, then use a transition that whets the appetite for the next visualisation and then click in this slide (*"So, that concludes x. What's interesting is how we proceeded and I'll show you that now."*). In this way, you focus the audience's

attention, carefully guide it through the presentation and make them curious about what is to come.

7.4.3.5 Make Use of a Short Speaking Pause When You Have Faded in the Next Slide

Allow the audience a moment to take in the new slide before you start speaking. This increases the impact of what you are saying.

▶ Only perform one task at a time. Do not speak when clicking on, or searching for a slide and vice versa!

7.4.3.6 Improvise if Necessary When Dealing with Technical Problems

- Inform the event organiser by phone or via a personal message in the chat.
- Deactivate your video if you have any problems with the network.
- Have a break to rectify the problem.
- Dial in again or restart the programme.
- Use the substitute computer.
- Use the chat if there are any problems with the audio function.

7.5 Conclusion

7.5.1 What Remains the Same

- Announcement of the conclusion
- Summary of the main points and implications
- Strong conclusion with thanks to the audience
- No "Thank you for your attention slide"

7.5.2 What is Different

You should pack the announcement of the conclusion into 2 speaking pauses in order to hold or gain the attention of all viewers for the summary if possible.

Keep the conclusion short. Bear in mind that a virtual presentation is more tiring than a lecture in a face-to-face format. Avoid providing a lot of details and additional information at all costs.

7.5.3 What Additional Elements Are There

Thank the audience for their attention and, if applicable, for their commitment during the activating elements.

Actively hand over to the Chair so that it is clear that you are passing on the baton.

Alternatively, formulate a friendly invitation for members of the audience to ask questions and share comments. Give your audience time to formulate a question or a comment and to unmute. Also check if questions have not already been asked in the chat.

▶ Wait if you have invited members of the audience to ask questions and make comments! Endure the silence!

Remember that classical applause is not possible. Mostly virtual symbols or the sign for applause from sign language are used for this purpose.

7.6 Discussion

7.6.1 What Remains the Same

- Thank your audience for every contribution.
- Make a note of any feedback and copy any notes from the chat.
- Ask more in-depth questions and ask for details if you are not sure you have understood everything correctly.
- Address people in the audience by name if possible, then everyone knows who is meant. And what's more: People like to hear their names.

7.6.2 What Additional Elements Are There

Virtual conferences are often recorded and made available for asynchronous viewing. Presenters can use this to analyse their own performance and identify opportunities for improvement.

7.7 Follow-Up After a Virtual Scientific Presentation

7.7.1 What Remains the Same

- Incorporate helpful feedback into your paper and adapt the slides or your talk. If necessary, inform people on social media about any changes made.
- Share your impressions of the conference on social media.
- Maintain, and, if possible, extend the network.

References

Bailenson, Jeremy N, 2021, Nonverbal Overload: A Theoretical Argument for the Causes of Zoom Fatigue, https://tmb.apaopen.org/pub/nonverbal-overload/release/2, last retrieved: 27.12.2023

Bradbury, Neil A, 2016, Attention span during lectures: 8 seconds, 10 minutes, or more? https://journals.physiology.org/doi/pdf/https://doi.org/10.1152/advan.00109.2016, last retrieved: 27.12.2023

Ewers, Robert M, 2018, Do boring speakers really talk for longer, https://www.nature.com/articles/d41586-018-06817-z, last retrieved: 27.12.2023

Fauville, Geraldine et al., 2021, Zoom Exhaustion & Fatigue Scale, https://papers.ssrn.com/sol3/papers.cfm?abstract_id=3786329, last retrieved: 27.12.2023

Hey, Barbara et al., 2021, Virtuelle Veranstaltungen in Wissenschaft und Lehre: Eine praxisorientierte Einführung (essential) Taschenbuch, Springer

GPSR Compliance

The European Union's (EU) General Product Safety Regulation (GPSR) is a set of rules that requires consumer products to be safe and our obligations to ensure this.

If you have any concerns about our products, you can contact us on

ProductSafety@springernature.com

In case Publisher is established outside the EU, the EU authorized representative is:

Springer Nature Customer Service Center GmbH
Europaplatz 3
69115 Heidelberg, Germany

www.ingramcontent.com/pod-product-compliance
Lightning Source LLC
LaVergne TN
LVHW022037260326
834688LV00060B/821